FAMILIES AND POV

Everyday life on a low income

Mary Daly and Grace Kelly

First published in Great Britain in 2015 by

Policy Press
University of Bristol
1-9 Old Park Hill
Bristol
BS2 8BB
UK
t: +44 (0)117 954 5940
pp-info@bristol.ac.uk
www.policypress.co.uk

North America office:
Policy Press
c/o The University of Chicago Press
1427 East 60th Street
Chicago, IL 60637, USA
t: +1 773 702 7700
f: +1 773 702 9756
sales@press.uchicago.edu
www.press.uchicago.edu

© Policy Press 2015

British Library Cataloguing in Publication Data
A catalogue record for this book is available from the British Library

Library of Congress Cataloging-in-Publication Data
A catalog record for this book has been requested

ISBN 978 1 44731 883 5 paperback
ISBN 978 1 44731 882 8 hardcover

The right of Mary Daly and Grace Kelly to be identified as authors of this work has been
asserted by them in accordance with the Copyright, Designs and Patents Act 1988.

The statements and opinions contained within this publication are solely those of the authors
and not of the University of Bristol or Policy Press. The University of Bristol and Policy
Press disclaim responsibility for any injury to persons or property resulting from any material
published in this publication.

Policy Press works to counter discrimination on grounds of gender, race, disability, age and
sexuality.

Cover design by Hayes Design
Front cover image: Getty
Printed and bound in Great Britain by CMP, Poole
Policy Press uses environmentally responsible print partners.

Contents

List of tables

Acknowledgements

The study on which this book is based was undertaken as part of the Poverty and Social Exclusion in the United Kingdom research project. The project was funded by the Economic and Social Research Council (ESRC Grant RES-060-25-0052) under the leadership of Professor David Gordon of the University of Bristol. We thank the members of the team for their interest and helpful comments on the research, especially Professors Mike Tomlinson and Paddy Hillyard of Queen's University Belfast.

We would like to record our thanks to Michelle Crawford from the Analytical Services Unit of the Department for Social Development, who arranged access to the Family Resources Survey. The work of departmental staff in carrying out the initial screening exercise is also gratefully acknowledged. Dermot Donnelly of the Central Survey Unit of the Northern Ireland Statistics and Research Agency deserves special mention for his work on extracting the required sample from the Family Resources Survey and arranging delivery of the initial research material.

We also note the key role played by the Community Foundation for Northern Ireland, which put us in touch with a number of local community groups through which we recruited some of our respondents. The West Belfast Partnership deserves recognition for also facilitating contact with local centres and groups for the purpose of recruiting respondents.

There are some people in particular who deserve special thanks for believing in the research and facilitating access to participants. These are people who work on the ground within their local communities, whose work is quiet and unassuming but whose contribution to their communities is immense. To name these people individually would be to jeopardise the anonymity of the respondents. Instead, they have been thanked in person.

Finally, our greatest thanks go to each and every respondent who agreed to take part. They gave their time willingly and spoke openly and honestly in a genuine desire to further knowledge about what it is like to live in a situation of poverty and low income at the present time. Their accounts were insightful and arresting, and have stayed with us over the passage of time. We hope we have done justice to their stories, not least because they deserve to be heard.

Introduction

The central interest of this book is the nature and significance of family in a context of poverty and low income. The book reports findings from a study carried out in late 2011 and early 2012 based on interviews with 51 respondents (most often mothers) in Northern Ireland. It aims to contribute to a sociological perspective on poverty by exploring and problematising how family-related exigencies, norms and relationships take effect in the context of an inadequate income. The ordinary and extraordinary practices of constructing and managing family life and relationships in circumstances of poverty and low income are the driving set of interests. The research on which the book is based was funded by the Economic and Social Research Council under the Poverty and Social Exclusion 2012 study.[1] While the empirical material is from Northern Ireland – and there are of course unique aspects to family life there, as everywhere – the book proceeds from the conviction that what is being revealed has wide application and speaks to aspects of contemporary life in conditions of poverty and low income that are generic if not universal.

Aims and objectives

Investigating the relationship between poverty and family gives the book four main objectives:

- to contribute to the theoretical literature on family by offering a theorisation of the relationship between family and poverty/low income;
- to explore how decisions and practices around resource utilisation are influenced by family-related considerations and especially the well-being of children;
- to examine the support networks (if any) that people have available, the role of (near and distant) family, friends and neighbours in regard to support and the norms and expectations attending support;
- to elucidate how income shortages influence and affect people's local and wider engagements and interactions and the actions and representations people undertake to maintain an acceptable 'local face' and 'public image'.

---

[1] See www.poverty.ac.uk

Developing and applying a theoretical framework to understand the relationship between family and poverty is a primary goal of this book. Family life under conditions of poverty is far less theorised as compared with poverty in general or the household as a unit for the purposes of poverty analysis. Household-based studies help our understanding of poverty in a context of family in several ways. For one, the household is a collective unit and so as a basis for poverty calculations can help to complement estimates derived from individual income. Second, the household as a unit of analysis highlights aspects of the collective use of resources – in the sense especially of the relative economies of scale and expected patterns of allocation and consumption associated with households of different sizes and types. The household, therefore, gives a better basis on which to make adjustments to income so as to try to get a better approximation of people's actual income and living situation. Both are helpful but it is necessary to move beyond the household if we are to better understand poverty. Why?

A primary reason is because people tend to live in families rather than households. Hence, their expected patterns of resource accrual and use can be anticipated to be governed by relationships, bonds and preferences rather than utility. Whereas a household is a functional arrangement, a family is an arrangement of personal life. Family is one of a small number of primary social institutions characterised by emotion and affect and embedded in kinship-based norms, relationships and identities. Seen from a perspective of income, family is a form of economic and social organisation that provides for care needs and welfare, especially of the youngest generations, and governs relationships and resource exchanges among people of different generations and genders (Daly, 2011). Rather than being a matter of economic fact, people's actual income situation and their well-being are filtered through the complex of relationships, norms and practices associated with family. Hence, the rationalities implied by studies of households are unlikely to apply to families where moral and relational considerations predominate. This kind of sociological understanding suggests that the family's relevance for poverty lies not only in the accrual and use of material resources but in how ontological, relational and social factors are implicated in these processes. This highlights a second drawback in work on households and poverty, which is that it has no particular interest in – or often capacity to examine – relationships, bonds and norms between members and how these influence decision making, practices and outcomes.

Examining people's perceptions of and practices in regard to the operation of family life and family relations is the study's second key interest and goal. While there has been a lot of research on the material dimensions of poverty, relatively little is known about how people living on low income actually conduct their family lives, what they prioritise about family life and to what extent they can live up to their own (and others') ideals given the circumstances in which they find themselves. The study seeks not only to make visible some of the family-based processes and decisions about the use and distribution of resources but to locate these in familial interpretations and relationships. The way that people cope and the priorities that they set are guiding interests, especially when it comes to decision making and practices around resource distribution. Finch and Mason (1993, p 170), concluding their study of family responsibilities in England, say that it is not possible to understand family responsibilities or how they operate in practice if one concentrates only on material dimensions. The moral dimensions are also vital, in the sense especially of how people's identities as moral beings are bound up in the way that they make decisions about resource use and the exchanges and support they offer to and receive from others.

Third, the study is interested in identifying the kinds of support networks that people have, where family figures in these and how people engage with familial and other networks in a context of need and potential dependency. For these purposes, the book examines the use and exchange of goods, money, emotional support, advice/information and practical assistance within families and across wider networks. Research has found that, while family support is important across all social classes, it is more acutely so for those living in precarious situations and neighbourhoods. Moreover, given that existing research underlines that moral and emotional support may be as important as that of a material and economic nature (Daly and Leonard, 2002; Olagnero et al, 2005), this study takes an open approach to investigating the range of support available and its sources. Throughout, though, we want to ascertain the extent to which familial and other personal ties involve support when people need it and how this is received, interpreted and reciprocated.

How people view their local relationships and social engagement more widely and how they manage the social and public aspects of being on a low income is the fourth point of investigation. Here the two driving interests are localness and representation. In regard to the former, the book investigates the extent to which and how people's lives are locality-based. This directs attention to their contacts with friends and neighbours, their use of local services and their engagement in life locally. The second driving interest here is how people engage in public encounters, especially in situations where their low–income status is a key element. These encounters are taken as an opportunity to consider respondent agency, especially in regard to how they 'represent' themselves and their family in situations where reputation and well-being may be at stake (for example, in encounters at the benefits' office or their children's school). This directs attention to how the respondents see themselves and their family reflected in others' eyes and how they manage their behaviour in this kind of situation and seek to negotiate and shape their 'public' relationships and engagements (if at all). Managing reputation and avoiding embarrassment and shame are of primary interest here.

Designed to augment existing theory and knowledge about both family life and poverty, the book breaks new ground in several respects. In the first instance it fills a gap in knowledge about the texture and conduct of family life in a context of poverty and low income. Most existing work focuses on households and/or individuals and generally fails to explore family as a factor mediating income-related processes and relationships. There are, of course, publications illuminating the nature of family life, but some of these are old (for example, Brannen and Wilson, 1987; Finch, 1989; Finch and Mason, 1993) and most are not specifically focused on family life in a context of poverty and low income. While there has also been quite a number of studies on the lived experiences and situations of those living in poverty (Daly and Leonard, 2002; Ghate and Hazel, 2002; Hooper et al, 2007; Katz et al, 2007), these have not generally theorised family as a factor in poverty. Further, the breadth of its focus on family and its theoretical intent in this regard also act to distance this book from existing work.

The book is topical in several respects. Given the radical cut-backs of the welfare state that are underway in the UK and elsewhere, one can expect the topic of poverty and how people manage their income and personal circumstances to retain a prominent place in intellectual, public and policy discourses. Indeed, even before the recession, one could identify a family focus in social policy in the UK and elsewhere (Daly, 2010a). From the late 1990s 'think family' became part of the policy orientation under successive Labour governments (Cornford et al, 2013). A familialistic orientation, which has continued somewhat under the Conservative/Liberal Democrat coalition government that took office in 2010, has rendered family relationships and family practices an increasingly important area for policymakers. As a result, there is greater intervention in family life and ideals about good family life and good parenting are more prominent in public discourse and public policy than they used to be. State policies seek especially to

increase people's self-sufficiency. But it is a very qualified form of self-sufficiency – interpreted not as independence from family but more as independence from state benefits. The thrust, in a nutshell, is to get people to rely more on themselves and their families and less on the state. This book contributes evidence around these and other issues, and in its penultimate chapter engages in a reflection about the role and contribution of state policy in regard to easing (or worsening) people's circumstances.

The book is also well placed in regard to a strong current in recent British sociology around family as a frame of analysis (Morgan, 2010; Edwards et al, 2012). A debate is underway about the trend in UK-based scholarship in prior decades to de-emphasise family as an analytic category. Scholarship moved away from 'the family' out of a concern about its rigidity as a category of analysis. The depiction of family as a distinct social universe and a reality that transcends its individual members was also heavily critiqued (Bourdieu, 1996). A new understanding has emerged, with scholarship being taken forward by the view that personal life (Smart, 2007), intimacy (Irwin, 2005) and family-related practices (Morgan, 1996; 2010) are not restricted to any particular relational form or location. Family is not something that one has but rather something that one does (Cornford et al, 2013, p 14). That said, while it is probably more or less accepted nowadays that family should not necessarily be privileged as a unique space in which to study intimate relationships, it is also increasingly being recognised that there are particular and enduring aspects to family as a normative sphere, structural unit and set of relationships that merit investigation in their own right (Edwards et al, 2012). Pierre Bourdieu (1996), for example, pointed out that even if one regards family as a myth, social activity has to be engaged in to reproduce the family as a category of existence and meaning. There is, he says, a labour of institutionalisation involved – a set of engagements and activities whereby the feelings, dispositions and commitments necessary for the integration of the unit as a whole are engendered in each individual family member. There is great merit, therefore, in retaining family as a focus of analysis (Atkinson, 2014). This book fits itself into this kind of space. In its nuanced and differentiated conceptualisation of family and its investigation of the working out of family life and family dispositions in a specific economic situation, it will advance knowledge of family as both a collective entity and individual experience, while bearing in mind the insights from existing scholarship about not reifying family and not relying on old – structuralist – standards to analyse today's family.

Theoretical background

Two main bodies of work inform the book. The first is scholarship on family; the second is research on poverty, particularly that on poverty as a lived experience.

Family as a structure and arrangement of collective and personal lives is one of its most familiar features and representations in intellectual work. The systemic view of family, originating mainly in structural functionalism, emphasises the functions performed by the family and how family evolves and changes to fit the surrounding conditions, especially economic conditions (Parsons and Bales, 1955). It tends to view family in relatively singular and unproblematic terms, both in regard to how people become organised into families and the role and place of family in social life. The focus is on the links between family and society: the nuclear family form is said to dominate because it is the most efficient and suitable for prevailing economic and social conditions. Its emergence and development is regarded as a specialisation of the family as an institution, with the modern family mainly oriented to functions such as socialisation, emotional needs and the provision of support (as the family's direct economic production and employment functions have withered). An entire economic and social arrangement is involved, whereby at macro level family helps to organise a series of structural relationships between the economy, state and society, and at micro level family is a unit organising and governing everyday life and intimate relations. This work privileges a particular view of family. The family is a cooperative unit, resting on shared interests and mutual support. In this understanding of family, poverty can only be the result of some kind of dysfunction, either in the family's structure (inappropriate or deviant family form or size) or its operation (maladjustment at a personal and/or institutional level).

This perspective is not widely subscribed to today. This is so for numerous reasons: partly because it is out of date and out of fashion; partly because of its representation of family as devoid of power dynamics or internal diversity; partly because it over-generalises and over-relies theoretically on a particular form and type of family; and partly because it privileges continuity to such an extent that change has to be perceived negatively as some kind of systemic failure or dysfunction (Chambers, 2012, p 22). That said, however, one should not be blind to the extent to which structural functional notions and the idealised vision of family that flows from them – the heterosexual, nuclear, two-parent family – continue to inform debate and policy. Nor should one jettison the structural aspects of family entirely because

they have continued relevance, not least because individualised forms of living are often not possible for those with inadequate incomes. But work and thinking have moved on to highlight other aspects of family.

From the 1970s onwards, the focus of academic work changed and the thesis of family as changing only when pressure to do so was exerted on it from the outside (that is, from elsewhere in the social system) underwent a revision. A view stressing interdependence between family and other social institutions emerged (Berger and Berger, 1983). One of the consequences was not just a re-evaluation of the functions of the family in contemporary society, but a reconceptualisation of family to recognise its forms and behaviours as diverse and strategic. This meant according the family a theoretical status equal to that of other political and economic institutions (Sgritta, 1989, p 74). Gender scholarship was very important here in opening up the internal life of families to scrutiny and suggesting that families are sites of power struggles (especially along gender lines) (Barrett and McIntosh, 1982; Marx Ferree, 2010). Empirically, this kind of critique led to the examination of the internal lives of families, with special attention to the material and non-material resources and exchanges constituting the everyday life of families. The concrete accomplishment of these activities and the relationships and inequalities (of class, gender and generation) which they actualise became of key interest. But so also was there recognition of the significance of varying forms of family organisation and structure. Among the relevant developments to be highlighted here are: increasing diversity in family structure and form; the emergence of two-income families and the changing nature of gender and generational concerns as they affect the organisational and emotional life of families; and the increasing mobility of families within a context of insecure economic and social conditions and global migration.

This brings us towards the 'doing' of family life, reflecting a movement in scholarship away from institutional or organisational features and towards family relationships and behaviours. The newer scholarship on family is animated especially by the richness of family life, the elective nature of much kinship activity, family as constituted by the predispositions, needs and concerns that people bring to their interpersonal relationships, the significance of individualisation, and how family ties are altered and recreated through discourses, relations and interactions (Irwin, 2005; Smart, 2007; Dermott and Seymour, 2011). While it has not been specifically developed in relation to families on low income, the scholarship invites one to witness the complex exchanges involved (whether relating to money, support, care, information/know how or control) in family life and in sustaining family-based relationships within a network of other relationships and commitments. This has been a very strong current of recent sociology in Britain, taken forward by scholars such as Janet Finch, David Morgan, Carol Smart, Ros Edwards, Jane Ribbens McCarthy and Val Gillies. A leading concept has been that of family practices, which focuses on the everyday interactions of those with whom people are close and how these act to create the meaning of family (rather than it being a given). Scholarship examines how boundaries – of co-residence, marriage, kin status and so forth – are not fixed but fluid (Williams, 2004, p 17).

The second guiding body of work for the book is that on poverty. This is a very large scholarship, dating back at least 100 years. As one might imagine, poverty is a concept that has undergone considerable change, if not transformation, since its early days. A significant part of the challenges and debates around poverty is captured by questions around whether poverty should be seen and understood in a quantitative or qualitative way. In the former regard poverty is a lack of material resources; in the latter view poverty is a negative or substandard quality of life experience associated with inadequate material and other resources. While the quantitative approach to poverty has dominated the field, over time this has also become more 'socialised'. Of signature importance in this regard was the work of Peter Townsend in the 1970s and 1980s. Townsend's approach was heavily sociological – he was interested in the meaning of poverty and believed that poverty could only be understood in terms of a denial of customary standards of living and normal life of society. Moving away from a purely economic conception of poverty as living below a minimal income threshold, Townsend (1979, p 31) argued that poverty should be seen as a 'lack of resources to participate in activities and obtain the living conditions and amenities which are customary or are at least widely encouraged or approved, in the societies to which they belong'. The idea of poverty as exclusion from the customary lifestyle of one's peers was born. This has been an influential approach, especially in Europe where the European Union has adopted it as its approach to poverty (Daly, 2010b). Yet, quantitative conceptualisations of poverty dominate the field.

An argument can be made that a quantitative perspective is best at providing a snapshot of poverty, whereas if one wants to get to the core of poverty, and especially to examine poverty as dynamic and diverse rather than fixed, qualitative methods – including interviews and focus groups as well as more experiential and creative methods along the lines of diary keeping, life histories and mapping of experiences and situations – are to be preferred. These seek to reveal what it means to be poor.

Existing work in this vein highlights two dominant narratives in people's accounts of everyday life in poverty. One focuses on money and its management and the other on the way people living in poverty feel they are treated by others (Kempson et al, 1994; Daly and Leonard, 2002; Flint, 2010). In the former regard, daily life is described as living constantly from hand to mouth – going without, putting off even small expenditures, not celebrating family-related or other events, constrained and being characterised by constrained and very micro-level decision making. Sacrifice and compromise are commonplace. Budgeting and money management loom large over the conduct of daily life and become almost survival skills. Exploring how they manage suggests not only that people living in poverty have diverse coping skills but that they also have many strategies to make money and resources stretch as far as possible (Flint, 2010). A second dominant theme in people's accounts of their life is how they are treated. Poverty is for many people an experience of disrespect, humiliation, powerlessness and denial of rights (Lister, 2004, p 7). Those who are living in poverty report stigma as part of their everyday experience (Vincent et al, 2010; Chase and Walker, 2013).

There is, however, no simple way of depicting those living in poverty or on low income and one should resist negative depictions – people may and commonly do have access to other 'resources' or protective factors. Like everyone else, they often have very firm friendships and family relationships, for example, as well as support in their community or locality, especially if their living situation is similar to that of those with whom they closely interact. As Pemberton and colleagues (2013) put it, the presence of family, friends, neighbours and community can all serve to soften the harsh realities of life on a low income. However such networks can also be fragile because they are often over-stretched, something that can easily happen given that the people called on to help tend to be in a similar low-resource situation. And there are also many people who have no-one to call on.

Following a qualitative line of analysis, it is not so much the existence of poverty that is studied in this book as the experiences and conditions of life associated with poverty and low income. Hence the focus is on people's accounts of their situation in an everyday context. This approach is justified by two main rationales. The first is epistemological – to better investigate poverty and low income people's own accounts and interpretations of their situation are the best evidence because we know too little about how people use the resources that they have to make a life for themselves. The second reason has political overtones – to allow the voices of people in this situation to be heard. For these and other reasons, first-hand accounts are to be valued in their own right. While the research reported here does not claim to be fully participatory, it is in the general tradition of work that examines poverty or low income in the terms in which those living in the situation themselves identify and understand their situation (Norton et al, 2001).[2]

There is also a third set of literature informing this book: theorisation of the connections between family and poverty. This is a much smaller literature and so cannot be treated on the same basis as the two bodies of work just discussed. Nevertheless, it merits some discussion.

To the extent that it has been theorised, the relationship between family and poverty has been primarily viewed as determined by either structural factors or cultural factors.

With regard to the first approach – the structural – this has mainly been conceptualised in terms of the impact of the demographic and structural composition of family on poverty. It is known, for instance, that families with certain types of structure and composition have a higher risk of poverty as compared with the population at large. A recent review (Culliney et al, 2013) highlighted the following types of family as being particularly at risk of poverty in Great Britain:

• lone parent families;
• large families, that is, those with three or more children;
• cohabiting families;
• families with at least one disabled adult;
• families from minority ethnic backgrounds.

Poverty in this view, then, is mainly associated with factors in the family's structure or composition that lead to either an over-demand on the family's resources (like too many children) and/or an undersupply of resources (through too few earners, for example).

A second theorisation of how poverty and family are connected focuses on the way in which family culture and orientations is implicated in poverty and its transmission across generations. While originally oriented to revealing the beliefs and practices of people on a low income (as in the work of Oscar Lewis [1959]), studies of the culture of poverty tend to prosecute the view that culture is implicated in causing poverty (for example, Harrison and Huntington [2000]

---

2   See the approach developed by the World Bank called Participatory Poverty Assessments (Norton et al, 2001).

among others) and that family can be a significant conduit of poverty by virtue of the values and practices that certain families engage in. The intergenerational transmission of poverty debate has some elements of this perspective. Cultural approaches tend to locate their explanation in the characteristics and behaviour of people as well as their beliefs and cultural practices (Miller, 1996, p 570). People lack a work ethic, have no proper male role models and live in communities where benefit dependency and anti-social behaviour are widely accepted. Others have used cultural or sub-cultural arguments to suggest that 'the poor' form an underclass. This is an argument that has had wide currency in the USA, associated especially with the work of Charles Murray (1984) and Herrnstein and Murray (1994). The underclass theorists suggest that there is a class of people – with all the sense of permanence and coherence as implied by the use of the term 'class' – which is set apart from the rest of society. The underclass hypothesis sometimes dispenses with the definitional and measurement intricacies that characterise the poverty field, identifying 'the poor' as those who live in areas affected by such factors as large-scale unemployment, housing degradation and extensive 'dependency' on benefits (Wilson, 1987). It is an approach that categorises and objectifies 'the poor' and in this and other ways is very different to the perspective adopted in this study.

Definitions and theoretical framework

This book takes a relatively open approach to family and to poverty and low income.

Family in this book is defined quite loosely: to refer to an arrangement that, at its most basic, involves at least one parent living with one or a number of children who are below the age of 16 (or older if in full-time education or ill or disabled). Family is therefore defined structurally, but, as will be made clear in the proximate discussion, the structural aspects of family are not treated as uniquely interesting but rather as one element of a complex social formation. In short, family for the purposes of this book is viewed as diversified, having no singular form or structure and seen as worthy of study not for its structural or organisational aspects alone but for these together with the countless acts of family affirmation – what Bourdieu (1996, p 22) calls the 'constant maintenance work on the feelings', and (one might add) relationships – that are involved in maintaining family.

With respondents' accounts and experiences as the evidence of poverty in this book, the study is not tied to a particular conception or definition of poverty either. Rather than a fixed state or condition, poverty is viewed as a set of processes and relationships relating to the accrual and use of resources that are inadequate to meet need. The book also employs a conception of those who are in a situation of poverty as actors with leverage; people whose lives and experiences are diverse, changeable and guided in key ways by their own agency. Poverty understood in the sense of an income cut-off was used only as a criterion for sample selection. As will be explained later, an income threshold was set in order for families to be eligible for the study. However, because of difficulties obtaining a sample on a strict income cut-off basis, some of the respondents in the study were not strictly income poor. All were on a low income, though. Hence, poverty and low income are referred to simultaneously throughout the book to reflect that the respondents were not always technically below the poverty line and also because many respondents would not use the term 'poverty' to describe their own situation.

The book develops and applies a theoretical framework that views the relationship between family and poverty or low income in terms of four elements:

• family structure and mode of organisation;
• cultural specificity, meaning and identity;
• relationships, activities and processes;
• family as object of public representation and local life.

Before getting on to the details, there are a number of general points to note in regard to the framework. First, the framework has a dual purpose: to understand the relationship between family and poverty/low income at an experiential level; to contribute to causal thinking about poverty and low income in a familial context. Having said that, the framework does not view poverty as originating in the family but recognises that family may play a causal role (for example, in regard to particular constraints and/or practices regarding resource levels and the use of resources, the significance of caring-related responsibilities associated with family in a context of low income, and so forth). Second, the family is not viewed as a self-contained unit; each of the four dimensions reflects and refracts societal influences on family.

The structural approach highlights the need to take account of the composition and organisation of the family unit within which people live and the ways that this influences and affects access to resources and decisions around resources. With this dimension, we are suggesting that the demographic, structural and economic aspects of the family play an important role in both why people are poor or on a low income and how they become or remain so. An idea of a life-course effect – in the sense of the individual's or family's stage in the demographic cycle – is also implied here. However, in this study, family structure per se is only part of the story and is of most significance in terms of its impact on resource access and use. Unlike a lot of other studies then, here structure is treated as only one element of a more complex configuration of factors.

The second dimension – the cultural and cognitive – draws attention to how people interpret their situation in a context of norms and values. A broader sociological understanding of culture informs this book than that used in the culture of poverty literature outlined earlier. What are of interest, following Small and colleagues (2010), are people's values, the frames through which they interpret and understand their situation, their repertoires or strategies of action and meaning and how their narratives reveal elements of their identity and the knowledge or information they have acquired through their experiences. Drawing from this understanding, an interest in culture and cognition directs the book to the ways in which people conceive of and understand family life and family relationships and how they reason and make moral judgements about the management of resources and the conduct of family life. Of interest especially is a desire to identify and understand 'this family' through the instantiation of how people create rules, rituals and practices to organise their lives and their relationships in a familial context (Lamont and Small, 2010). Instead of claiming that culture causes poverty, culture is of interest because it allows access to people's subjectivity, which is crucial to understanding what it is like to live in circumstances of poverty and low income, and reveals how people's understanding of their situation and their cultural predispositions affect their use of resources.

The third dimension – relationships, activities and processes – draws attention to the exigencies, tasks, interactions and relationships associated with the maintenance and governance of family life. David Morgan's (1996; 2010) concept/approach of family practices is a useful lens here. This directs attention to the everyday, to the way that family members organise their lives and the manner in which they 'do' (that is, perform and live out) family life, family roles and family relationships. Morgan suggests that this approach is preferable to one that focuses on 'the' family, which in his view reifies family. Instead, agency and openness as regards the conduct of family life are emphasised. Drawing from this perspective leads the current study to consider how family life and family relationships are lived, managed and organised in a context of poverty and low income. The book looks especially at daily practices such as budgeting, shopping, meal preparation, seeking and receiving support from others (especially family) and especially providing care to other members of one's family.

Finally, the fourth dimension conceives of family as an object of public representation and image management. The underlying idea here is also sociological in that it recognises that both self and family do not just exist but have to be constantly created and recreated especially in the public domain. One might name the endeavours involved here as 'representation work'. This opens the way to study, first, local-level engagement and the extent to which and how life is localised for and by respondents. Second, it directs attention to how people maintain a particular public image, among those whom they meet every day but also in situations in which their low income may be exposed. There are sets of encounters that are crucial for everyone, but there may be much more at stake in those encounters for those living in poverty and low income. Encounters such as those in benefit offices, schools, and so forth may be high risk for those on low income, in that the outcomes are crucial to their well-being. But so too are 'image' and reputation crucial in a more general sense, for self-worth, for family integrity, and for the way children are treated and feel about themselves (to name just some). Maintenance of an acceptable public image may be more difficult in a context of poverty and low income because social opprobrium and negative imagery towards people in this situation are widespread.

In summary, in this book both structure and agency – in the sense of how respondents approach their situation and the actions they take in the context of the resources they have available, their family circumstances and the situations they face – are of central interest. The book takes an open approach to the capacities of people in low-income families – looking for the skills, orientations and dispositions available to people to utilise existing and generate further resources (or, if not generate, extend them) and the practices and relationships they engage in for such purposes. This is a counter perspective to that which views people's lives as determined by a scarcity of material resources. This interest in the resources and dispositions available to people to take action draws from Amartya Sen's (1984) theorisation of capabilities – the freedom that people have to do and be what and who they value. According to Sen, it is not resources or command over commodities per se that matter overwhelmingly in determining quality of life or even justice, but rather opportunities that can be taken up and acted on. While the concept of capabilities is not specifically employed in this book, its agency-oriented sensibility and its resistance to drawing a line between those living in poverty and the rest of the population influence the research in key ways. In addition, Sen's broad understanding of resources and their role in regard to agency is also useful to bear in mind.

Methodology

Given the study's purpose and leading interests, a qualitative methodology was followed. Face-to-face interviews were used to gather the evidence, mindful of the strengths of the interview method in exploring sensitive subjects and allowing participants opportunities to develop and communicate their points of view.

Two criteria governed the sample selection: to be eligible, respondents had to be living as part of a family and the family had to be living in poverty or on a low income. For the purposes of the former, a family was defined mainly in terms of the presence of dependent children (aged up to 16 years or older if in full-time education or experiencing an illness or disability). Both one-parent and two-parent families were deemed eligible. For the purposes of defining low income, an income threshold for family income was taken of 60% of median household income. This is the customary cut-off for income poverty measurement in an EU context. This threshold at the time of study, based on the households below average income (Northern Ireland) report of 2009/10, was £193 (after housing costs) a week for a lone parent with two children aged under 14 years (Department for Social Development, 2011a, p 24).

The initial sampling frame was drawn from that of the Northern Ireland Family Resources Survey (FRS) in 2009/10 and specifically respondents to that survey in 2009/10 who had given their permission to be re-contacted for the purposes of other research. Like its counterparts elsewhere in the UK, the Northern Ireland FRS collects detailed information on the incomes and general circumstances of private households from April to March each year. The sample size for the Northern Ireland FRS is 3,600 households (of which approximately 1,900 usually agree to participate in the survey). Because it collects very comprehensive income data alongside personal and household information, the FRS was considered to provide the most rigorous sampling frame possible for the present study. Permission to use the FRS was granted by the Department for Social Development once its internal comprehensive and detailed ethical regulations were satisfied. The study also obtained ethical approval from Queen's University Belfast.

A list of 90 respondents who matched the two main study criteria (family, income) was derived from the respondents in the 2009/10 FRS who had agreed to take part in further research. A letter was sent at the beginning of October 2011 to each of these inviting them to take part in the study, together with an information sheet, researcher contact details, a consent form asking permission to contact, and a stamped self-addressed envelope for return of the documents. Potential respondents were also informed that a £15 shopping voucher would be given as an expression of gratitude for taking part in the study. All initial contacts with potential respondents were initiated by the Department for Social Development in order to preserve anonymity and confidentiality.

Subsequent to the mail shot and one follow-up contact either in person or by phone call, a total of 14 interviews were secured from the 90 contacts. This represents a response rate of 16%, which is relatively low. We attribute the low response rate and the high refusal rate partly to the climate of uncertainty and fear surrounding the cuts in welfare and public expenditure, including the reassessment of the entitlements of benefit claimants going on at the time the study was being planned and carried out. The response rate was also further depleted by the fact that the original list contained errors or was out of date (with several invitation letters being returned because people had moved address) and a significant subset being unobtainable via personal or phone contact. Table B.1 in Appendix B gives the reasons for the non-responses.

To generate further interviews, it was decided to approach voluntary and community organisations to ask that they act as a contact point with local groups and, via these, potential respondents. The Community Foundation for Northern Ireland – which supports community-based activity through targeted grant funding and is the largest independent charitable grant-making body in Northern Ireland – was approached for this purpose. The study rationale, aims and objectives were explained in full at a meeting at the Foundation premises in late November 2011. Attending the meeting were representatives of a range of voluntary and community groups located across Northern Ireland, thus providing an opportunity for the researchers to make direct contact with community-based groups and for them to ask questions and request further details about the study. Four groups expressed interest in participating in the study and agreed to act as a point of contact at community level. The geographic spread of these groups encompassed the west (Derry and Tyrone) and east of the region (Antrim and Belfast East). The areas were a mixture of rural and urban locations and they also included areas of different religious composition.

In order to broaden coverage and increase diversity, the West Belfast Partnership was also approached. This is a broad-based social partnership organisation working at community level in West Belfast, a mainly Catholic area of the city that is economically and socially under-developed. Bringing together community, statutory, political and business interests, the West Belfast Partnership supports neighbourhood renewal in West Belfast, working alongside locally-based neighbourhood partnerships in designated areas. Full study details were presented at a meeting with key personnel and local community workers. Interest was expressed by a number of groups and contact numbers were exchanged.

Through these different channels, a further 40 respondents were recruited to the study. This brought the total study sample to 54 families. Three of the 54 interviews were not subsequently used since they failed to match the study criteria (either because the income was too high or because there were no dependent children living at home). In fact, once we departed from the original FRS sampling list, it was difficult to ensure that the respondents met the two criteria before we interviewed them. To a large extent we were dependent on the 'gatekeepers' in the different organisations to represent and interpret our criteria accurately when they were circulating information to potential respondents and fielding questions about the study. In the end, the narratives of 51 respondents provide the empirical basis of the analysis presented in this book.

The interviews

We adopted an approach to interviewing that allowed participants to tell their stories in their own ways as far as possible. A semi-structured interview schedule was used that was structured on a thematic basis but allowed both interviewer and respondents a degree of freedom over the sequence of topics and degree of depth (see Appendix A).

The face-to-face interviews were carried out with respondents either in their own homes or in the premises of the contacting group or organisation. The choice of location was based on respondent preference, comfort and convenience. Interviews lasted approximately one hour. A digital voice recorder was used to record the conversation with the signed permission of the respondent. Field notes were written within a short period of each interview. The interview recordings were downloaded onto a password-protected secure server. All interviews were anonymised and assigned a code number. No identifying information (such as names and addresses) was stored with the interview files, and identity records, such as signed consent forms, were kept separately from other interview material.

Interviews were carried out in the latter months of 2011 (October to early December) and the early part of 2012 (February to April).

The interview schedule is reproduced in Appendix A. The following are the main themes covered:

- *resources/capacities:* access, volume, usages of a range of resources (including income and other material resources as well as a range of non-material resources);
- *management of resources, coping strategies, decision making:* the practices and skills utilised in the management and deployment of resources; the trade-offs made and how respondents think about these trade-offs and decide on them; the ways and extent to which considerations relating to family and kinship figure in these decisions and whether family is seen to offer protection against current and future risks;
- *family practices:* values, norms and responsibilities prevailing in the family around the conduct of collective life; the extent to which decisions and behaviours are guided by considerations for the family unit as a whole and/or individual members;
- *strength and meaning of familial ties and relationships:* the meaning of 'family'; the positive and negative emotions and images associated with family; the degree of closeness of family ties; the implications of low income for the practice and quality of family life;
- *exchanges and reciprocity/family support:* the resources (advice, information, financial help, labour, other material help, emotional help) exchanged among family members; the nature of and norms around intra-familial aid; the nature and understanding of reciprocity;
- *local life and reputation:* feelings about the local area; degree of involvement with the local community; contacts and relationships with friends and neighbours; use and degree of satisfaction with a range of services; occasions and experiences that have caused embarrassment and shame.

All interviews were carried out by one or both authors. Both have extensive experience of qualitative interviewing, including in sensitive situations. This experience was drawn on throughout the study from preparation to fieldwork, analysis and writing up. It was anticipated that some topics might be emotional for people and that some of the issues covered might result in respondents considering availing of help or advice from professional services such as the Citizens Advice

Bureau or the Northern Ireland Housing Executive. A list of relevant organisations offering supportive services was prepared in advance of the interviews and offered to all participants.

Of the 51 families, 30 were couple families and 21 were lone-parent families. Mothers dominated the respondents, with only five male interviewees. We did not specifically set out to recruit mothers; the ideal respondent was envisaged as either the female or male partner or household head who could speak about family practices. It may be that women were over-represented as respondents because of their greater engagement in the community sector (which, as mentioned, was targeted for accessing respondents) or because women are generally more likely than men to 'volunteer' or self-select for this kind of 'conversation'.

Analysis

The interview narratives were analysed using a 'thematic framework' approach (Ritchie and Lewis, 2003). Data management/analysis was assisted by the use of Excel spread sheets and Computer-Assisted Qualitative Data Analysis Software NVivo 10. All transcripts and field notes were searched both manually and by examining the nodes emerging through NVivo. The analysis was therefore 'grounded' in nature. The process of analysis comprised three main stages:

- *Initial analysis:* This involved familiarisation with the raw data, listening to the interview recordings and reading and re-reading the interview transcripts for the purpose of analysing systematically the replies to each set of questions. This was followed by an initial descriptive 'coding' stage, whereby a set of themes, sub-themes and concepts was elaborated.
- *More in-depth analysis:* Following refinement of the thematic framework, a more in-depth analysis of the interconnections between key questions, themes and dimensions of analysis was undertaken. This involved grouping similar statements/themes together so that the main forms and variations of the themes were readily identifiable.
- *Explanatory analysis:* At this stage, patterns of association were looked for, together with regularities and irregularities of association for the purpose of identifying explanatory factors. This was mainly done manually, although the pattern or tree of relationships as identified by NVivo was a central tool throughout.

Before presenting the study's findings, it is important to note the backdrop in Northern Ireland (and the UK in general) in the period when the research was taking place. This was a period of substantial cuts in social security benefits and public services introduced by the coalition government through the June 2010 budget and the comprehensive spending review in October 2010 (HM Treasury, 2010). Most of the cuts in benefit expenditure were directed at short-term housing and disability benefits. The budget and comprehensive spending review together announced a reduction in social security expenditure of some £18 billion for the UK as a whole. Further cuts to public expenditure were announced in successive budgets and the 2013 Spending Review (HM Treasury, 2013). It has been estimated that local government and social security benefits bear over 50% of current and imminent cuts (Duffy, 2014). The plan announced in the Budget 2014 to introduce a cap on future welfare spending will limit expenditure on Employment and Support Allowance, Disability Living Allowance, Housing Benefit and Tax Credits. This will have its main impact on those reliant on sickness and disability benefits and low-paid workers reliant on Tax Credits.

The economic and social structure of Northern Ireland makes the region especially vulnerable to cuts in welfare and public sector spending. A higher percentage of average household income in Northern Ireland comes from social security benefits – 3% as compared with the UK average of 1% (Department for Social Development, 2010). Northern Ireland also has a high rate of disability and therefore a higher number of people receiving disability-related benefits. For example, around the time of study, receipt of Disability Living Allowance was over 10% compared with the UK average of 6% (Department for Social Development, 2010). Another relevant point to note is that the higher proportion of people employed in the public sector in Northern Ireland (as compared with elsewhere in the UK) makes Northern Ireland more vulnerable to reductions in public sector spending (Browne, 2010).

Running alongside the macro-economic and political conditions, there has been a noticeable increase in public rhetoric reminiscent of earlier underclass discourses (for example, Murray 1996) that places emphasis on cultural as against structural factors as explanations for poverty and apportions blame to individuals for situations like unemployment, family breakdown and homelessness. The hardening of attitudes against people who are not economically active or self-sufficient is seen to have facilitated the decision making around cuts to the welfare budget (Baillie, 2011). Furthermore, people are now generally less supportive of public spending on all types of benefits including those for older people in retirement and the belief that welfare spending increases dependency is now widespread (National Centre for Social Research, 2012).

Limitations of the study

The first point to make here is that the evidence about family processes relies on information from one individual only. It is therefore just one view of family processes. Ideally, family processes should be studied from the perspective of all those involved, whereas here we rely on the account of just one family member to tell the 'family story'. In the absence of interviews with all family members, speaking to mothers or fathers alone is the second best option.

Since a commitment was given to both the contact person/organisation and the respondents that only outline details would be requested on household income and benefit receipt, the reported collective income of families is an approximation based on the income band into which the respondent placed their family. That said, there are grounds to suggest a generally accurate representation of the family's finances. For example, there was a high degree of congruence in the incomes reported by similarly-constituted households, and the levels of income that respondents reported receiving from benefits were also generally accurate. A further possible study limitation derives from how the sample was obtained. About two-thirds of respondents were recruited via community and voluntary sector contacts. Since these people essentially self-selected to take part in the study, it is possible that the results represent particular views or situations. An area of investigation that might be skewed is the extent of engagement with community groups – this might be over-estimated, given the numbers of respondents secured through local contacts. However, it was also clear that some of the respondents who were contacted through local groups had responded to the information about the study sent out and did not necessarily have strong contacts with the local group or centre through which they were recruited.

Structure of the book

Following this introduction, the book is organised into eight main chapters followed by a conclusion. The chapters are structured loosely around the four elements of the theoretical framework outlined earlier. However, they do not follow it exactly, mainly because the dimensions are overlapping and are closely interconnected in practice. The book follows the general structure, though, in terms of the sequencing of themes – moving consecutively through structure/organisation, culture, relationships and representation.

Chapter One introduces the participants. It focuses especially on what might be called 'structural aspects' of individual and family life, setting out personal and familial characteristics such as the number of dependent children and the economic status of different family members and also detailing people's situation with regard to housing and health. As well as outlining people's circumstances, it considers something of their life course trajectories, in terms of how they got to their current situation. Vignettes of a small selection of respondents' stories will also be presented so as to convey a sense of the substance of people's lives.

The next four chapters treat of the processes and relationships associated with family life and the cultural specificity and meaning of family.

Chapter Two is one of two chapters probing the economics of everyday life in both a functional and interpretive way. It examines family as a unit of expenditure and consumption. It first outlines how money and spending are viewed and organised and where the priorities lie in these regards. This leads to a discussion of how people organise their essential spending, especially that on fuel and food. The chapter then moves on to more existential elements, detailing how money and family are intertwined in individual psyche and frame of reference. Having set out how money looms large in individual and family life, the remainder of the chapter probes processes around the organisation of finances, the distribution of resources and the general patterning and practices of family life in these regards. As a whole, the chapter explores how people seek to manage the family's financial circumstances and the ways they imprint familial considerations on everyday life in this context.

Chapter Three takes these themes further. It focuses especially on family culture and values by examining the sets of understandings around family that prevail – depictions of the 'we' of family – and how these are enacted in everyday activities and interactions, especially in relation to money. The first part of the chapter explores how people understand and characterise their family and what they understand to be the most significant features of their family situation. More cognitive aspects are considered in the second part of the chapter. One of the key questions here is how family has a positive or negative impact on people's capacity to deal with their financial circumstances. The third part of the chapter investigates people's sense of their capacities to realise the personal and family lives they would like to have.

The focus of Chapters Four and Five is on the modes of relating within respondents' families. The role and place of children is the lens through which this is examined in Chapter Four. The first part of the chapter uncovers the extent to which children are the source of their parents' most meaningful relationships. The chapter then goes on to offer a detailed exploration of the meaning and practices of parenting in conditions of low income. It particularly explores the ethical basis to parenting in respondents' opinions and the struggles that parents on low income have in this regard. There is also in the final section a brief exposition of the lives of children in these families and the kinds of roles that they play in their families.

Chapter Five turns to relationships with adult family members, and especially those with parents and siblings (including in-laws). It examines the main resources – both material and immaterial – that people may access through their family and the characteristics and conditions of such support. As well as revealing the support received, the chapter enquires into the meaning and significance of familial exchanges, by examining norms and practices around reciprocity on the one hand and ambivalence on the part of respondents on the other.

The next two chapters are oriented to the fourth dimension of the theoretical framework: family as an object of public representation.

Chapter Six explores poverty and low income from a perspective of place. Its aim is to uncover both the local lives and engagement of respondents and the 'localness' of their lives. One of the threads running through the chapter is the extent to which people are socially isolated or locally engaged. The first section considers the extent to which people are embedded in and engaged with the locality in which they reside and how they regard the locality. The second section looks at people's local social networks, especially their engagement with friends and neighbours. We are especially interested in these relationships as evidence of local engagement but also in terms of the support that they make available to people. The chapter then moves on to people's use of a range of local services. Finally, it reveals respondents' evaluations of how they and their family compare with others in terms of aspects of standard of living.

Chapter Seven adds another dimension to the locational aspects of life by investigating how respondents interpreted and engaged with a range of 'public encounters', especially those involving perceived negative constructions and expectations. It tells of people's accounts of key interactions in 'public' settings, and especially 'formal' encounters with schools and benefit office(r)s. The chapter is especially interested in revealing situations where respondents felt embarrassment either for themselves or their family and how they responded to this kind of situation. Occasions of felt shame are also explored, in the belief that these are revealing of key elements of poverty and low-income experiences, from both the perspective of those living in this situation and the way society regards them. The chapter also looks at how people engage in 'othering', that is, distancing themselves from others and underlining their own distinctive characteristics. The emphasis throughout is on how people seek to convey an image or impression of themselves and/or their family and how they respond to and even counter negative depictions.

Chapter Eight seeks to put the findings in a policy context. It offers a discussion of both the relevant policies that are in place and the main policy-related considerations to arise from the study. It especially devotes attention to the ongoing welfare reforms in light of some of the key findings and reflects on these and other policies from the perspective of the families studied. Among the specific policy topics considered are illness and disability, childcare provision, income adequacy and employment, fuel poverty and an integrated set of local services.

A short conclusion draws the book to a close. Its purpose is to take an overview of the main findings in their own right and with reference to the theoretical framework. This is followed by a list of references and two appendices. In the first appendix, the interview schedule is presented and the second outlines the key details of the response rate and the procedures used to equivalise family income.

ONE

Introducing the respondents

This chapter introduces the respondents and outlines key elements of their living situation. The chapter will concentrate mainly on the objective or structural conditions, detailing people's situations with regard to family composition and make-up, economic status, income, housing and health. The chapter also aims to convey a sense of the nature and trajectory of people's lives in order to reveal the roots of their current circumstances. Two types of evidence are presented for this purpose: people's own explanations of how they came to be in their current situation and real-life profiles of circumstances, organised in the form of vignettes. The latter, chosen to represent different situations and intended to give a sense of personal circumstance and trajectory, are presented at different points of the text so as to give greater depth and meaning to the more quantitative information. Key details that might identify people have been omitted from this chapter as elsewhere.

Personal and family characteristics

There were 21 lone-parent families in the sample and 30 couple families. This type of characterisation does not take one very far, however, for to describe any family simply in terms of family structure is to underplay the diversity of what goes to make up the family's situation. These are families with diverse experiences of family life. Of the 30 couples, 26 were married and four were living together unmarried. The couple families involved some 'reconstituted families' where the male partner is not the father of all of the children. This was the case in four families. The lone-parent families, too, were a diverse grouping, with mothers who had never married or lived with a partner (two) and others who became lone parents either through the break-up of a relationship, divorce or separation (18) or widowhood (one). Only one lone father was represented among the study population, reflecting the general societal pattern whereby children being reared by one parent are mainly to be found in lone-mother families.

As mentioned, women were heavily represented among respondents, with some 46 female respondents as against five male respondents. Respondents were spread across the age range, with most aged between 25 and 44 years (Table 1.1). The sample also contained some older parents, however, many of whom were grandparents, so this allows insight into cross-generational relationships. As can be seen from the table, about two-thirds of respondents were living in cities (Belfast or Derry), with the remainder divided between towns and rural localities. All except three respondents were born and bred in Northern Ireland. The three respondents in question migrated to Northern Ireland mainly for relationship reasons. Apart from these only a fraction of people had ever lived outside Northern Ireland.

Table 1.1: Family characteristics

	All (n)	Couple family (n)	Lone-parent family (n)
Family type	51	30	21
Gender			
Male	5	4	1
Female	46	26	20
Age group			
18-24	4	1	3
25-44	37	22	15
45-64	10	7	3
Location			
Urban (large city)	32	15	17
Urban (town)	10	7	3
Rural	9	8	1
Number of dependent children per family			
1	19	7	12
2	18	11	7
3 or more	14	11	3

Thirty-two respondents had two or more dependent children and 14 had three or more. In all, there were some 101 dependent children in respondent families. Family size tends to underline the close relationship between larger family size and increased risk of poverty. It also reflects the fact that Northern Ireland has the highest percentage of families with children of any region of the UK (34% compared with the UK average of 29%). Northern Ireland also has the highest percentage of families with three or more children (5% as opposed to a 3% UK average) (Department for Social Development, 2010). Here as elsewhere, the more children in a family the greater the risk of the family being at the lower end of the income distribution (MacInnes et al, 2013). Around the time this research was carried out, over half of children in Northern Ireland lived in households with incomes in the bottom two quintiles of the income distribution – two-thirds of families with three or more children fell into the bottom two quintiles (Department for Social Development, 2010).

Economic status

Economic status was interpreted as 'in paid work' if the respondent and/or partner had any current labour market attachment, and 'no paid work' if there was no engagement in the labour market. In almost two-thirds of cases (29 families), either the respondent and/or a partner was in paid work. The employment situation was quite diverse, though, including full-time, part-time, short-time (one day a week or less) and time-limited government training schemes such as Steps to Work. The details are set out in Table 1.2. In general, the lower propensity of the adults in lone-mother families to have no engagement with paid work should be noted.

Table 1.2: Economic status of adults

	(n)
Couple family	
Both in full-time work	2
One full time, one part time*	7
One full time, one not in paid work	6
Both in part-time work	2
One in education, one not in paid work	1
One part time, one not in paid work	4
No paid work	8
Total	30
Lone-parent family	
Full-time work	3
Part-time work	3
Education/training	1
No paid work	14
Total	21

* Includes one case where partner is in part-time training.

The vulnerability to job loss and job insecurity is reflected in the high numbers of respondents working in service industries like retail, taxi driving and hairdressing, which are either insecure, stop–gap-type jobs or ones that have seen a general drop in demand since the onset of the recession.

Vignette 1

Joanne is a 48-year-old married mother of three children – she has worked since she was 16 years of age and was made redundant last year. She is totally devastated by the redundancy, describing it as 'the biggest shock of my life'. Her job as a senior manager earned her some £31,000 a year in salary as well as a company car. She had been the main breadwinner for most of her marriage, as her husband was disabled by an accident at work nearly a decade ago. He receives ongoing medical attention and was due to have a serious operation shortly after the interview was conducted in March 2012. Joanne has added responsibility because her husband is, she says, on the autistic disorder spectrum (as is one of her children, who has also been self-harming), and so she is the family's 'social face'. Apart from the family's financial circumstances being affected by the redundancy, she saw her identity as being strongly invested in her job. She has applied for over 100 jobs since being made redundant and has not secured a single interview ('not even for a job on the till at Tescos'). She feels embarrassed and a failure. With the family income plummeting to about 40% of what it formerly was, her redundancy money has been used up, as have all the family's savings just to pay bills, including the mortgage, and keep going. "Now everything is gone", Joanne says. She still has credit card bills and is trying to come to an arrangement with the creditors with the help of the Citizens Advice Bureau. She found it almost impossible to work out the benefit system and the different entitlements and in fact only did so with the active involvement of the Citizens Advice Bureau. In order to keep herself busy, she has thrown herself into volunteer work in the local community. She tries to keep her concern hidden from her children, her husband (of whom she says 'if he worries the world ends') and her wider family and friends. She therefore takes on all the worry and feels relatively isolated with it. She broke down on a number of occasions during the interview. She never thought she would be in this position but she is very proud that she and her husband are still together given all that has happened to them.

Twenty-two families in the sample had no one in paid work but only three of the respondents had never worked at all. The reasons for not being in paid work varied and can be classified as shown in Table 1.3:

Table 1.3: Reasons for not being in paid work

Status	Couple family (n)	Lone-parent family (n)
Looking for work	5	4
Sickness or disability	2	5
Young children/no accessible childcare	1	5
Total	8	14

It will be obvious that the majority of respondents in couple families are currently working or looking for paid work. The situation of the lone-parent respondents in this position is more complicated, in that a third are faced with sickness/disability issues and a further third are not seeking paid work for child(care)-related reasons.

Household income

Table 1.4 sets out the approximate monthly income, after housing costs, for families taking part in the study, as reported by the participants.

Table 1.4: Approximate level of net household monthly income (after housing costs)

Approximate monthly income	All (n)	Couple family (n)	Lone-parent family (n)
Less than £500	3	1	2
£501-£750	13	4	9
£751-£1,000	16	8	8
£1,001-£1,500	16	14	2
£1,501-£2,000	2	2	0
£2,001-£2,500	1	1	0

It will be seen that net family income ranged quite widely, from less than £500 a month up to £2,500. The data also indicates that couple families had generally higher incomes than lone-parent families, unsurprisingly perhaps, given the higher level of labour market engagement by the former. In addition, there was an age gradient. Those in the lowest income band were all aged between 18 and 24 years. This is related especially to the fact that, at the time of the study, personal allowances for all the main welfare benefits for young claimants were some 21% less than for people aged 25 years and over.

Three families had higher than expected income levels (of between £1,500 and £2,500 a month). One of the respondents may have over-estimated her income because during the interview she described how she had just experienced a severe drop in income when she lost eligibility for Working Tax Credit after her recent marriage. The remaining two participants with higher than expected incomes were part of a couple family where both partners worked full time. However, in both cases a large percentage of the income was apportioned to servicing debt that had been incurred when they were earning higher incomes; so while their income was nominally high, the sums they had available were very constrained.

In order to measure poverty, it is customary to adjust household income for family size and to select an income threshold for the purpose of separating those above and below the poverty line. Key to the adjustment process is the use of equivalence scales that adjust household income for different household sizes and composition so that income levels are comparable across households. For example, the more people there are in a household, the more resources are required to maintain an equivalent standard of living – an income of £300 per week for a single person is not equivalent to £300 for a lone parent with two children. The adjustments most widely used in the UK and other countries of the European Union are those of the modified Organisation for Economic Co-operation and Development equivalence scales. The procedure is as follows. Household incomes are divided by household equivalence factors that take account of the number of adults and the number and age of dependants in the household. Two separate scales are usually used – before housing costs and after housing costs. The resultant income is then used to compare the living standards of households (although it is based on the assumption that all individuals within the household experience the same living standards).

In the present study, the 2009/10 equivalisation scales (after housing costs) were used to calculate what the median income would be for households of a similar size to that of respondents. This was then compared with their reported income. The equivalised income below 60% of median household income was taken as the poverty threshold (Department for Social Development, 2011a).

On the basis of these approximations, the majority (53%) of participants had incomes in or around the poverty threshold for the Northern Irish population as a whole in 2009/10. However, 29% of respondents reported their income as being in one income band below the 60% equivalised poverty threshold. Table 1.5 gives an indication of their circumstances. It can be seen that those who are poorest had particular characteristics. The majority had no current attachment to the labour market; lone parents were just slightly more likely to report having the lowest income; and all the poorest families lived in an urban area. There was no particular patterning with regard to numbers of children.

Table 1.5: Families with income considerably below the 60% equivalised poverty threshold

	All	Couple family	Lone-parent family
Below 60%	15	7	8
Families in paid work	3	2	1
No paid work	10	4	6
Disabled	2	1	1
Families with 1 child	7	4	3
Families with 2 children	7	3	4
Families with 3 or more	1		
Urban	15	7	8
Rural	0		

Just under a fifth of families had adjusted household incomes that placed them in one income band above the 60% equivalised poverty threshold. Of the nine families reporting such circumstances, it is noteworthy that eight were couple families and only one of these families had no labour market attachment. The remaining respondent was a lone parent who was also in paid work. While no families living in a rural area reported incomes below the poverty threshold, three families from a rural district reported their income as just a bit above this level.

Vignette 2

John is 61 years old and a father of four children. He has had two families in a way, two young sons and an older son and a daughter in their twenties (who live very close by with their own families). He lives with his wife and two younger children in a local authority house in the city. He is on Disability Living Allowance, being unable to work due to a back injury sustained at work some 15 years ago. Formerly he worked as a driver. John says his total income is in the region of £635 a month. He is very worried about being able to manage the costs of gas, electricity and food and to get by has to have a regular loan from the Provident Society. He is very critical of politicians, both local and national. Locally, areas like his are completely neglected, he says, and nationally he wonders if the current government is trying to kill people with the welfare cuts. He says he feels suicidal sometimes and is on anti-depressants. One of the dominant themes in his interview was the local area. This was reserved for very negative comment: 'it's a dive' and 'people fight each other'. He is thinking of his younger children and others of the same age who have nothing to do locally, other than hang around street corners. He paints a dark picture of the area. Nevertheless, John reports quite good relationships with most people locally and he appears to be well known in the area and to be engaged with what goes on locally. He has a Disability Living Allowance car, which he describes as 'heaven sent', as it allows him a degree of freedom and comfort and also to help family and neighbours out with errands now and again. Other than that, he appears to live a very home-based life.

Table 1.6 sets out the position of respondent families in regard to their connection to the paid labour market and their main source of income (as identified by themselves in response to a question about main source of income). It shows how few respondents can rely on employment alone for their main source of income. The data underlines the crucial nature of provisions such as Tax Credits and their effect on the everyday

Table 1.6: Primary source of income

Source	(n)	%
Employment	3	6
Employment + Tax Credit	23	45
Disability-related benefits	6	12
Means-tested benefits (Income Support/Job Seekers Allowance)*	19	37
Total	51	100

* Includes one respondent in full-time education.

lives of low-income families – 45% of the sample relied on Working Tax Credit and/or Child Tax Credit to supplement the income they received from labour market sources.

Only three families reported relying on employment alone for their income. In two of these families, both partners were working full time and the third was a lone parent working full time. For over a third of families, the main source of income was means-tested benefits such as Jobseekers Allowance or Income Support. One wonders about how these families are faring in the current climate of widespread welfare reform, with the majority of means-tested and tax credit benefits for working-age claimants due to be phased out with the introduction of Universal Credit (UC) from 2014 on. The scale of the planned reforms, the ambitious time schedule and the uncertainty surrounding the implementation and administration of UC are to be noted given the critical role played by these benefits in the lives of these low-income families.

Housing tenure

The majority of respondents lived in rented accommodation, with nearly four out of every 10 in social rented housing (renting from the Housing Executive/Housing Association) and a fifth in accommodation rented from a private landlord (Table 1.7). The relatively high numbers in the latter situation can be taken to reflect the significant changes over time in housing tenure in Northern Ireland, the effect of which is to bring about an increase in the private-rented sector (Northern Ireland Housing Executive, 2011). In the province as a whole, lone-parent households are highly represented in this sector, with 37% of all lone-parent households in Northern Ireland renting privately (Northern Ireland Housing Executive, 2011); in the current study, almost even numbers of couple and lone-parent families were renting from a private

Table 1.7: Housing tenure

Housing tenure	(n)	%
Owned outright	1	2
Buying with mortgage	17	33
Renting from housing executive	18	35
Renting from housing association	2	4
Renting from private landlord	11	22
Living with parents	2	4

landlord. The number of households in the private-rented sector in receipt of Housing Benefit in Northern Ireland doubled between 2001 and 2006, making Housing Benefit increasingly significant for normalising this form of housing situation. The profile of the private-rented sector is also characterised by an over-representation of unemployed tenants, with 19% of Household Reference Persons being unemployed compared with 8% in the total housing stock (Gray and McAnulty, 2009).

Making up the remainder of respondents were some 17 who were buying their home through a mortgage, one who had already done so and two who had moved back in with their parents (in both cases lone mothers) because they were waiting to be housed by the authorities and could not afford to rent privately.

Rents are higher in the private-rented sector than they are in the social housing sector, resulting in the majority of tenants in receipt of Housing Benefit who are renting privately having to make up the shortfall between what they receive in Housing Benefit and the rent they have to pay. Such a shortfall has risen year on year and was recently estimated at £20 a week (Gray and McAnulty, 2009). Entitlement to Housing Benefit for people who rent privately is decided using Local Housing Allowance rates and is based on rent levels in the area in which a person lives. As of January 2012, the Local Housing Allowance rates were reduced to cover only rents in the bottom 30% of local rents. For the beneficiary, this means having to make up an even greater shortfall than formerly. For families with children who have seen their Child Benefit frozen for three years, it means their rent takes up a greater proportion of an ever-decreasing income. This was exemplified by a number of respondents whose main struggles focused primarily on housing, as will be clear as the analysis of the findings progresses.

Vignette 3

Ruth is a 25-year-old mother of two young children, aged six and three years. She is now a lone mother – she had been married but the relationship was a very violent one and she made what was for her a very hard decision and left her husband two years ago. She describes him as the children's father (rather than her husband) and frames her decision to leave in terms of 'keeping my children and myself safe'. She says, "My story started from two years ago." While she was in the marital home, money was not a problem. Her husband worked and they had a good standard of living. She said she knew it was going to be difficult being a single parent but is still wracked by guilt about whether she has done the right thing for her children. The split from the children's father has turned very acrimonious and over the course of it he asked for a DNA test to prove paternity. She has therefore had to go to court. The children's father has refused to pay maintenance. She worries about the impact of all of this on her son especially, who at six years of age she feels is old enough to know what is happening. He is being tested for attention deficit hyperactivity disorder (ADHD), being very behind at school. Ruth now lives on benefits. Her income is very low, mainly because she has to pay a large amount of it in rent to make up the shortfall in Housing Benefit. After paying the rent she has about £500 a month for everything else. She is embarrassed because she has no money and cannot give her children what other children get. The weight of the responsibility she feels for the children is almost palpable. She said she had contemplated suicide because of the money situation. As well as skipping meals herself, there are days when she has no food and has to ask her parents if she can go to their house to eat. Her parents do not have much money either. She is conscious also that both have mental health-related problems and her mother's condition in particular means that she cannot have the children in her company for long. Ruth feels people look down on her because she is on benefits. Her doctor recommended she attend the local women's group. She said members have been a great help to her and other than the group she is quite isolated. Looking to the future, she feels poorly educated and ill equipped to face the jobs market and yet feels she cannot live any kind of life with only £500 a month to keep a family of three going.

Health

Respondents were asked how they rated their general health. Table 1.8 shows that the majority reported their health as either good (43%) or very good (31%). Only four considered their health as 'bad' and a further nine rated it as 'fair'.

Table 1.8: Evaluation of own health

	(n)	%
Very good	16	31
Good	22	43
Fair	9	18
Bad	4	8

This is at odds with the way people discussed and evaluated their health over the course of their interview. In fact, on the basis of the latter information, only 20 of the 51 respondents do not have a serious health problem, making ill health a widespread experience among the sample. People suffer from both mental and physical ill health. Seventeen respondents reported experiencing depression and two had attempted suicide. Respondents also report a range of problems relating to physical health – including back- and joint-related illnesses, asthma and anaemia. The poor health of partners also emerged during interview, with serious conditions such as heart disease, high blood pressure, brain injury and cancer being reported.

The discrepancy between people's evaluations of their health and their actual health reflects people's views of their situation and the degree of priority they attach to their personal well-being. It was not uncommon for a respondent to reveal but then discount psychological problems such as depression, anxiety and stress. For example, this is the response from Cathy, lone mother to two small children, when asked how she would rate her health:

> 'Ach, it's alright. It's good. It's not like I'm really bad or anything. I'm good, I'm alright. I'm on depression tablets and all, like, but I still have to get up and do things and take it day by day. I'm on depression tablets because of stress and stuff.'

Another participant (Marie who is rearing one child alone) replied that her health was 'very good' but during the interview spoke about having depression and explained how she tried to manage it. The situation had been so bad that at one stage she had called the Samaritans:

> 'I can get depressed at times, have had depression…. I don't allow myself to dwell on it too much because that's what happened before and that's how I got depressed. So, if I find myself dwelling too much on things I just have to be really hard and blank it out and start thinking about something stupid or something frivolous. That's my way.'

These two quotes give a strong sense of how respondents either discounted their own health-related problems or used cognitive means to try to control 'bad feelings'.

Two respondents brought up the matter of their suicidal thoughts. In both instances, financial insecurity coupled with a strong sense of insurmountable difficulty without any possibility of intervention to change the situation (despite in the first case the existence of good family support) is at the root of such thoughts. The first quote below is from John, an older interviewee who has a disability (and whose story is set out in Vignette 2 above), and the second from Ruth (Vignette 3), a young lone parent with two small children (who is responding to the question of what helps her to keep going):

> 'Depressed. Nobody about, nobody here to help you. As I said before, the politicians are doing nothing for us. But we have good family support, no doubt about it. I know that for a fact, great family support. I'll say it again, we help one another out but what do you do if the money's not there? Do you go and plan a robbery or something like that? And that's the way it's going to get with the way this government's going. They're bringing in pension cuts, they're looking at the DLA [Disability Living Allowance] to review it. I could get a letter any day to say I'm off the DLA and what do I do – throw a rope up? That's the way people's going to think ... throw a rope up.'

> My children, 'cause I'm the only carer they see, I'm the only person in their wee lives.... And they're the only ones keeping me here, they're the only ones keeping me here 'cause I've had suicidal thoughts about ... financially can't cope... financially it's been hard so I feel as if I don't even want to be here 'cause I can't provide properly for the children. It's got me on a low end where I just feel I can't do it no more. I just can't cope you know.'

Another very striking health–related finding is the number of references to the existence of poor health among children. While the study did not set out specifically to explore this, the evidence reveals that in 16 families at least one child had health-related difficulties and in two families more than one child had a health-related condition. The main conditions included chronic conditions such as Crohn's disease, diabetes and asthma as well as behavioural and developmental conditions such as ADHD and Asperger's Syndrome or autism. In a few cases, children had multiple problems. More than a quarter of people interviewed spontaneously brought up their children's health problems (although not always framing it as a 'problem').

Vignette 4

Roisin is a grandmother in her late 40s. She lives in a large town with her husband and severely disabled daughter. A non-dependent child lives at home also, and her eldest daughter and grandchildren live close by. Life has not been gentle on Roisin and the word 'carer' does not go far enough to describe her. She has lived with a painful debilitating auto-immune disease since her 20s that means that she has been unable to continue working. There is a poignancy in the way she describes her condition as 'cutting her short' and how her career 'was just taken away like that'. She is fiercely protective of her daughter, especially when they go out and other people stare at her but it is, she admits, emotionally draining. As her daughter gets older, her physical needs are becoming more complex and Roisin's husband has had to give up his job because Roisin is no longer able to cope with the physical demands – 'it's like having a 17 year old baby' is the way she describes it. This means that the family now solely depends on disability benefits and Tax Credits to get by. Financially it is a struggle but paid employment is not an option for either of them. In addition Roisin's elderly mother lives alone and has dementia. Roisin provides almost daily care for her along with care for her daughter. She fears that her mother may soon be incapable of living alone and is consumed with guilt at the thought that she might have to go into residential care. Her grandchildren are a source of pride and joy and she helps her daughter as much as she can with babysitting and childminding. But even here, Roisin feels guilty because she feels she is not providing her eldest daughter with as much help as she would like to. A major worry for Roisin at the time of interview was that when her disabled daughter reached 18 years she would come into the domain of adult social services. From what Roisin has been told, the demand for adult services is more acute and acquiring these services demands a high level of assertiveness. As Roisin says, "I haven't the energy to shout any more, do any more, fight any more."

There is a broader context for all of this revealed by existing evidence. Some of this is national or indeed global and some is specific to Northern Ireland.

Internationally, there is a well-established body of work regarding the association between poverty and levels of mental ill health, particularly in high-income countries where large inequalities in wealth exist (Pickett et al, 2006; Wilkinson and Pickett, 2006; 2009). The association between being born into families experiencing poverty and deprivation and a high incidence of poor health and outcomes in later life is well established (Dyson et al, 2010; Marmot Review, 2010; Bradshaw, 2011; Child Poverty Action Group, 2012). Taking a more local Northern Irish lens, there is evidence to suggest that health outcomes are worse in areas of high deprivation as compared with the region as a whole. For example, the prevalence of mood and anxiety disorders in the most deprived areas in Northern Ireland was two-fifths higher than the regional average, with the rate for the most deprived areas being three-quarters higher than the least deprived areas (Department of Health, Social Services and Public Safety, 2012). In regard to children, the scale of child ill heath found in this study is somewhat unexpected and higher than what the existing evidence indicates. The *Health Survey Northern Ireland* reports that in the majority of cases (94%), parents evaluated their children's health as good or very good (Department of Health, Social Services and Public Safety, 2011).

Ill health extends wider still in respondents' families, however. In addition to respondents' own health problems and the poor health of children in some families, ill health and disability was also part of the health picture of the wider family network for many. Almost a third of respondents raised the matter of the poor health condition of other family members over the course of the interview. In regard to parents and siblings, for example, difficulties mentioned included alcoholism, arthritis and diabetes. In two cases, both the respondent's mother and father were suffering from limiting health conditions. There were also a number of cases of congenital mental or physical conditions reported among siblings. Taking the situation of the wider family into account, just a fifth of all respondents had no serious health-related problems in their immediate and wider family. Poor health was a fact of life for the vast majority of respondents.

Vignette 5

Marie is a lone mother in her late forties. A city dweller, her family consists of a son aged 18 and a daughter aged 21 (who has been working for the past three months). She has always been a single parent, she says. She has a partner who is not the father of the children but they do not live together. He does not help her financially but occasionally buys her 'treats' (like a haircut). Her income comes exclusively from benefits and it is, she says, in the region of £750 a month. She finds she can just about manage if she budgets very carefully. Marie's story is dominated by her son who has Asperger's Syndrome and ADHD. He is attending college now and seems stable but his condition has stamped its imprint on her life and she has had to live through many crises on his part, such as involvement in petty crime, suspension from school, and a suicide attempt. She worries constantly about him and found it extremely difficult to manage his behaviour when he was growing up – he rejected the diagnosis once they finally got it and she says she has had to cajole him into accepting it. Having to manage her son's condition has brought out some strengths in her, though. She has learned about his condition, for example, and is adjusting his medication to 'wean him off the tablets' (with the approval of his doctor) as she thinks best. But generally she felt quite alone with the situation and suffers from depression. On one occasion, she even called the Samaritans for advice. She lives quite an indoors life – she has no friends to speak of, except one with whom she keeps in infrequent contact, she is not close to her family and has no ties to the local community. Other than her partner and her daughter, she has little or no support. Now that her son is in college, she expects her income to fall by half as she will no longer receive different benefits for him since he will no longer be classified as a dependant. She is extremely worried about this and has been trying to get some skills and work experience. Her daughter works in a shop and Marie has been doing some volunteer work there, expressly with the hope of getting some basic training and something to put on her CV (which is, she says, 'empty' because she has not worked in 18 years).

How did people get into their current situation?

One aim of this chapter is to ask why some people experience more extreme forms of deprivation than others and to gain a sense of the trajectories involved. Highlighting associations or relationships can help build more complex explanations for why such patterns occur and alert us to the interrelationships among contributory factors (Spencer et al, 2003). Trajectories into and out of poverty have been a major focus of recent poverty research; this has been especially facilitated by the availability of longitudinal panel data (Gardiner and Hills, 1999; Jenkins and Rigg, 2001; Marsh and Vegeris, 2004). A central concept here is that of transition highlighting a movement from one situation to another. Research often focuses on identifying so-called 'trigger events' associated with major life-course paths. For example, there is a body of work examining people's employment trajectories and experiences from benefit receipt to employment (Dean and Shah, 2002; Millar, 2007; Barnes et al, 2011; Sissons et al, 2011).

Taking the study population as a whole, we estimate that no more than a fifth of families could be said to be 'OK' in terms of being able to manage on their income. These families were set apart from the rest by virtue of the extent of their income from employment. Almost all had someone in paid work and some had two workers. Apart from these, two-fifths of families lived in a situation of quite severe deprivation. These had just about enough to manage on a weekly basis but over time their financial resources were insufficient and they were depleting the resources that they had by using them just to survive or get by from day to day. They were a diverse group and a range of factors rendered them vulnerable. Disability and/or ill health was a primary factor, as was unemployment and under-employment.

The remaining third of families could be said to be experiencing more intense forms of hardship as compared with other families. These 'worst-off families' were distinguished by both the nature and extent of the deprivation experienced. For example, while the high cost of food was raised by all respondents and almost everyone interviewed reported buying cheaper brands and lower-quality food, the worst-off families reported not being able to afford food and having to resort to family support networks for help to feed children on a regular basis (see Chapter Five).

The struggles faced by these worst-off respondents stem from a combination of factors. Most typically there is a 'toxic cocktail' of low-paid or no employment, an accumulation of debt and an inability to increase income through employment either due to the unavailability of suitable work or because of the presence of disability or ill health in the family. As mentioned, 31 respondents had a disabled or ill family member in their own household, including, in 16 cases, children with health, behavioural or other difficulties. A further 10 respondents had at least one member of their non-resident family who was ill or disabled (typically a parent or sibling). Care-related responsibilities and demands were therefore very common in these families. Among other factors making for hardship was debt, one family was dependent on what the wife and mother could earn, for example, because the entire earnings of the husband/father went to paying back debts accrued through the purchase of property at a time when property was seen as a high-yielding investment. In these and other families, financial pressure caused by routine expenses such as the children's school uniforms, school dinners and bus fares may make the difference between being able to function at an adequate level and barely surviving.

A good example is the assessment made by Lily (a young partnered mother of one child who was expecting a second baby), who needed to borrow £3.50 for transport to get to work:

> 'If you haven't got enough money to get to work, you haven't got enough money – you know what I mean?'

Lone parents were over-represented among the most hard-hit families. This and other results of the study underline the vulnerability of many such families. For example, more lone parents evaluated their health as either 'fair' or 'bad' compared with families with partnered parents and they were more likely to experience deprivation. Mental health conditions, in particular depression and nervous anxiety, were common illnesses among this group of participants.

The quality of employment rather than employment itself has been found to be a key factor in protecting people from recurrent poverty (Tomlinson and Walker, 2010) and this is the case in this study also. The fact that in the general population over half of all poor children have someone in employment in their household (Department for Social Development, 2010) strengthens this finding.

During interview, many respondents mentioned events that had precipitated a change in their circumstances. In the following example, Ruth, a lone mother, is describing how her situation was more financially secure when she was married but changed when she had had to leave her violent partner:

> 'My husband worked when I was with him so we were financially stable as a family, but because of my situation I needed to get out of it for my children and that's where it went downhill. But I wouldn't change it for the world because I needed to get my children out of that and I needed to get myself out of that situation.... I knew the sort of things that could be in front of me as a single parent, as low income is what you get ... but my children's the most important here and their welfare is what I was thinking of at that time.'

Lone motherhood is of course a well-known poverty-related trajectory. Katy, who had a teenage daughter living at home and three older children in their 20s, and who had been married once and also had experience of being in a long-term partnership, spoke in detail about the financial struggles she faced bringing up a family without a reliable male income. Her husband's departure was sudden; during the interview she explained how she had gone from being part of a couple to being a lone parent overnight when her husband 'went to a football match and never came back'.

A third significant life event with a strong association with poverty is the onset of a disability or serious illness. This can act as a turning point and set the pattern for disadvantage or deprivation for years to come. As mentioned, nearly two-thirds of families in this study are affected by disability or serious illness. For Roisin, the onset of a severe auto-immune disease at an early age changed the course of her life by ending her chosen working career and severely limiting her earning power, which contributed to experiences of impoverishment in later years (Vignette 4). Life had changed for another respondent, Sheila (a married mother in her late 40s with one dependent child and another aged 20 years), when her husband had an accident, leaving him physically damaged and mentally scarred. This meant not only that he could not earn but that he had become for her another mouth to feed.

It is important to bear in mind, however, that there was a lot of variation in the range of experiences reported and that the trajectories highlighted here fail to capture the individual and unique features of people's lives.

Overview

One-third of the families represented in the study could be said to be in severe financial hardship. Nearly half of these families had some attachment to the labour market – indeed, in two cases both partners were working. Hence employment per se does not offer a defence against financial need. While inadequate income was the overarching facet of deprivation and social exclusion, the situation of families was exacerbated by a high prevalence of health-related difficulties that not only made demands on people's time and other resources but created problems in accessing well-paid work. Lone parents' situation was generally worse than that of two-parent families; contributory factors here included the level of income available to single parents outside of the labour market (employment being inaccessible to many because their children are young or because of the unavailability or unaffordability of childcare) and lone parents' relatively greater propensity to report ill health.

While people's current income situation was roughly similar, the trajectories to their current situation varied. For some, people it was a failed marriage or partner relationship that was the initial trigger; for others, it was illness or an accident, or it was rearing one or more children outside of a relationship; and for others still it was the absence of the capacity or resources to earn a decent income through employment that first catapulted them into low income. While one factor may be the initial trigger, these families face accumulation of problems and difficulties that mount over time.

TWO

Family life through an economic lens

This chapter probes the everyday reality of lives marked by the background facts presented in the last chapter. Family as a unit of expenditure and consumption will be examined in detail. In many ways, money is the leading actor in this chapter and it is treated in both an existential and factual manner. The chapter opens by first outlining how money and spending are viewed and organised and where the priorities lie in these regards. This leads to a discussion of how people organise their essential spending, especially that on utilities and food. The chapter then moves on to consider more existential elements, detailing how money is part of individual psyche and family frames of reference. Having set out how large money looms in individual and family life, the remainder of the chapter enquires into the organisation of finances, the distribution of resources and the general patterning and practices of family life in these regards. These are important in their own right, but they are especially interesting for what they reveal about the tasks and rituals associated with the maintenance and governance of family life. We learn about the main priorities of the family budget and see what the major pressure points are in terms of competing pulls on financial resources. In essence, the chapter investigates not just budgeting practices but the extent to which these are affected by relational considerations. The chapter is therefore (like all the others) a mixture of fact and orientation.

Money and need

Respondents spoke at length – and with great fluency – about how they try to make ends meet. Words such as 'stretching', 'balancing' and 'minimising' peppered their conversations. The evidence makes clear that money management in a situation of low income is very intense. Here is a quote from Sheila, a married mother of one child aged 14 years and another aged 20, that conveys a sense of the constant mindfulness involved:

> 'You are always trying to think ahead, what you have that can be put aside. "OK, there's that and there's that."'...

You're so conscious of trying to ensure that you're utilising everything so that you can maximise what everyone else has.'

The following quote, from Lizzie, a lone mother with four children all aged under 17 years, gives a good sense of the mind play and resolve required.

'We're getting by. OK, we have to put aside wee things for a good week and on a bad week run to Mammy but do you know what? It's balancing it. It's knowing what you can have and what you can't have and if you can't have it you can save up for it. And it's setting aside. And it's giving you a good input. You're not running and being stupid with the money. It's OK to balance your money and it's OK to say, "No I can't get that." Because you're not full of yourself, going "I'm getting this," and "I'm getting that."'

In these few sentences alone, mention is made of doing without, saving up, setting aside and getting help from her mother. There is also an existentialist set of references: about not 'being stupid' or 'full of yourself'. And not only does Lizzie recognise scarcity's moral 'benefits' in terms of self-denial and character development, but she goes on to say that it is good for her children also to know that she (and they) have to save up for something. 'It balances them', is how she phrases it.

Austerity is the financial regime prevailing in these families. There is a sense in which the money is already spent before it is received. As Lily, a partnered mother of one child, put it: "All my money's wrapped up in bills and food." Moreover, as in other studies (Hamilton, 2012; Harrison, 2013; Hickman et al, 2014), respondents show stoicism and considerable resourcefulness in responding to their financial situation. The evidence confirms that poverty ratchets up the personal and social skills required to undertake successfully the basic tasks of domestic financial management (Walker and Collins, 2004, p 205).

Budgeting takes time, know-how and patience (Walker and Collins, 2004; Patrick, 2014). There is very little margin for error. Katy, a lone mother in her 40s with a daughter aged 16 years, put it as follows:

'You are always watching. You never have any freedom to make a mistake. You can't afford to have a wee wobbler and buy that extra wee thing because next week you suffer for it. So there's always the consequence for everything that you do and you have to be aware of that all the time.'

She then went on to explain:

> 'Monday to Monday is fine. If you have to do without, you're only doing without a day or two but if you make a mistake one Monday when you're paid fortnightly, you've a full two weeks so it throws you into a whole different set of stuff.'

Both of the quotes draw attention to how when living on low income one is faced with the consequences of one's actions more or less immediately. The contrast to the general societal practice of an increasingly more indirect relationship with money and its spending (through the use of credit, bank or other cards and online shopping for example) is very striking.

About two-thirds of respondents reported that they could not make ends meet on their existing income. One consequence of this is that there were days in the week when they had no money left. This was the case for both lone-parent and two-parent families, but it was more likely to be the case in lone-parent families. It is important to note that almost half of those who experienced days without money were in employment, although their links to the labour market varied, ranging from partial employment to a mixture of full-time and part-time paid work. As outlined in the last chapter, there were varied and sometimes complex reasons for the variation in working patterns. Included especially were situations where families had to reduce or tightly organise their working hours due to extra caring responsibilities associated with the illness or disability of a family member or the arrival of a new baby.

Low income in a context of high need was the main reason for money shortages. In fact, shortage of money to meet need has to have centre stage in any explanation of these families' situation. But 'need' is not simple or uni-dimensional. Many of the families had multiple needs. As Chapter One showed, they experienced disability and illness to a far greater extent than is the case for the population as a whole. Moreover, there were often other specific factors at play, such as paying a heavy mortgage or a high rent. But not being able to make ends meet was also caused by situations or expenses that might be regarded as routine – such as the extra expense of maintaining a car, which was essential for Maura who was employed in a call centre 20 miles from her home and regularly worked night shifts when no public transport was available. The car depleted her resources so much that she was close to the poverty line.

The remaining third of families that did not experience days in the week with no money characterised their situation as 'just about getting by'. Some families talked about having a few pounds left over – as Sarah (a 40-year-old mother of two teenage children, who lived with her husband and children in a rural area) explained: "I always make sure I've a couple of pound of loose change." However, such small amounts were only notionally left over, since they were usually used to give a small margin of comfort around future costs of essentials (most commonly by buying saving stamps for oil or electricity or gas).

Money and the rhythms and moods of family life

Money is not just a backdrop to family life; it is interwoven into everyday family life. It was ever present to a degree that is hard to understand by those outside the situation. It is no exaggeration to say that money exerted an iron grip on these families. The narratives are threaded through by money-related considerations to such an extent that one could say that daily life was to all intents and purposes 'monetised'. Let us consider what this means.

In effect, money defined the practices and rituals of family life in fundamental ways. One could speak of 'money rhythms'. These are daily and weekly but fan out also to encompass the entire year.

The daily/weekly cycle started for respondents not with a specific named day but when they received their money – with those receiving benefits also describing this as when they got 'paid'. For most people – recall that most of these families received some income from state benefits and about a half had no other income source – their money pattern was a mix of weekly and fortnightly arrangements. Child Benefit and Tax Credits were at the time of study paid on a weekly basis and the main social security benefits – most widely, Income Support and Job Seekers Allowance – on a fortnightly basis.[1]

---

[1]   The method of payment of the main income-based benefits was changed in 2009 under the Department for Work and Pension's 'periodicity programme' from being paid weekly to being paid fortnightly. This is due to change again with the introduction of Universal Credit (see Chapter Eight). At the time of the study, the benefit system had a degree of variation and flexibility built into it as regards the scheduling of payments. Child Benefit was normally paid every four weeks but could be paid weekly by special arrangement in circumstances of household income constraint. Tax Credits were usually paid every four weeks also or weekly if requested by the claimant. Almost every family in the study chose to have their Child

As is clear from the following quote from Rachel, a lone mother who was working part time and whose pay, together with some benefits, formed the main source of her income, people mark out the different days of the week through the availability or supply of money:

'Well … I have no money on a Monday. I have to borrow the money for his school dinners on a Monday. By the time Tuesday comes I have my bills and stuff to pay out, so when the money comes in it all goes out again on a Tuesday. Then, by Wednesday again I've no money, so I would probably have to borrow something to get through Wednesday. Then I would get paid on a Thursday, but by the time I take out my travel expenses to work and pay back whatever I owe out it's back to Mondays with no money again.'

The association between days of the week and money was repeated over and over again in people's narratives. Days were described as 'scarce' or 'short', and there was a striking regularity to the weekly cycle, which went from receiving, spending and then being either broke or down to only emergency funds until the next payment. The latter was a weekly occurrence for nearly two-thirds of respondent families.

There is a sense in which low income becomes part of one's psyche. Katy (unemployed lone mother of one teenage girl) explained how, on a bad day, when she needed a strong cup of tea she kept the teabag in her cup for longer, thereby foregoing the possibility of reusing it. On a good money day, she would just dip it in and out and keep it for further use. This became a social ritual also in that when family or friends called to visit she would attempt to gauge their disposition with the question, "Is this a teabag-in day or a teabag-out day?"

The absence of money on particular days could mean that the family made no public appearances on those days. One woman described what the family did on such days as 'hibernating in the house'. One could also describe them as 'lost days' in the sense that they are a form of putting down time, trying to get through the day waiting for the next day or

Benefit and Tax Credits paid on a weekly basis. This preference for weekly payment was seen by respondents as enabling people to put a feasible budgeting strategy in place and especially to give them regular access to money and protect against unexpected occurrences and expenses. They were effectively 'bridging' their access to money to avoid periods with too much and too little money.

days when the money will come into their accounts again. This is the voice of Mary, a lone mother of two children aged 16 and 12 years:

> 'I work it out until I come to Sunday and then it doesn't matter if I have no money on a Sunday because I get my money on a Monday morning. So Sunday you don't need any money – just to get the kids out to school on Monday morning.'

For some people, the money rhythm was monthly. Just read Conor's account (he was unemployed with one child and his partner worked one day a week). He starts by describing looking at the calendar on that day, which was the 23rd of the month:

> 'I've a loan of £100 due on the 15th of every month so I'll be looking ahead always to see if my benefits come in because they come in fortnightly and I need to make sure if I get my fortnightly benefits next week that I have the money left to pay that direct debit on the 15th ... because when you get your two weeks' money you think, "I'll go and get this and I'll go and get that" and then you check the calendar and think, "What did I do? I have that coming out on the 15th."'

It is striking how large the payment of £100 looms in his calendar as well as his thoughts and actions.

Money issues may fan out to frame the entire year. The following is how Lizzie (a lone mother with four children) saw the year:

> 'I think you have more bad weeks in the winter than you do in the summer basically because you are not turning on the heating as much. So I'll always find I can buy more clothes in the summer for the kids and myself than in the winter where you have heating and also Christmas. So you're finding it hard in October, November, December, January, February. Come spring you are getting out of your debt from Christmas but you are also coming into summer.'

And Cathy (a lone mother with two young children):

'It's one thing after everything. It's like you get them back
to school – it's school uniforms. And then it's Christmas ...
and then it's Easter. It's like a circle, you go round and round.'

As might be expected given the regularity of people's income,
different days and even weeks were associated with particular moods
or emotional reactions according to the availability of money. People
differentiated between their 'good week' and their 'bad week' in terms
of income. The good week was when they got paid their wages or main
benefits (such as Income Support or Job Seekers Allowance); the bad
week was the week when they got only the benefits that are intended
as subsidiary means (Child Benefit, Tax Credits). Here is how Katy,
an unemployed lone mother with a daughter aged 16 years, put it:

'Good days are fridge full, oil in the tank and nobody sick.
Bad days would be an over-run on the phone bill because
you have been socialising on it ... or the oil is running out.'

It is not only the money but how it translates into a sense of relative
calm or unease about being able to maintain family life that we see as
at the root here. To use a colloquial term, it could be said that money
gets into one's head. How, then, do people use money?

Family expenditure and consumption patterns

In the rational economy, three priorities had first call on the family
income: utilities, rent/mortgage and food. This is more or less a
universal finding, suggesting a patterning of budgeting first for essentials
that are conceived as being of three main types. Moreover, people
engaged in the earmarking of money – designating certain monies for
particular purposes and thereby not only setting particular funds out
as distinct, but constructing rituals and rules about their use (Zelizer,
1994).

Fuel and utilities dominated, especially given their rising and hence
unpredictable cost. The majority of families used electric and/or gas
pay-as-you-go meters and had a very precise idea of how much of their
money was consumed by these machines. 'Consumption' is the right
concept here – people conveyed a sense of these machines as 'eating'
their money. One woman described the machine as 'singing' when it
ran out of money. The rising costs of these commodities was a source
of widespread comment and concern and money was continuously
being set aside so as not to 'risk' the meter running out of money.

People were constantly involved in trying to 'beat the meter' and had a whole range of strategies to adjust their fuel consumption and restrict it. The most common form of saving on heating was to restrict it and the main metric in this regard was around the presence of children: the heating was on mainly when the children were at home and off when they were not. Hence, the heating routine was closely patterned on the school day: the heating would be on for a short time in the morning before the children went to school and on again when they were at home after school. In effect, many of these parents regarded heating as a collective good, especially in regard to children's well-being. For parents at home, then, donning extra layers of clothing to keep warm was the most common strategy for saving on heating. The sense of prioritising the children and of deprioritising self when it came to heating shone through many accounts and shows how moral elements saturate otherwise rational calculations. This is clear from Heather's comments. With two small children and another on the way, she considers heating the house for just herself and her husband as 'wasting it':

> 'I would rather sit with a jumper on when the kids are at school rather than turn my heating on 'cause you're just wasting it. It's different if the kids are in. I need it on then but me and him can sort of put jumpers on and layer up. I wouldn't have it blasting if it was just us in the house.'

Staying out of the house during the day to save on electricity was a saving strategy employed by more than a few respondents. One young couple and their eighteen-month-old baby told how they would go out for a very long walk or walk around the supermarket and the local shopping precinct; as Lena (unemployed, as was her partner) explained: "If we stay in the house obviously we use electric somehow."

Possessing a good but not being able to use it emerges from this study as a significant form of deprivation. People constantly self-censored their use of different goods and utilities. One woman (Susan, who had three children aged under seven, one of whom had ADHD) felt she over-used the clothes' dryer and castigated herself: "I'm terrible for using the tumble dryer."

Rent or mortgage was the second priority in the rational economy. People did not comment much on this, other than to point out how expensive they found their housing costs. The general lack of comment on housing costs was also due to the fact that it was seen as a necessary expenditure and one that they could not change in any way – for example, they could not vary the amount they paid as their circumstances changed. It was fixed in another way as well – not subject to seasonal variation.

As compared with heating and rent or mortgage, people exercised far more agency over their third essential type of financial outlay: food purchases. This was the area where people felt they had most leeway to make cut-backs. The interview narratives reveal how the vast majority of respondents strategised around food purchase. This started before they even went shopping. Some had strict rules, some made lists, and a small few even kept a diary around food consumption and shopping. To be 'thrifty', people employed both general strategies when shopping – such as Peter (unemployed father of two young children whose wife worked full time), who said he and his wife did not look at the brand name of the item but just at the price when they shopped for food – and specific strategies. The most commonly recounted examples of the latter included buying staples in larger quantities, availing of special offers even when the produce in question was out of season, taking the smallest trolley or basket, maximising the use of promotions such as buy-one-get-one-free, looking for food that was reduced in price because it had reached or was close to its sell-by date (and going early in the morning or near closing time for this purpose), shopping at cheaper shops and stocking up on frozen foods, especially when they were on offer. These are all strategies that have also been identified by other research on families living in a low-income situation (Kempson, 1996; Daly and Leonard, 2002; McKendrick et al, 2003; Flaherty, 2008; Flint, 2010).

The food was usually purchased for the week in one large shopping trip. As well as having the advantages of cutting down on transport costs and keeping an overview of spending on food, this pattern established the norm among family members that the available food had to stretch for the week. People reported purchasing more or less the same food all of the time. The regularity of their pattern made them very aware both of what they were getting for their money and what they were feeding their families. Although precise amounts of money were not discussed in great detail, it was clear that respondents had prices at their fingertips. They were also very conscious of how much food was consumed in the family. Similar to the findings of other studies (McKendrick et al, 2003; Horgan, 2007), these respondents felt they were better able to manage and control the food consumption of their younger children as compared with those who were older. This was not only a matter of food preferences, but was also about the amount of food. Older children were seen to eat like adults. This led to parents constantly trying to manage the food consumption of teenagers. Notions of what is a fair distribution of the available food were part of the everyday reality of family life. Families with older children seemed to struggle more.

Thriftiness was especially applied to the use of food and its purchase (Cappellini and Parsons, 2012). Emma, who had three young children and who was unemployed as was her husband, put it as follows: "You are not just lifting [items off shelves], you're thinking, 'Do I need teabags or will they do another week?'" This sense of mental pressure was very strong in some interviews, Sheila explains: "With Christmas you're thinking, 'I have to get that out of the way,' then when it is over, you're 'OK, what's next? I have to get that sorted, that organised.'"

The interviews give a strong sense that most people purchased food that would be cooked, rather than, say, readymade meals. However, this varied somewhat by age, with the younger respondents pointing out that they were still learning how to be economical when it came to food and its usages. Among the older respondents and those with larger families, though, cooking strategies were prominent as a form of cost containment – in this context, people valued preparing meals that would last for more than one day such as stews, casseroles and soups. Such meals also had the advantage that they could be shared with members of the wider family. Cathy, lone mother of two young children, told of inviting her family with the words: "I am sticking on a big pot of stew, want to come?" Using food in this way allowed people to extend hospitality that they could otherwise not afford, although some had to cope with the consequence of their children hating such one-pot meals. The latter underlines how managing family members' food likes and dislikes is an integral part of coping in low-income households (indeed in all households) (Cappellini and Parsons, 2012), and that even the children have to do their bit by accepting food that they do not necessarily like.

People showed great resourcefulness. Lizzie, lone mother of four children aged under 17 years, describes how on the days when she has no money left she "goes to the back of the cupboard where you have never been … or to the bottom of the freezer for the food that's been there for weeks … or for the tin of beans at the back of the fridge …. going 'til the cupboard is bare". Katy's family even had a name for the kind of dinner that would be produced in these circumstances: they called it 'a bitz of a dinner', whereby Katy would go to the freezer and take out everything that was in it, defrost it, cook it and serve it for the next two days. This, Katy explained, meant that the family could be eating pizza and cabbage or two sausages with a fish finger.

Not only were food and cooking objectified through strict control and management, they were also a source of learning and skill development. Food and diet were among the most common themes when people talked about how they were getting by and what skills they saw themselves using and developing. Much of this brought a sense of self-achievement. Scouring for bargains and being able to make good food for their children out of limited means were particular sources of pride and self-worth. People prided themselves also on their food-budgeting skills. Two respondents commented on how there was nothing on a recent television programme about saving money – Superscrimpers – that they were not already doing.

For almost a fifth of families, the strategies employed to save on food bills were more extreme than cutting back. In these instances, getting fed by other family members – especially parents – was a common recourse. For example, here is how Lily, a young expectant mother with a partner and a three-year-old child, spoke about how she managed when she could not stretch her finances enough to cover food expenditure:

> 'I would stretch stuff out if that's what you mean. I would
> ... if I'd run out of food and didn't have the money to cover
> it, I would visit more houses, let me put it that way. I would
> go down and see my Mammy or my partner's Mammy or
> ... I find if one week we haven't got enough money to
> cover food, I'd be down in Mammy's that whole week and
> you'd get by that way there.'

The most extreme case of restricting food strategies was relayed by Ruth (a young lone mother with two small children), who admitted that there were days when they went without food and she had to ask her parents for food for herself and her children. The main cause of her predicament soon became clear:

> 'Financially I struggle with trying to figure out what I'm
> going to make on a day-to-day basis for them. There's
> times I have to ask my parents to help me and can I go up
> and get a meal from them because financially the money's
> tight. I'm in a private-rented house so I have to pay £192
> rent shortfall.'

Three main themes are obvious in the excerpt from this interview: food poverty; the crucial role of family support networks in dealing with the worst effects of poverty; and the ramifications of housing costs and policy for low-income families.

Meeting needs over and above absolute necessities proved a daunting challenge for people. The two-thirds of respondents who said they had days in the week or fortnight when they had no money responded to their situation in one of two ways: either they borrowed money from a close family member (commonly parents but also in-laws, non-dependent children, sisters and an aunt) or, if they had enough food in the cupboard, they basically decided to sit tight and ride it out until they next got their money.

The rational economy versus the moral economy

The narratives leave no doubt but that respondents were generally very active in the management of their money. It is important therefore to recognise their agency in this and other regards. Considering the decisions people make around what to cut back on gives further information on this form of agency as well as people's practices and how they think about and rationalise different decisions.

When people were asked about the savings and cut-backs that they make, their accounts suggested that they tended to prioritise four main areas for cut-backs. These were: social participation; personal items and activities; travel; and leisure/communication. Table 2.1 sets these out in the order of their frequency of mention and/or occurrence across the sample, together with the main examples given of each.

Participation in social events such as a family holiday, socialising with family and friends and family days out were the activities that were most frequently identified for cut-backs or non-purchase. The second most widespread recourse was to cut back on personal items such as buying new clothes and make-up or getting one's hair cut. Making fewer car or other journeys or giving up a car altogether was the next most frequently mentioned form of cut-back, with cut-backs in such things as mobile phone and television subscriptions (which we label as 'leisure/communication') being the least common. These types and frequency of privation tend to reflect similar findings reported by other research. In a study focusing on areas in London and Yorkshire, Hooper and colleagues (2007) found that family-based social activities (family holidays and family day trips) were what the greatest percentage of parents said they could no longer afford. Similarly, a general sample of the population identified social activities as the domain they would cut back on first (Ofcom, 2010). In this same survey, communication services were the least likely to be cut back on.

Table 2.1: Areas where respondents have cut back on spending

Social participation	A family holiday A night out with friends Family days out
Personal	New clothes Sweets/chocolate Make-up A hair cut
Travel	Fewer car or other journeys Car-related
Leisure/communication	Sky TV Newspapers/magazines Mobile phone

Almost two-thirds of respondents in this study mentioned a family holiday as something they would like to be able to do but could not afford. Included here were people who had never been away on a family holiday as well as those for whom the year of interview was the first year a holiday had not been possible because of money difficulties. Discussions around a family holiday raised a mixture of emotions in people. Some parents talked about holidays longingly, as a very welcome break from routine. Others framed their discussion in terms of feelings of guilt about not being able to give their children a holiday. One unemployed lone father (Brian) with a six-year-old daughter told how he felt bad because he knew that when his daughter went back to school in the new term she would be asked to write a composition on 'What I did and where I went on my holidays' and would not be able to do the exercise or say that she had been on holiday.

This sense of loss around a family holiday was partly related to it being an occasion for family togetherness and family building. Jenny, a married mother of three young children and an older son, explained how the family had not had a holiday in three years and that it made her sad because she believed by the time she would be able to afford another holiday her oldest son would most likely not want to go with them any more so the 'family holiday' would not be a 'family holiday' because 'it's not the complete family'.

In relation to socialising, the typical enforced deprivation was cutting back on nights out with a partner and/or friends. Ciara, a young partnered mother with two children, explains:

> 'We probably would've gone out once a month with friends but I haven't been out in months, months. Just can't afford it now. We just sit in the house now. Most weekends we're

never really out at all unless it's maybe his birthday or my birthday we'd make an exception for it. But now – I haven't really been going out at all with my friends.'

However, being unable to afford to go out socially with a partner and/ or a friend did not arouse the same intensity of feeling as children missing out on a holiday. While people did miss socialising, there was a sense of this as a 'normal' or expected deprivation given their circumstances and the fact that many of their friends were in a similar situation as themselves. Such a sense of 'normalisation' of enforced deprivation was a strong undercurrent in the study as a whole. It was almost universal for parents to forego buying items like clothes or shoes or other goods for themselves. And most commonly this 'sacrifice' was for a child. While essentials were prioritised in this regard, parents engaged in self-sacrifice even to give the child a leisure activity a trip to the cinema or a sport-related event or activity being the most common examples given. A small number of respondents represented giving up smoking as an act for their children. This was not a matter of risk avoidance but rather one of financial necessity. Lizzie (a lone parent with four children between the ages of 2 and 17) made her sense of morality very clear: "I don't feel a packet of cigarettes at £6 odd should come first before my children having a cinema trip."

All of these decisions are located in a complex moral frame. In this moral frame the interests and needs of children outweigh personal considerations. As much as they might wish to make a clear differentiation between essentials and luxuries, this is for low-income parents a boundary that is tricky and continually shifting. In general, expenditure in relation to such needs of children as food, shoes and clothing, nappies or basic health- and school-related items was readily identified by respondents as something that could not be cut back on. Beyond these 'essentials', decision making is more complicated and one sees a tendency for what might be 'luxuries' in another context to emerge as 'essentials'. We might say that there is a blurring of absolute needs and relative needs. Expenditure on children's social activities is a good example. It presents low-income parents with a major moral dilemma – people are torn between not prioritising them because they are not essential and yet feeling that in today's world they are necessary for their children's growth and development.

'I suppose like I would love to send my wee girl to gymnastics or singing lessons or things but they're just too expensive. I would love to send the boys to karate and things, they go to football and it's only £1 but karate and judo and all them things is more expensive. And they're looking to go to them but you're sort of saying, "No." You're palming them off, "Maybe next year, no you're at football now just stick to one thing," that kind of a way. One of my wee boys ... he was kept back a year ... and I would have loved to have sent him to a tutor but I couldn't afford it so we're just trying more at home with him.' (Emma, mother of three young children whose husband was unemployed)

Out of similar kinds of rationale and sense of responsibility, people were very reluctant to drop their internet and TV subscriptions (although these were one of the rational economy cut-backs that were mentioned). The internet was regarded as essential for the children's schoolwork. Molly (a young partnered mother with four children, one of whom had ADHD and another – the daughter in question – who was two years behind at school) described how she would retain the internet at all costs so as to avoid her daughter experiencing any embarrassment. She explained how her daughter's school had sent out a letter asking parents to have a computer with internet connection available at home. Those parents who did not or could not provide this were advised to contact the school for special homework to be set for the pupil. As Molly said:

'... well as if that's not going to mark her out in class or anything!'

There are clearly different elements involved in decisions around what is an essential good and what is a luxury when it comes to children. At least two can be identified. One register is about children's development and learning; a second relates to children's 'social face' or reputation, drawing on classic ideas about 'relative deprivation' (Runciman, 1966). In the latter regard, it is seen as vital that the children do not stand out as 'different'. All of this means that people faced with these decisions are visited not just by feelings of guilt but an inability to rid themselves of moral dilemmas. They are never free of the conflict between economic and moral views of value because they never have enough money to have freedom of choice (Hohnen, 2007).

The importance of television for people in low-income situations as compared with households higher up the income spectrum has also been established (Kelly et al, 2012). For the respondents in the current study, television viewing was the most popular form of family entertainment – it was valued as being relatively inexpensive compared with other forms of entertainment and one that all members of the family can enjoy. Furthermore, people could enjoy it together as a family. Helen, a lone mother of five children aged between eight and 17 years, explained:

> 'A good day is when everybody comes home from school or we all sit down to watch a DVD. Family time or whatever, sweeties and wee drinks of juice … so if we sit in with a DVD we'll have juice that night and have crisps or something. That's a good night in for us.'

A more nuanced interpretation of how people use and consume the internet and television is needed than its common depiction as a sign of apathy and withdrawal on the part of the low-income sectors of the population. The last quote demonstrates a point made by Savage (2012, p 152) to the effect that television can be part of a collective act and provide a modern-day 'electronic hearth', or, in the words of one of the respondents, a 'bit of social'. People in this study often felt they had to justify why they had television and internet connections and why they exercised agency to create small spaces or pockets of freedom for themselves in the face of their own low income and public attitudes about what people in their situation are entitled to have.

For a few respondents, freedom inhered in allowing themselves a small luxury. But people felt this too had to be justified. There is a mental process involved, as in the following quote from Katy (unemployed lone mother of one teenage girl and three older sons), who continued to smoke despite identifying cigarettes as something she could cut back on:

> 'I justify it by it's all I do. I don't do anything else so I am entitled to have something. That word "entitled" is not right but do you know what I am saying? That's the only thing. Because my money is exact, bills exact, everything is accounted for … at the minute I am still able to smoke.'

It is insightful to consider the thought processes involved for parents in this kind of situation. Here is a snippet of the conversation between the interviewer and Katy, who had raised her four children more or less single-handedly through 25 years of economic and emotional hardship and knock backs.

'That does sound like you put such a strong limit on yourself really that you never allow yourself to dream about things.'

'Yeah because you're not going to get it so you'd just be torturing yourself really. You don't realise. It's a very slow process and you don't realise that that's happening because as you're asking me questions I'm thinking, "Do you know what? I don't really think about that now."'

So how did families manage the money and who in the family took on the role of household budget planner?

Money management

The main point of interest here is the degree of control that adult members of the family have over budgetary management and the extent to which patterns in regard to money and its management are shared. Obviously, in the 21 lone-parent households, there was no other adult to take responsibility and so much of the discussion that follows is limited to couple families.

In more than half of the 30 couple households represented in the sample, one partner assumed the role of the budget planner and manager. It was overwhelmingly women who undertook this role. There is no single explanation for the gendered pattern. Sometimes it was a pattern passed on to respondents by practices in their own families – these women undertook the role without great thought or deliberation. Sarah (married mother of two, husband and self both unemployed) thought of it in the following way: "I feel it's my job to have everything organised, to have the bills organised, the wee ones for school, I would do the clothes and all that." But in most of these cases, the female partner managed the money because she felt the other lacked either the ability or the reliability to do so. In a few cases, women voiced a lack of trust in their partner's money management patterns. The missing link here was both a lack of skills and a perceived lack of focus and capacity to prioritise when resources were scarce. These respondents did not voluntarily assume the role of money manager, but they held onto it firmly in order to avoid financial disaster (in their eyes). Both quotes below are from mothers of two small children (Leah (whose husband was in full-time work) and Connie (whose husband was unemployed).

'I would trust myself more than I would trust him.'

'He's not a selfish man but I think I think about the kids more than he would.... Not that he doesn't think about them or love them, he does and he does look after them. But if there's a spare £10 or something he would say, "Let's get a chippie." I would say, "No, James needs vests and socks." He probably didn't notice that he needed vests and socks. Silly things like that. He's not selfish. And then I would say that to him and he would go, "Oh right, I didn't know that." And that's it. We would get the vests and socks. I would be more alert on what everybody in the house needs.'

There does not appear to be an especially gendered structure to money management in the remaining families – rather, responsibility tends to be shared. Here again, however, what may appear to be a similar pattern masks diversity. Sometimes women took responsibility for smaller everyday expenses, while their partner took charge of the larger household expenses such as mortgage, rent, rates and insurance; in other families, responsibility for both small and large expenses was shared between members of the couple more or less equally. These couples tended to go shopping together and to communicate fully about money.

In families where women carried the main responsibility for financial budgeting, most of the women said they were happy enough with this role. However, their reasons were often negative, such as taking responsibility because they believed they were better with money than their partners or not having a choice because they feared what might happen if they did not.

'I like the control. Before he would lift a penny out of our bank he'd be on the phone going – he smokes and I don't – "Can I afford tobacco?" He would say to me on a Tuesday, "I'm going to need tobacco tomorrow," and I'm, like, "Good luck with that, we need to eat tomorrow."' (Molly, four children, husband working full time and she part time)

'I've said to him loads of times, like, for instance, see if ... like we were going out, even though he knows we don't have the money, he'd say 'What about going out?" and I go, "You haven't even stopped to see where we're getting the money from," ... because I deal with the money.... I'd be scared to let him take over 'cause we'd probably not have a house ... 'cause that's something I will never do.' (Anne, three children, both partners working part time)

In general, the pattern of decision making showed no clear connection between earned income and control over decisions regarding money. For example, people who were main earners in their family were equally as likely to exert primary control over decision making as they were to share control. What did emerge, however, was a clear gender patterning in the control and decision-making process. In families where the role of budget planner was the sole responsibility of one person, this was overwhelmingly the woman. This is in line with existing research that underlines the significance of women's role as money managers, especially in poorer households (Pahl, 1989; Bennett and Sung, 2013; Bennett and Daly, 2014).

In the current study, even though very few women with total responsibility said they were unhappy with the situation, there was evidence of an implicit acquiescence in a few cases. For example, the following quotes are responses from women who were asked if they were happy taking sole control of the budgeting:

'I am, but sometimes I say to him, "Can you not just take it?"'... Like the last holiday we had, he automatically handed me all the money: "You deal with it." And it was like, "We're on holiday, can I have a break, you deal with it."'... No, he's quite happy just to hand his wages over.' (Jenny)

'Well my husband isn't very good when it comes to money. He's great when he has it for handing out but I'm the one that has to kind of budget it all so it all comes down to me in the end. I'd love it if it was the other way round, but it's not, unfortunately.' (Maureen)

Jenny, mother to three dependent children who was employed as was her husband, agreed immediately that she was happy, with responsibility for budgeting, but, as the quote shows, once she began to reflect on the pattern she showed more ambivalence. The second woman, Maureen, had five children and an older son; her partner was employed full time and she was employed on a part-time basis. She began her reply with a factual piece of information that implied inevitability about her role as budget planner, but then went on to express a wish that things were different, although she ended with acceptance.

Being responsible for money in a situation where there is too little of it takes its toll, however. Sheila (who worked part time and whose husband was disabled) said: "You feel as if at times you don't know whether you are man, woman, or beast, you are just trying to negotiate that many things." Women did feel burdened and a small number implied that their husbands or partners withdrew – as Sheila put it, "He goes into a retreating thing." Whether this was out of pique – often the women had to discipline the men over their spending – or shame was not clear. This and other findings signal that money and its management was a source of tension in the relationship between couples.

But some female respondents also expressed concern about how their menfolk felt about earning. The following is how Emma (mother of three young children whose husband was unemployed) put it:

> 'I think there's more pressure on men, because I suppose they feel it's their job. I would worry. I hope my husband's not worrying as much. I always say to him, "We'll be grand, we always get by no matter what." But he probably feels it's his job to make sure, his responsibility.'

Overview

This chapter has outlined the practical processes of managing family life on a constrained income and some of the associated cognitive and relational processes. All the evidence suggests huge energy being expended on money and its management – one might call this 'poverty work'. Money is a dominating influence on family life and family practices. The payment rhythms associated with income from different sources exerted a significant affect on family life. People's daily and weekly patterns were organised centrally around money coming in and going out. The fact that different benefit payments came in at different stages of the week or month was generally highly valued by respondents. This was seen to allow them to budget better but it also had the impact of bridging different parts of the week. Other research on Northern Ireland confirms this, finding that for some, staggered, multiple payments helped them to budget more effectively and 'get by' more easily (Hickman et al, 2014, p iii).

Throughout the interviews, a pattern of very tight money management was confirmed. This was a very gendered pattern in some families, mainly for perceived utilitarian reasons (women saw themselves as better at it). Most people believed that they were taking every possible opportunity to curtail spending, make savings, and rein in household expenditure. Only in five cases did the narratives suggest that people felt they could make additional savings. In many cases, the process of cutting back was cumulative and layered and it was possible to see people at different stages of the stripping-back process. In general, the roads that people were on converged more or less on the process of gradually (although sometimes more rapidly) stripping back their lives. Respondents' accounts clearly demonstrated that, in order to make ends meet, sacrifices had to be made. Family holidays, socialising and family days out were the first things forfeited. Not being able to take children away on a family holiday was a genuine 'deprivation' for people and one of the aspects of life on low income about which they expressed the strongest negative feelings.

It is possible to say that a family/familial economy exists, that is, the family was the unit of budgeting, essential items for the family as a whole were prioritised, there was a low level of individual resource holding and a strong sensibility that resources were collective. The decision-making patterns of these families cannot be captured fully by the notion of a rational economy, however. There was also a moral economy in play. This is characterised by three features. The first is a hierarchy, mainly along generational lines. This sees children and associated expenditure prioritised over that of adults. In fact, prioritising children and minimising their social deprivation was the most widespread child-related norm among the sample. The presence or absence of children was the key determinant of how people used heating and energy, for example. Moreover, communicational and educational items such as the internet and television emerged as the items people made significant efforts to retain in the face of falling real incomes. These were deemed absolute necessities, mainly for educational reasons, but also because they were used in a way that contributed to family building and family enjoyment. Second, the moral economy sees a lot of 'leakage' between what is seen as an absolute need and a relative need, especially when it comes to children, and third, it comprises selfless giving of parents to children – their own needs become suspended, for later.

THREE

The construction, possibilities and limits of family in conditions of poverty and low income

This chapter further explores the everyday processes of family life in conditions of low income. Chapter Two used economic and money-related processes as a prism through which to view family life. Here we look at cognitive and cultural processes. The chapter has two main aims: to explore further the meanings of family and the ways in which people try to build 'a sense of family'; and to better understand the emotions and attributes that are connected with keeping families going under adverse circumstances. The chapter is divided into four sections. The first focus of discussion is the sets of understandings around family that prevail – depictions of the 'we' of family – and the ways in which everyday activities and interactions contribute to realising prevailing senses and ideals of family. This part of the discussion revolves around the question of what is being evoked by the language of family and the actions engaged in to construct family in the context of everyday strains on income and resources. The chapter then goes on to examine some instances whereby people engage in family building. As well as routine examples, it also looks at what people do at Christmas and birthdays. The third and fourth parts of the chapter investigate people's sense of their capacities to realise the personal and family lives that they envision for themselves. Among the themes to be investigated here are the impacts of living on a low income on people's sense of themselves and their capabilities and whether they feel empowered to bring about change. Throughout the chapter, a key interest is in family as a mental and cultural category – respondents' sense of 'this family' as it emerges from how they describe their family, especially in terms of the characteristics of family life that they identify as positive and negative, and how they situate family resources and responsibilities in a context of both continuity and change.

Views and understandings of family

As Ribbens McCarthy (2012, p 69) says, it is important in the various debates about how to understand 'family' in contemporary societies to include close consideration of how people themselves use this term. What words do people use? What or whom do they refer to when they speak of family? The discussion here looks first at how people reply to a question about what family means to them; it then turns to looking underneath this to see how people's replies to other questions reveal their meaning systems around family.

The first thing to report here is that family is interpersonal in meaning. It is not a place or a locale, but a set of people. There were two classic responses when respondents were asked to describe their family in their own words. The first was to list the members, usually starting with children and a partner (when there was one). Those who went beyond members of their resident family ('just in our own house') in describing their family usually included their parents and siblings (and in a few cases in-laws). People used the term 'immediate family' to sort or order their replies, but this had different meanings. Some meant by this family of residence, whereas others included family of origin also (and especially parents). So there is variation in how immediate family is interpreted. The reference in the following quote from Sheila to 'tiers of family' offers a way of thinking about the fine-grained differentiations involved.

> 'My family are my son who's 20, my daughter who's 14, and my husband. But although they're the immediate family I automatically think of my Mammy and Daddy and that's my family. You think almost like in tiers of importance. There's your own immediate ones, my Mammy and Daddy, my sisters and their youngsters and like it kind of goes out from that.'

The second register used by people to identify their family was how it is (rather than who it consists of). Here the references were predominantly affective in a positive sense: 'happy', 'great', 'close'.

> 'I don't want to come across as big-headed, we have four sons and we're always complimented on how well-mannered they are and how loving they are and how family-orientated we are.' (Margaret, partnered mother of four children)

> 'I would say we are a really, really close family and people would say to me, "God, I wish we had a family like yours," and that's not just me and the kids and Joe. My husband

always says to me that he has a good family too. His is a big family and they're good. But he would always say, "I've the best family in the world," and I would say, "What? Me and the kids?", and he would say, "Yes, us, but also my extended family." (Carmel, married mother of five children)

What does 'good family' mean? Closeness is one constituent meaning and what closeness in turn signifies is sharing or being able to share. The sub-text in the quotes above – as in many other narratives – is of family 'being there'. There is an existential meaning to this – being able to share information about one's situation with one's family – and also a practical register – being able to get help should one need it (as will be discussed in Chapter Five).

Positive references to family far outweighed negative references. But in a few cases people used terms such as 'mad', 'crazy' and 'broken' to describe their family. That said, they tended to inflect these terms with a positive resonance, especially in the sense of overcoming structural and functional problems.

There were other registers to family in the narratives also. In some cases, the financial strains on the family were highlighted as a descriptive feature. A particularly widespread undercurrent was the sense of responsibility that people felt in relation to their family (children especially). Below are Ruth and Rachel respectively, two young mothers describing what they understand by family. They are both parenting alone. Ruth is a 25-year-old lone mother of two young children and Rachel a 30-year-old mother of one child aged five.

'I'm responsible for them, I have to protect them, I have to look after them, they're mine. I have to meet their needs. I have to look after them and if I didn't it would fall to bits.'

'My expectations and hopes are just to be a good provider for Gavin, especially now that he's coming from what would be a broken home, for him not to feel that he's different or losing out or missing out. That I can be that one well-rounded person that he needs for him to grow up and be stable and still achieve and not let anyone like … because I know a lot of things I've went through have come from being from a really unstable family and I don't want that for him. So that's what my expectations and dreams are, just to try and be the best that I can for Gavin, emotionally and I suppose financially and try hard to get everything that he deserves.'

These and other narratives confirm how the bonds with children are seen as a defining characteristic of family (Ribbens McCarthy, 2012).

Asking people to compare their own families with those of others proved a useful way of probing further the meaning of family. In reply to a question about how they thought their family compared with that of others, only three people were unable to answer and the majority answered in a normative way (usually in terms of 'better' or 'worse').

Two main lines of comparison were used by respondents: for some people, the focus was their financial situation; for others, it was the emotional interior of family relationships and family life. Using one or both of these yardsticks, about half considered their families to be better than comparator families, a further third saw no real difference, and the remainder considered that their family compared negatively with others. There was no real pattern to the latter instances – one respondent expressed resentment at what others had (but was the only person to reply in this mode), while another spoke of how her situation had deteriorated compared with what it had been (indicating that the comparison was really with her own family at an earlier period).

As with other work, the research reported here conveys a sense of the family as a unit to which an individual feels they belong: 'we're tight', 'we're close'. The extent to which people find in their family a reason to be positive about their situation is very striking, especially in the context of their financial circumstances. Comparisons with others are used to represent one's own family in a positive light. The first quote below is from Nora (a young lone parent with a three-year-old child) and the second is from Katy (a lone parent of four children, one of whom still lived at home).

> 'See ... people I talk to and the way they say, like, they've been fighting with their Mummy and I'll go, "How can you do that?" I am dead amazed.... It's just when they don't talk to half of their aunts or their uncles or cousins and all. They all fight and I'm, like, "Oh my God, I wouldn't like a family to be like that." I like mine the way it is. Just everybody being close and never falling out and always there for each other. I just love it. I wouldn't change that for the world either. And then everybody says, "I'm so jealous of your family I wish mine was like that." I'm, like, "I know" [laughs].'

'The closeness of us and that they [the children] are all extremely caring, good human beings. That they do have values, that's what I'm really proud of them for and money doesn't achieve that. Money won't pay for that.'

Apart from the generic, two main positive representations emerged from people's accounts. One is people representing themselves as 'lucky', as described by Sarah:

'We're lucky ... we probably have things that other families don't have – families that are broken, for example.'

By 'things' here, Sarah, a 40-year-old mother of two teenage children whose husband had been unemployed for five years, meant qualities or characteristics – like being together or having a supportive network of relations – rather than physical things or goods.

A second source of positive evaluation around family is stability. For some, this had strong moral overtones, and for others, it was associated with security. Here are two quotes. The first is from Conor, who was unemployed and a father one child; the second is from Rachel, a lone mother of a five-year-old child:

'A stable household means a lot, so it does, because there's so many single parents, kids growing up not knowing their father or their mother... stuff like that, you know. As I say, it sort of makes you feel good knowing you're trying to bring your child up in the right environment.'

'Yeah. I think the one thing that no one can take away from you is that you love your family and circumstances can't take your family away from you no matter what ... if all else fails, you'll still have your family and it's always the one thing you should be most grateful for.'

But there was also a significant minority of respondents who saw no real difference between themselves and others in regard to family. The general tenor of replies here was not to deny familial specificity, but, rather, to represent people as being in the same boat or, in a more defensive stance, to represent one's family as no worse than anyone else's ("we're all in the same big boat trying to stay up"). The recession has given people a 'cover' to see themselves in a similar light to others.

This was how Paula, a lone mother of a three-year-old child who was studying for a degree at university, put it:

'As I said before, I think because there's so many people now in the same boat, even people that were earning big money a while ago and then the recession hits and suddenly they're not.'

Quite a number of respondents' narratives contained references to their central or special place in their family of origin. The following (from Alice, a married woman aged 50, who had three children and who worked full time) is typical:

'If anything happens, say my Mammy wants to discuss something, it's ... "Oh, I'll talk to our Alice in private," "I'll see our Alice." If she wants to do something, "Oh, I'll see our Alice first." Or the girls [sisters], if Mammy's not well, like today, it was, "Mammy is in bed, you better go over and see what's wrong with her, she won't tell us what's wrong with her." You know, they depend on me for all that sort of thing. I hope I'm not another Mammy figure, though, you know.'

Or here is Cathy again, a 25-year-old lone mother of two children aged six and three, in response to a question about her family:

'If they were stuck or were in trouble, they would probably come to me and ask me for a bit of advice or things, like, or stupid things, like. I'm like my Mammy's secretary, I know everything about her, you see. When we're out, it's like, "What's my date of birth?" She's stupid some days, she forgets. I'd fill in forms and stuff like that.'

Constructing family life

On numerous occasions throughout the interviews, it became clear how central family was to respondents' identities. 'Provider', 'mother', 'father', 'guardian' were the identifiers that sprang most commonly from the replies here.

People tried to generate a sense of the specialness of family by placing a distance between themselves and others. This was often done with physical imagery, such as "Inside these four walls, this wee family, we're a team, we're a tight unit," or "We have our wee nest here to huddle in when we want to."

The following are telling representations of the process of boundary marking. The first is from Helen, a lone mother of five children, and the second from Rachel, a lone mother of one five-year-old child:

> 'As I keep telling the kids, it doesn't matter what goes on outside, as long as we're all alright in here. And we are not starving you know.'

> 'I know me and my Gavin can be very settled because I never had a settled life coming up as a youngster and that's what makes me happy about family, to be settled and to be part of that wee unit and to have those people in your life ... just close a door and people out there let them go on by.'

In these and other families there were echoes of an emotional retreat by the parent(s) from other relationships apart from those with their children (which will be considered further in Chapter Six).

Apart from the discursive, there are other ways in which family is a site of continuous construction or work in progress. We came across many instances of people acting to create a sense of family, especially for their children. This centred on trying to compensate children and for this purpose parents engaged in a range of activities and adopted dispositions that were, among other things, oriented to incline children and others to identify their particular interests with the collective interests of the family (Bourdieu, 1996, p 23). Let us consider a few examples.

One of the most common ways was for people to create 'oases' or small freedoms for building and sustaining family relationships, and making what might otherwise be routine occasions special in some way. Here is Helen again, lone mother of five, who refers to her oldest son as 'the big boy':

> 'We wouldn't go out, say, once a week for dinner or anything ... our quality time is spent at home. We stay at home and we'd have biscuits and tea or a girly night in when Sean [son] is away out or whatever. When the big boy's away out we have a girly night, get make-up on the kids and things like that, you know. That's a good night in for us, if you understand what I mean.'

Family occasions are a good opportunity to institute collective patterns and deepen loyalties. In this regard, the prominence of birthdays and Christmas in people's discussions and in their activities is quite revealing.

Both birthdays and Christmas involve a considerable amount of forward thinking. When one is on a low income, a big advantage of birthdays is that one has advance warning. The most common way of coping with this kind of large forthcoming expense was to put away a few pounds, maybe three to four weeks in advance. It is interesting to note, however, that it was only the children's birthdays that were celebrated in these families – there were hardly any references to respondents celebrating their own birthday. Birthdays were effectively a child-specific event in these families. Furthermore, there was no decentring of tradition in regard to children's birthdays – in fact, it was the obverse. Children's birthdays had to be 'celebrated' and were so important that they led to cut-backs on other areas of spending. This is how Emma, a young partnered mother of three children, explained it:

> 'Coming up to birthdays and things, that's when you really have to pull the reins in because you know if it's one of the kids' birthdays, they're so important … you have to get their birthday presents. So I suppose you're doing without other things, hoping the electricity will last until next week, for example.'

As might be expected, Christmas was a particularly significant time of year. This, too, has a strong familial resonance. In low-income families, it is the one special occasion in the calendar of family life that is guaranteed to happen. To ensure that it could be celebrated, it was carefully planned for. Christmas was not a one-off event in terms of planning, but was spread across a number of months. It was not a matter of casually looking out for suitable gifts, but, rather, of picking up bargains and meting out the expenditure on gifts for a period longer than a month or two. Sheila started preparing for Christmas as early as January. She was unusual, though – most often people started putting money by (if they found it possible) from the middle of the year onwards, and actively picked up gifts and foodstuffs from September/October. In the words of Lizzie, who is repeating what her father said to her as advice and sometimes as admonition, "You've got to space your money out."

Overall, then, for both birthdays and Christmas, money was often 'sneaked' from other costs or allocated when available because of some unexpected savings in other areas.

All of this 'money–family work' takes a huge amount of work and energy. Emotional energy is as prominent as physical energy here. A considerate degree of strength is called for. What do people identify as strengths of their situation and how empowered do they feel in regard to what daily life requires of them?

Dispositions, resources and capabilities

This research seeks to add to the small but increasing number of studies that are beginning to shift the focus from a deficit model of poverty and low income to one that acknowledges the strengths of individuals and families in this situation, and indeed the positive factors generated by people themselves when under pressure due to lack of income. In contradistinction to the tendency to focus more or less exclusively on material factors, interest is directed here to the affective sphere and the emotional resources that people see themselves calling on or generating. The intention in this section, then, is to examine what people themselves identify as assets and how the way they conduct their lives acts as a set of protective measures against the stresses and strains of economic hardship, especially for other members of their family.

One question put to people for this purpose asked them about what they saw their family as being rich in. While some had difficulty with the framing of the question – especially the use of the word 'rich' – only one person could not provide a response. The overwhelming majority of people referred directly to an emotional dimension of family richness. The responses, all affective, were dominated by four themes: love, closeness, support and happiness. These themes were so widely referred to that they suggest a set of shared assumptions about family life that is deeply rooted.

The significance attributed to each varied. Love was by far the most universally identified trait of respondents' families. Most people believed their family to be rich in love. This is the voice of John, who was long-term unemployed, in receipt of Disability Living Allowance, and whose youngest son had learning difficulties together with a physical disability:

'Love, one hundred per cent, that's it, Love, trust....'

Others were a bit more reticent at the beginning and somewhat shy about saying the word 'love'. Lily's voice is typical of these responses:

'What would you say your family is rich in?'

'Without sounding corny?'

'Yes.'

'Love for each other, to be honest. Love Jack, love him there [son], love the two of them. They crack me up, both of them, crack me up, but I love the two of them.'

Another theme to emerge from people's depictions of their family was feelings of pride. This was sometimes respondents' pride in themselves. The findings point to an ontological connection between money and sense of achievement. People achieved a sense of security and well-being from having used money well. Consider the following from Molly, mother of four, who is describing how you should always make sure you pay the essential bills:

'I can sit safe in my living room and know that my electric is not going to run out and I'm not going to run out of gas.'

The association between money management and pride in achievement was quite a strong underlying theme; in an insecure and generally inadequate income situation, people try to generate some sense of security by ensuring that the bills and essential items are covered and that their children have a safe place to call home.

However, when and if people framed their family in terms of pride, it was much more likely to be pride in their children rather than in themselves. Respondents made frequent reference to how polite and respectful their children were, how they 'never bring trouble to the door', and, in particular, how well their children were doing in school. Here is a sequence of dialogue between the interviewer and Susan, a 34-year-old mother of three young children, one of whom had ADHD:

'What makes you most proud about your family?'

'The wee ones.'

'Could you just tell us a bit about that?'

'I don't know.'

'Like what it is about the family?'

'I suppose it's just the wee simple things about your wee ones that make you feel so proud. My wee girl at school last week, she got pupil of the week and I could feel myself like I was going to cry and my friends were sitting beside me and they said, "Susan, it's only pupil of the week." And I said, "I know but it means a wild lot to me." Just wee simple things that they do and things like that there.'

Biography and life course can be a profound context to feelings of pride. Here is Lizzie again, lone mother to four children:

'I would say what we've been through, the ups and downs of what we've been through, the divorce coming up, the separation of the Daddy, all the things that we've been through that I feel that I still have that connection with them that they can still come and tell me anything and that I've taught them nothing is too big or small that you can't talk about ... we're still communicating, thank goodness. If I see one backing off, I can also reel them back in and say, "Mum's here, Mum and Dad is here, don't feel that you can't speak to us." They're good kids and I'm proud that they're good kids ... that they can come and talk to me and they haven't brought trouble to the door, if I'm honest.'

As well as being proud of the children for managing hardship, other themes to emerge included respondents being proud of remaining with their partners, the happiness of the family, parenting skills, and providing a good life for the family under adverse circumstances.

The narratives gave a strong sense of how managing in circumstances of poverty and low income is not just about keeping a household functioning, but is also about keeping a sense of family alive and strong. While this has functional elements, it is primarily about emotional well-being and maintaining a sense of family integrity and loyalty to family. It is also in crucial ways about balancing the needs of individuals in a larger group, as well as balancing the needs of particular individuals and more collective exigencies.

It would be plausible to frame the guiding question here and also the findings thus far in terms of resilience. Indeed, this is an increasingly common framework in studies of individuals and families living in conditions of low income (Garmezy, 1991; Vandsburger et al, 2008; Canvin et al, 2009). The concept of resilience has many constructive features. One major benefit is that it shifts emphasis from the deficit model towards positive outcomes and the individual factors that help people overcome adversity (Howard et al, 1999). Focusing on assets and positive attributes as we have done here allows one to portray people as active agents as opposed to passive recipients (Batty and Cole, 2010). However, when viewed against the results just presented, the framework's serious limitations are revealed. For a start, resilience is an individual trait. Second, given that it is theoretically anyway possible in every situation, it is not very discriminating as a concept. There is a tendency also to idealise resilience, and with this comes a risk of 'blaming the victim' and labelling a person who does not display resilient behaviour as having individual failings (Luthar and Zelazo, 2003). The potential for imposing a set of middle-class values and assumptions on the framing and measurement of resilience (Frydenberg, 2002; Delfabbro and Harvey, 2004) is another reason to be wary of the resilience concept.

There is also the fact that the interviews contained many negative references to family. Respondents deal with trouble every day (especially around the health-related and behavioural needs of their children) and many come from family backgrounds where these and other problems were widespread. People therefore voiced real challenges, not just in remaining positive, but in generating a positive emotion in themselves about their family.

In many cases, there were negative overtones to the construction of self. The following are two revealing sections of narratives. The speakers are, respectively, Rachel, a 30-year-old lone mother of one child aged five years, and Alice, a 50-year-old married mother of three (aged between 15 and 24 years):

'I think maybe the big thing would have been for it to have worked out with his father and everything that I tried there ... I would like that changed. To be able to be more financially settled and not have to go and say, "Oh, we're here and or we're there", to be able to live together as a family unit because it doesn't pay for us to live together as a family unit.'

'Well, I'm sorry the day I was so protective of the boys because they haven't got the confidence ... to me they wouldn't have the confidence to go out and do the things for themselves. They need to be pushed and I'm sorry they weren't pushed more. And I would have done things you know, if they had to go to the doctor I was ringing the doctor, I was taking them to the doctor, I'm still doing it. I'm sorry that way.'

As is obvious from the latter quote, some approach their children with a sense of guilt. These are the words of Katy, a lone mother with two broken relationships behind her:

> 'When I tried to explain to Conor about the whole break-up and I said to him, "I have to apologise to you, son, for what I allowed to happen. I thought I could fix it. I thought I could get through it." And he said, "Mum, you thought you were protecting us ... the only person you were protecting was him [former partner]."'

Katy's apologetic, guilt-ridden tone here is not unusual. But it is not necessarily a discourse of personal failure (as found by Flint, 2010). Many respondents recounted this kind of incident as an exemplum of strength. In the case in question, the respondent wished to convey how she had come to terms with what had happened in the past – her journey into and through poverty and low income, if you will – and as demonstration of this felt able to voice it openly with her son.

That said, respondents' accounts were replete with perceived failures around money and achieving independence through paid employment. One can see here evidence of how respondents defined themselves in the terms used by conventional society. Women especially struggled around the reconciliation of a good mother role in a context of poverty. These people struggled every day with what is 'right' in their situation and family-related considerations played a large role in this, as the following quote shows:

> 'I feel less of a Mammy because I can't buy my child Timberland boots or I can't buy my child Diesel jeans or because he's not standing head to toe in Nike, you know what I mean? I don't like being in that situation, I don't like having my child compared to other kids.' (Lily, a part-time employed married mother of a three-year-old who was expecting a second child)

The following is an account by Lizzie, lone mother of four children – as can be seen, she had to 'learn' that caring for her children was valuable and that being on benefits was acceptable as a way of doing that, in the short-term anyway:

'The women's group taught me, you know, you are worthy of this, the best job that you're doing is rearing four children on your own. Look at what you're doing – it's a wonderful job and it's the most heaviest and most stressful job anybody can do.... It was them that empowered me to think, "Oh, you know, I am worthy of this and I can do this, I am a good person because I am doing this on my own" ... it's not permanent because I want to go back to work when the youngest one goes to school, but it's there for to help me get by these three to four years while I am out of work.'

In fact, the most widespread role that respondents had was that of carer – of their children, but also, in a significant minority of cases, of adults. Fiona Williams (2004, p 8) has pointed out how care involves a moral and social weighing-up of a given situation. Duncan and Edwards (1999), too, in their study of lone mothers, pointed out how the decisions of such mothers around paid and unpaid work were made with reference to moral and socially negotiated views about what behaviours were right and proper. The present study confirms this. Against a backdrop where many respondents had heavy caring responsibilities, change (and especially change in relation to employment) always had to be put through the needle's eye of family, in the sense of whether it was possible or positive in light of considerations relating to family responsibilities and especially those relating to care and well-being. This is another example of a moral economy.

Some people seemed to suggest that lack of money effects a change in one's personality. Here is Sheila describing what it is like to be constantly thinking about money:

'You seem to be always worried. You seem to be always counting. You seem to be always serious when maybe your basic personality wouldn't be like that at all.'

Speaking of money Rachel, a lone mother of a five-year-old who, although employed part time, was living on very low income, said:

'I just feel like none of it belongs to me, it's all other people's borrowed money I live on because I'm constantly having to pay this one back, pay this back, pay that back, so by the end of it there's nothing that's actually mine. It's always somebody else's.'

Sheila doubted whether there was any item in her house that was bought at full price. She went on to describe herself (in a self-deprecatory if not derogatory fashion) as "queen of the bargain bucket. If I am wearing it, you know somebody else didn't friggin' want it because it was cheap somewhere."

Anxiety caused by the constant stress of managing finances and budgeting on a low income were among the main negative consequences mentioned by respondents. Anne, a married mother of three who worked part time, as did her husband, likened it to being a policewoman 24/7, constantly on alert:

> 'I never let my guard down, and that's the only thing, I would love to be able to let my guard down now and again, so I would.'

The following is how Sheila (an older married mother with two children, one dependent) expressed her thoughts on the relationship between money and worry:

> 'It's very trite to say money's not important because money absolutely is important and to say it's not it's almost an insult ... it's not important if you have it and it certainly doesn't buy you happiness, but not to worry does bring you happiness.'

One can see evidence of an anxiety trajectory. First, constant cutting back on consumption may adversely affect health. Second, cut-backs are a cause of stress and strain on the self and on relationships. As mentioned already, quite a number of respondents spoke about how being constantly on alert about money sets up not just a disposition towards watchfulness on their part, but also tensions and even rows within the family. Third, while engaged in the activities that enable them to cope, people may well be undermining their own health and relationships, disposing of assets and eroding their future capacity to respond.

Relative (dis)empowerment

Despite such anxieties, most respondents did not seem to feel disempowered. Only 12 of the 51 respondents felt that it was not possible for people in their situation to change their circumstances. These respondents, a more or less even mix of lone and partnered parents, had a number of reasons for feeling like this. The main reasons were related to employment and health. Employment – or lack of it – played a very powerful role. It seems that most, if not all, of these respondents were of the view that long-term benefit receipt means a life of penury. Hence, paid work is the only way out. But given that such work was not available either in the quantity or quality needed, they considered their situation to be one of relative disempowerment. Their circumstances tended to be quite entrenched, in terms of both employment and health/disability. A few were in employment, but on a part-time basis, and generally in low-paying jobs; a few others had recent experiences of either long-term unemployment or redundancy and were weary of searching for jobs in a very difficult market. Others could not take up employment mainly because of disability; in six of the families involved, for example, there was at least one family member with a disability. Depression was present in a few of these cases and at least one respondent had experienced an abusive relationship. These people tended not to see any way out of a situation where negative factors cumulated one on another. One respondent described it evocatively: "It's like a brick wall right in front of me."

These were a minority, though – the vast majority felt that someone in their general situation could overcome their circumstances. These were drawn from right across the sample. They tended to attribute the power of change to either positive attitudes ('positive thinking') or a feeling that people are empowered if they feel in control of their situation. Examples depicted as empowering by respondents included taking charge of debts and actively negotiating with creditors, or receiving access to professional medical help either for self or a family member.

If there is one thing that separates the more positively disposed respondents from those who were more negatively disposed, it is that a significant number of the former were already on a trajectory of change. The nature of these trajectories varied. Education was central – in nine cases, either the respondent or husband/partner was involved in some kind of formal education. Most usually, this was a form of short-term training but a few respondents were pursuing degrees or professional qualifications, sometimes with many challenges. This is how Paula, the mother of a young son who was attending university, described her attitude and aspiration:

> 'I'm positive, I want to teach. People scoff and say, "You'll never get a job teaching." If I had that attitude, there's no

point in me being at university. I just believe that something
will come of it ... what you give out you get back.'

There was an equally large group of respondents whose trajectory
of development was through local community involvement. This
probably reflects the fact that some respondents were recruited through
community groups. Nevertheless, the capacity to undertake short
courses or to get mentoring support is hugely significant for those who
can access it. The respondents themselves spoke of this as a turning
point in their lives. The fact that some of the training was in the area
of basic skills underlines its significance. Here is how Ruth, a lone
mother of two children, framed her reply to the question of whether
someone in her situation can change their circumstances:

> 'I feel as if one can ... if one puts a budget on things and
> sticks to a budget and gets what they need on the days they
> get paid and stick to that, then they know they're covered
> for the week. Which is what I'm trying to do at the minute
> because of the women's group helping me in that situation,
> showing me the way.'

Another respondent echoed a quite widespread feeling when she said
that in her view people could change their situation but only when they
had support. The support of family was mentioned in this context (see
Chapter Five), but this was especially meant as a comment on public
and voluntary services. The extent to which people felt they were
starting from a negative standpoint – especially in regard to education
level, skill levels and work-related experience – was striking.

Respondents were also asked whether there were things about their
own situation that they would like to change. Thirteen respondents
replied in the negative. This should not be interpreted at face value,
however, because people responded to the question in very different
ways. For some, to bring about change would require even greater
energy than they were currently expending, and so they felt that their
resource levels at present were insufficient to change their situation.
There were also people who felt that their current situation was
acceptable, in a few cases because it was an improvement on their
former situation. These were people who had left a violent relationship
or were taking charge of their debts or other difficulties, or had recently
secured a job or access to a training programme.

Among those who said that there were things about their lives
that they wanted to change, employment or job-related factors were

mentioned most frequently. This desired change tended to have two roots: the 'respectability' and status that comes from being in work (a value orientation that was quite widely shared by respondents) and the hope that a job would increase the income level and hence the family's standard of living. Apart from employment, other dominant themes were related to either health or changing house or locality.

Overview

This chapter has examined some of the processes associated with creating and sustaining family life in conditions of low income. It has revealed especially that in a situation where money shortages create instability and insecurity, the construction of an image and reality of 'our family' can be very important. Another major finding is that family, generally conceived of in terms of children, is a source of some deeply-felt and very clear references. Respondents know what family means to them, they can readily define and depict their own families, and they used both negative and positive descriptors to invoke their sense of their family. The positive references were primarily used for good familial relations, whereas the negative characterisations invoked the constraints on family life occasioned by people's straitened financial circumstances. Aspects of the family's biography – or respondents' own biography – also occasioned negative comment.

Second, it was clear that family did not just happen, but was something respondents consciously strove to create. While 'a sense of family' might sound vague, it is an ideal that was evident both in people's dispositions and in the way they managed their actions and activities. An example here is people's decision to celebrate family occasions (such as children's birthdays and Christmas) even when this took careful planning and resulted in privation in other regards. A further example is the many ways respondents sought to create the family as an 'oasis'. The sense of binding children to the family and of creating a family 'in here' was quite a strong tendency. Third, while people were readily able to identify assets in, and strengths of, their current situation, the negative personal consequences of living the way they did were huge. Such negative feelings were not restricted to an isolated event, but were ongoing and to some extent ontological, as when, for example, people felt demeaned by the poor quality of their possessions and their 'failure' to provide their children with the goods, resources and opportunities available to children in other families.

It is important, though, to point out also that respondents did not generally feel disempowered. For the minority who did feel this way, difficulties around securing employment and overcoming health-related problems were the major factors mentioned. Those who felt they could change their situation made reference to both psychological characteristics (a positive frame of mind, a sense of taking control) and also getting help. But the main difference between those who felt empowered and those who did not was the fact that the former were already on a course of change, either by being involved in further education or through local community involvement.

FOUR

Parents and their children

This chapter and the next explore the modes of relating within respondents' families. The role and place of children is the lens through which relationships are examined in this chapter. We will investigate the extent to which children are the source of their parents' most meaningful relationships. The chapter then moves on to hear parents' accounts of their child-rearing practices. The interest is not in parenting as a mediating factor on outcomes for children, but rather in the parenting-related perceptions and practices of people as they play out in everyday life. It should be noted that there is insufficient information to compare female and male parenting practices and that the generic 'parent' is usually a mother. Given that all the respondents are parents and that the interviews were with them rather than their children, the chapter mainly explores parenting practices from the viewpoint of the parents. However, some evidence from parents does give a sense of the lives of their children and the kinds of relationships that children have with parents. This is explored in the chapter's last section.

The significance of children

Respondents' children dominated the interviews, despite there being few specific questions about them. One could even say that for about a fifth of respondents it was as if the purpose of the interview was to discuss their children's lives and their own feelings about their children. People's accounts conveyed a very strong sense of the centrality of children in their lives and, as evidenced already, indicated the existence of a hierarchy along generational lines, whereby children and their needs were prioritised. The significance of children was so profound that it was impossible to pin a single meaning or interpretation to it. There was, however, a number of striking aspects to how people described and discussed their children: one was their children as a source of pride, a second was the extent to which children conferred meaning on their lives, a third was about prioritising children for the purpose of sharing family resources.

By far the most frequent mention of children was as a source of pride. There was even an existentialist side to this: "I just look at them and go, 'Goodness, that's what I have created' — it makes you proud looking at them, you're sitting looking at them at night," says Heather, (young mother of two with another baby expected). Most widely, what respondents seemed to admire in their children was their ability to meet public expectations, in effect to be able and willing to conform to what conventional society values in children and young people. In respondents' eyes, theirs are 'good children'. Good has a number of references, but most are behavioural. Respondents made frequent mention of their children's politeness, for example, their good manners, their capacity to 'know their place' and conduct themselves properly. As Molly said of her four children:

> 'My kids can go anywhere and they're the most polite kids you'll ever meet and everyone comments on it. ... I can take them and leave them anywhere and they'll not let me down.'

There is a strong sense here of children representing their parents and the family more broadly.

It is important to be clear, though, that 'good' has a wider meaning than not being naughty or mischievous and that politeness is actually a signifier with more than one register. Above all, 'good' means children not causing trouble or engaging in 'anti-social behaviour'. "They never give me any trouble or any grief, you know; they bring no bother to the door," explained May (a widowed mother of four children). Parents appreciate this especially because they feel 'trouble' is another call on an already over-burdened set of coping resources. There is also a consciousness of the family's 'place' and reputation in the locality (as will be seen in Chapters Six and Seven). References to manners and politeness shade into children acting with respect, which in turn shades into respectability. Therefore, as well as the psycho-emotional benefits of people being able to relate more easily to their children because they are 'good', there is both a functional (being able to manage the children) and a social or sociological dimension to politeness in children. These parents need their children to be good in a context where the children are like mini-ambassadors in the family's struggle to cope and also to get respectability.

The children's achievements are another source of pride and pleasure. Nina, a 25-year-old lone mother of two young children, talked about the pleasure she got from her children getting rewards in school, and said how "it makes your day knowing they're smarties". But intelligence is valued beyond its currency for academic performance. As the following quote shows (from Sandra, a lone mother of two young children), it is seen to equip children with coping skills:

'They're doing brilliant in school. They're in the top reading groups and they're flying and they have brains on them. You tell them one thing and they take it in really quick, very smart. I'm just very proud of everything they are doing and how they deal with things. Life's hard and they can put up with it.'

In the following quote from Sheila, a married mother of two whose partner had been disabled by an accident that she said had changed his personality and left him with mental health problems, one gets a strong sense of the challenges that children (and their families) are faced with.

'My two kids are doing so well now and I'm happy because my son's on the range of Asperger's and autism spectrum and there was a long time when he seemed quite removed from other people which was really compounded by his daddy's odd behaviour ... it has been a real labour of love trying to get him to a stage where he completely fits in. When I see him now, I think, "I'm so happy for him." He sings in a band and he's doing well and he's a very happy character, although he has wee foibles, like.... And where Lorna [daughter] is concerned, our girl is a very self-contained person and almost quietly confident and gets on in her own wee way. And I look at them and think they're very, very different people but they're very, very close to each other, very supportive. And in a way, although the situation in our house is difficult, it has given them an insight that in a way I think they've been lucky to have, you know. Life doesn't always work out so good at times and you learn to roll with the punches. I think it's given them an empathy for people that most young people their age wouldn't actually have.'

Another respondent framed resilience in her children in terms of their being "very wise children". For Joan, a married mother of three children whose husband was disabled, intelligence is the lack of any sense of entitlement in her children – "They don't expect stuff." Another respondent (Margaret) described this kind of realistic orientation in her children by saying that they were "very grounded", which seems like a description more appropriate for an adult. People appreciate loyalty in their children as well. Of course, looked at another way, child loyalty is an essential element of family cohesion, which seems to be a root of idealisation of family life. Mary, a lone mother of two children, praised her children for all sticking together, especially given the family's straitened circumstances.

A further striking dimension of respondents' accounts — albeit less common than the references to children as sources of pride — is the extent to which their children give meaning to their life. These children are 'emotionally priceless' in their parents' lives (Zelizer, 1985). In quite a few cases, it seemed that children are respondents' most fulfilling relationships and in a few cases their only meaningful ones: "They're mine ... they're all mine 'cause they only know me." The sense of ownership here is palpable, although the quote is suggestive also of the urge to protect (which was the strongest overall theme in this particular interview). While a protective orientation to children was more or less universal, it had an added edge and sense of poignancy among lone mothers, most of whom were parenting alone. Sandra, who had two young children and who had left their father because of an abusive relationship, put it like this: "I'm dead protective of them. They're my responsibility 'cause there's nobody, you know." As well as a certain sense of loneliness here, there is an undertone of guilt (confirmed by other passages in the interview). But in other family situations, too, the sense of closeness between parent and child was very striking. More than one parent, for example, when answering the questions about the quality of family life, adopted the voice and perspective of the children: "Now my children would probably answer a 4 to that question."

The significance of children was also underlined when people were asked about their aspirations and priorities for the future. Providing well for children was the single most dominant theme here and in it education dominated. The latter is sometimes refracted through a negative lens around respondents' own achievements. Here is Anne, a married mother of three who worked part time as an assistant in a small company:

> See, if you can read and write decent enough — 'cause I can't read and write very well — if you can do that, you can nearly do anything, so you can. Everything else comes after that, so it does, and you can work on anything else after that. And my Jane [daughter], she's doing childcare at the minute but she has to do her wee GCSE again 'cause she never passed it. I says to her, here's me, "More than anything, focus on your spelling and everything else." And that's what I want for my kids — able to read and write properly. I know it

doesn't sound much – it's 'cause I have the problem of it – then they won't be scared to face anything, so they won't.'

The findings generally reflect those of Hooper and colleagues (2007, p 70) in that only a few respondents expressed the concern that their children would remain disadvantaged throughout their lives. Most parents expressed the belief or hope that their children would overcome the various disadvantages they had faced, of which poverty was one, and achieve a more financially secure and happier life than they themselves had had.

Some respondents also made sense of their own efforts towards achievement in terms of their children's future. Paula, a lone mother currently attending university, put this in terms of trying to make a better future for her son. Setting a good example – in other words, being a role model – for children was a recurrent theme.

Parenting in conditions of low income

There is only a small body of evidence on parenting in a context of financial shortage. This work is guided by two main theoretical orientations (Katz et al, 2007). One is stress theory. This holds that parents who are stressed – and stress is generally seen to be part of the low-income experience – are less likely to be able to provide optimal home circumstances and more likely to use coercive and harsh methods of discipline (Katz et al, 2007, p 13). A whole range of factors is investigated, but those that are most widely measured as 'outcomes' in this context are birth-weight, diet, emotional well-being and behaviour of children and adolescents, life chances and educational success. This, the most prevalent theorisation of the relationship between parenting and poverty has been criticised for failing to take into account the reciprocal relationships and interdependence between parents and children who are facing adversity together (Katz et al, 2007).

The second prominent theoretical orientation in the field is the culture of poverty theory (discussed earlier). This, in contrast to stress theory, downplays the primacy of parental psychological attributes and upgrades the impact of cultural beliefs, practices and backgrounds in determining outcomes for children from disadvantaged backgrounds. Learned behaviours are the 'problem' here. This scholarship makes reference to the term culture of poverty mainly in a pejorative sense, especially in regard to the persistence of poverty and low achievement across generations. It tends towards the view that parents living in poverty have a different 'culture' from that of middle-class parents, and that their style of parenting is generally negative and acts to transfer bad habits across generations. One of the classic studies here is that of Fram (2003).

There is also a more open view of parenting in low income and other circumstances. This approach is found in the work of some sociologists who wish to know how parenting is practised, to fill in the many blanks around agency left by the tendency to treat family behaviour as self-evident or unremarkable by functionalist sociology (Ribbens, 1994; Lareau, 2003; Edwards and Gillies, 2005; Gillies, 2008; Ramaekers and Suissa, 2011). This study follows that line of enquiry.

In their discussions, parents emphasised that they brought their children up to be well-behaved: 'manners, please and thank you'. While there is variation, there was a sense of relatively strict child-rearing practices in a lot of families. Margaret put it like this: "My boys know the lines not to cross." People's accounts of their child-rearing practices also made reference to instilling values in their children, which in some families meant passing on the values taught to respondents by their own parents. There was a notable sense of continuity here, although this was far from universal. When people were asked specifically about whether they had any rules or norms about family life that they were strict about keeping, most people said that they did. The most common references were to rules about the children's demeanour or attitude (not being 'cheeky') and control over their behaviour. In the latter regard, respondents made reference to the children having to be home by a certain time and not 'roaming about the streets', going to bed when they were told, doing their homework, and so forth. Some respondents mentioned making it a priority that the family ate together or that the children and parents had some leisure time together (either activities outside the home or within). The building in of family ('we') rituals was notable. Parents especially tried to do this for young children – it was harder to see it through with teenagers, however. With older children, the constant struggle between care and control was more difficult to manage.

There were many references to caring for children throughout respondents' narratives. Children's health and well-being, as well as their safety, were predominant themes here. As outlined earlier, many of these children had an illness, disability or some kind of functional difficulty, and this was a predominant concern of the parents. There was a wish to 'get children settled and on their feet', and indeed also to ensure that other children in the family were not too affected by the illness or disability. It seems that both the rewards and stresses of parenting are amplified in low-income circumstances.

Listening to the parents in this study suggests that in conditions of low income with many calls on the available money, parenting requires a careful and repeated weighing up of the morality around different alternatives. There is an active search for ethical parenting. Not least here is the worry that the child might be being 'spoiled'. This is not spoiling in the conventional sense, but 'spoiling' in the sense of not readying the child to face the harshness of life. Here is how Paula, lone mother of a two year-old boy, who is attending university on a degree course, described her complex feelings:

> 'He's very demanding in shops with toys and stuff and he would be very tantrumy ... because I suppose he is spoiled with small things.... If I can afford it and if I am feeling particularly guilty, he'll maybe get a wee toy or DVD. But I would never spend more than £3 or £4 on him for no reason. I bought him a DVD at the weekend there and he just loved it and walked around Tescos with it. It was £2.50 and I thought, "How could I not because he gets so little?".... You would walk into his bedroom and there's so much toys and stuff, but it's just because things are cheaper and it's three years' worth of toys. It's not last year.... In comparison to other children, he gets a lot less. So I don't mind the small things, but I try not to do it that every time we are in a shop he gets something.'

Here we see justification piled on justification, underpinned on the one hand by feelings of guilt (occasioned by the fact that since Paula had been attending university, her son was in childcare for a number of days a week) and on the other by self-doubt about her own principles and exactly how her child compared with others. Of course, there is also an apparent contradiction here between the perception of the child as having at once too little and too much.

The kind of 'weighing-up' process that is revealed in this quote was found again and again, so much so that the interviews suggested that a continual self-argument around morality is a condition of life for those rearing children in conditions of poverty or low income. Respondents seemed to be in continual conversation with themselves about what was right or what should be done in the circumstance. Among other things, this was evidenced by the frequency with which their narratives posed questions to themselves, and the listener.

The sense of prioritising children was ubiquitous (as was evident also in the last chapter). Sometimes this was expressed in the most bald manner – "My kids eat first"; "You leave yourself with nothing to give them something." At other times, respondents recounted specific situations where children would be put first. Trying to enable the children to avail of leisure and educational activities – such as to become a member of a local sports or educational club or to partake in a school educational trip – were commonly mentioned instances of prioritising children for what might seem, at face value anyway, like non-essential items. However it was expressed or realised, the principle that children should be prioritised was the single most common child-related norm among these parents. This spells a departure from the rational approach to budgeting that was so prominent elsewhere in the narratives. The moral principle involved pertains not just to children's access to essential goods and activities. For many parents, it extended to enabling their children to be as 'normal' as possible – hence the desire for them to participate in activities or to have a lifestyle that approximates to that of their friends or schoolmates. This is a very important register of children's consumption in the respondents' families. A core parenting norm, then, is that children's social deprivation should be minimised as much as possible. Wanting your child to be able to participate is, in effect, akin to wanting them not to be socially deprived or socially excluded. In the words of Katy, a lone mother of a 16-year-old daughter as well as older children, "They kind of feel left out, they feel different because you can't afford it."

One of the parents' moral 'conversations' centred around what is fair to each and all of the children. In a context of low income, the search for fairness is to walk a complex line between privileging one child over others and yet not denying any child important opportunities when they become available. But fairness was not generally seen in the individualistic terms of *this* child. Rather, people made comparisons between their children in terms of a generic or general benchmark, worried that some had it harder (especially linked to the time when the family's circumstances worsened) than others and usually striving for a balance that was fair to all. To set this in context, it is important to note that family circumstances change and that, for some of the families, low income was a relatively recent occurrence (associated especially with the recession) or had not been constant throughout the family's life course. Hence, different children in the family might be being reared in varying financial circumstances. Here is Alice describing her feelings about not being able to afford to give one of her children £500 or £600 for a school trip in the context of the others' needs. Both Alice and her husband were in employment, she full time and he part time:

'We could never afford it. It was hard because they never did ask for much. And you tried, you tried your best but you just couldn't stretch it. I mean you had three of them and you couldn't stretch it to let one get £600.'

Overall, the findings on parenting in conditions of low income have little in common with either the family stress theory or the culture of poverty thesis. There is no evidence of poverty having a direct relationship with poor parenting.

The impacts of parenting in low-income situations

There is, however, evidence to suggest that living on a low income has a negative effect on parents. Feelings of parental guilt abound. Such feelings are intensified if one parent is absent. For example, the following quote is from Sandra, who was in an abusive relationship and made the decision to leave because she believed it was the right choice for her two young children:

'I'd like to get them away on a wee holiday. I constantly feel guilty 'cause I can't afford to do all these things. So I beat myself up and because their daddy's not there I beat myself up even more because I feel they're missing out. But I know it's best for them.'

Compelling here is the tension between simultaneous negative and positive feelings regarding Sandra's family situation – she feels bad because she took a set of actions that has resulted in her children not having their father present in their lives and because the resulting situation means she cannot give them a holiday. This and other things she can or cannot provide are framed through a compensatory lens, in terms of making up to them for the deprivations they have suffered. But, at the same time, Sandra drew some comfort from suggesting that it was better for them that their father was not there.

What is the source of parents' guilt? Along with Hooper and colleagues (2007, p 40), we find that parents' inability to live up to their own ideals around how they should be as parents was a significant source of anxiety. Children suffering privation is especially hard to take. Parents felt they were failing in the duty to protect their children when they exposed them to the negative consequences of being on a low income. There are two senses of exposure here: one has an experiential sense, as is clear from the following quote from Emma's interview:

'If it's one of the kids' birthdays … they're so important, you have to get their birthday presents.... You're doing without other things, hoping the electricity will last until next week … buying the bare necessities for groceries so that you can get this wee present. Because you can't make them suffer. They don't understand. You can't not get them a birthday present – you're not getting them what they want and you're tightening it, but it has to be just something to give them.'

The second is the sense of exposure in revealing a negative situation to others. This reveals the societal norms framed around childhood and how, against this backdrop, parents struggle to spare children from suffering embarrassment. Listen to Helen, a separated mother of five children, discuss how she felt about a skiing trip organised by her daughter's school:

'I couldn't afford it. I felt embarrassed for myself and her because she wasn't going and other ones were. But in the end I found out there was a few not going, so that made me feel better. But I was really, really embarrassed for myself and her because she couldn't go on that educational skiing trip. It was hundreds of pounds … £300 and something.... I couldn't do it.'

And here is Heather, a young expectant mother (aged 25) of two quite young children whose partner was employed, who felt the need to buy things for the children to compensate them for the low-income situation:

'Every time my kids go into a shop they need sweets and I feel I need to buy them to sort of replace what I don't buy them.... And then I try and put them into clubs and stuff. Like Lisa is in the Brownies and it's £17 a year.... See, even trying to get that it's hard 'cause you don't want her being different from any other wee girl, you know … you want them in the clubs, you don't want them that they're left out.'

Another mother spoke in terms of her children not having 'freedom' – by which she meant freedom from worry. In a few of the narratives, there was a strong theme of self-blame – these parents somehow felt that they 'caused' the privations of their children.

Parents struggled also to cope with the negative emotions induced by saying no to their child's requests. Two respondents mentioned specifically that it made them feel 'mean' to refuse their child. This is how Sheila, a married mother of two, framed how she felt about denying her children small treats:

> 'If I was writing down traits that I don't like, meanness is one of them. And yet I don't consider myself mean. I just think, "This is all we have and I am doing the very best I can so they don't feel as if they are missing out." Do you know what I mean?'

Parents' self-image is affected by their financial restraints. Lizzie described her interaction with her children since she stopped working (and hence had less money) in terms of "no, no, no". Sheila said she felt like an "ould crank" and frequently castigated herself for getting upset ("losing the head") about mundane things. She tried not to give her children a hard time if they did not take care of their clothes or whatever, but "the pressure of knowing you're having to replace stuff makes me impatient". Sheila went on to explain further:

> 'What I wanted was that my kids would not have felt deprived, wouldn't have felt as if you were watching every slice of bread. You know you wanted them to feel as if "certainly, eat away there, son"... but what I was conscious of was the amount of food he was eating....'

And Katy wondered if life might be different for her children if "I wasn't so on the ball all the time about being so strict."

Parents can be hurt by their children as well. Here is Caitlin, a lone mother talking about her four-year-old daughter:

> 'If you were to get her something small, she would say, "Well that's not really anything, is it?" And you're thinking, "Well, Jenny that's just not nice." No matter where you go, she wants you to buy her something.'

For parents who were unable to afford to allow children activities they had previously engaged in, this was a major sense of loss. For example, Joanne, who had recently been made redundant and whose husband was disabled, explained how people did not fully understand the human cost of unemployment, including the effect it has on children's social development. Guilt was a major factor in her perception of being unable to provide for her son's social needs:

> 'If my son comes home from school and says, "All the guys are going down to [roller blading] and I'm not going" ... I have to walk away. That just kills me because it's like £6 or something. But that's nearly a third of the gas for the week and I can't give him it. And that's where all his wee friends are and he has no social life and that just brings me to tears. I can't cope ... I feel bad that I'm not providing for my kids and to me providing is, you know, food, a roof over their head, a warm home and a strong family. But providing for them is also to let them have their life and be individuals and I feel that I'm taking that away from them because I can't provide money for them to go and socialise and develop socially and grow up with people ... because they're losing contact with their friends because they can't socialise and that's just mean.'

Joanne's questioning of whether she was an adequate provider or not shows how torn she was. The breadth of responsibilities involved in her view of providing is notable, including a strong family and warm home as well as allowing her children to be individuals and to have a social life. The stress caused by having to deny children things that others can afford has also been noted by a number of other studies (Ridge, 2002; Hooper et al, 2007; Horgan, 2007; Athwal et al, 2011).

But parents do not always say no. This is the reply of one such parent – May, a widowed lone mother of four children – to the question about whether her kids put pressure on her for designer clothes.

> 'No, no, my kids aren't like that. They know if I have it they get it, if I don't have it, they don't get it. I friggin' have them ruined, don't I? [directed at her father, who was present at the interview]. I went out yesterday – cupcakes, gingerbread men, buns, everything from that bakery. I spoil them [father adds: "She's very good to the kids, I can tell you that"]. Every day they have to have their buns, crisps, chocolate and all ... that's every day they come from school. I have them ruined.... My daughter goes, "What are you doing? Junk." The majority of it is junk, but you have to ... I like them to have their wee treats coming from school.'

And here is Alice, mother of a teenager as well as two sons in their 20s:

'Well, I do try, I suppose, I do try to make sure they, even if it's only once a week or twice a week, feel a wee bit spoilt. You know, they would feel spoilt that we would ... I don't do desserts, really, but even a dessert once a week, even on a Sunday, it's like a wee highlight of the week. They enjoy things like that.'

We see here how May maintained her relationship with her children and defined her role as mother through the ritualised provision of treats for the children. There is a strong sense in both cases of compensating the children and trying to counteract (or even deny) the reality of the low-income situation, even if, as in May's case, it brings opprobrium from her oldest child.

In almost all cases, putting children first requires sacrifice and altruism from the parent (confirmed by Hickman et al, 2014). This, one could say, is a third principle of ethical child rearing in conditions of low income (along with prioritising children and fairness). In one extreme case, Katy (an unemployed lone mother of four children, only one of whom still lived at home) told how when money was very tight in the family she used to not prepare any food for herself but wait to eat what her children did not finish (if they left anything). In fact, she said she had forgotten this until her daughter reminded her of it in a recent conversation about the family's past when they were 'poor poor'. This is a common finding in studies of low-income families such that mothers often compromise their own needs to ensure their children do not go without (see, for example Kempson, 1996; McIntyre et al, 2003; McKendrick et al, 2003; Anderson et al, 2010).

Kochuyt (2004) gives a context within which to view this kind of behaviour. He says that self-sacrifice is an act of upholding one's honour as a parent and it develops at the same time a relationship with the children marked by affection, care and loyalty: 'This altruism clearly shows that consumption is not a simple deduction of the available income, nor is it a strictly utilitarian business' (Kochuyt, 2004, p 139). Altruistic behaviour on the part of the parent also constructs the family as a unit of internal solidarity. As Kochuyt explains it (2007, p 149), the 'gift' gets across care and affection to the children and therefore the gift becomes a basic constituent of the family bond. This has the effect of generating or sustaining ontological security for the parents (and presumably also the child). It may also imply expectations of future return of solidarity from child to parent. Moreover, there is evidence to suggest that the giving of goods and money to children is, as a cultural norm, more important among low-income households than among those that are better off (Komter and Vollebergh, 2002).

Altruism is never one-dimensional, then, and in fact the narratives of some parents indicate that their relative disinvestment in themselves increases their emotional investment in their children. This is how Fiona, lone mother to a nine-year-old boy, responded to the question of what makes her most proud about her family:

> 'When Jason was born, I was all, "Oh my God, I can't believe he's mine." But his Daddy is never there. He would come once in the blue moon. But, you know, at the end of the day I've got my wee man and I'm very proud of that.'

Isabel, also a lone mother to one son who was aged two-and-a-half at the time of interview, described her son as her shadow, and recounted how she took him everywhere (see the quote below). Another lone mother (Rachel) said her five-year-old son was a "wee rock through everything I have been through". In a context where she saw her son as coming from a broken home, she went on to say: "We're just a team, we stick together and we're able to talk … the two of us love each other and we are really, really good together." In part, this level of attachment to the child may stem from the parent's need for love and affection in an otherwise difficult and sometimes barren emotional setting. In other respects, it may be rooted in a desire to gain self-worth through the child and the act of mothering. Here is some interview dialogue from Isabel, a lone mother of one child who left her partner (because of domestic violence) some years ago.

> 'Well, I have to say, like, I brought my child up on my own for two-and-a-half years and I am proud of that because I am a good Mummy.'

> 'You're a good Mummy.'

> 'Yeah [laughs]. Well everybody tells me I'm a good mummy 'cause he's my main focus and I've to be Mummy and Daddy because his Daddy's not really involved with him so I think I'm most proud of bringing him up.'

> 'And when you say you're a good Mummy, tell me a little bit about what you mean by that.'

'Just like I give all my time, 100% to him. I make sure he's eating properly, I make sure he's developing well. I get on the floor with him, I be as silly as ... we just play. We just do everything together, he really is my shadow, I just take him everywhere.'

But of course constant engagement and self-sacrifice also cement the parent's control over the child and key aspects of the child's environment. And it places the demand of loyalty on children. Hooper and colleagues (2007, p 106) point out that investment in the identity of mother may also be defensive and idealised, appearing to offer not only a valued role, but also a new start after troubled childhoods.

People struggle with ethical parenting in conditions of low income in other ways also. One matter of great relevance to respondents was how much they should reveal to the children about their situation. This was quite prominent as a concern in respondents' narratives. The respondents were loosely divided between those who level with their children at a relatively young age and those who try to keep their children from knowing the family's financial situation. The latter was usually represented as a wish to 'protect' the children's innocence. This seems to be a personal preference of the parent, although it is also a contextualised behaviour affected by the extent to which children ask for or expect things and the parents' capacity to supply what is being requested. Whatever course parents choose, the evidence suggests that it is a deeply moral path.

While the urge to protect the child is strong, it is challenged by the desire for realism and openness about the family's situation. Here are two accounts by parents of how they have responded to the situation describing how they level with their children. The first is from Lizzie (a lone mother of four children), and the second from Molly (a married mother with four children):

'I don't hide anything from them. I explain, "You know, there's only me. We don't have Mammy and Daddy here, there's only one Mammy in this house."'

'I just thought, "They're old enough." Obviously, I didn't want to hit them with financial matters because at that age they don't need any more because they've got school. But I thought, "No ... because I'm having to keep saying no to you I need to sit you down and explain it." So we sat the both of them down and explained to both of them and they seemed to take it on board.'

To give children knowledge of the situation was seen to burden them with the responsibility, and indeed, in the second respondent's view, to add to the burden of school.

Managing the children's expectations is part and parcel of being a parent in a situation of low income. When asked if their children wanted or possessed brand-name clothing or goods, most people rushed to qualify their replies to the effect that their children were 'good' in this respect. However, there were a number of exceptions. Here is Susan, a married mother of three children:

> 'My Mammy bought him a LuckyJoes, she rang and said, "Tell Boyd I got him a LuckyJoes hoodie," and I said, "God, Mammy, they're wild dear, why did you buy him that for?" She said, "I only paid £15 for it." I never said nothing to her, but I thought £15 for a LuckyJoe top? And I knew it must be one of the fake ones. So she gave this to Boyd and he said, "That's not even a real LuckyJoe's jumper." And I thought, "I'm going to kill you when I get you home" [laughs]. He wears it now, like, but he'll tell you he wants a real one and I always say, "Don't you tell Nana that's not real because Nana spent a wild lot of money." He says, "Well, she didn't spend all the money because it's not real." He's terrible, he listens to all the other boys in the street, he knows what he wants, he's terrible.'

This meaning of being 'good' – not being demanding or self-centred – is another dimension of the behavioural values discussed earlier (around children not bringing trouble to the family and around the family fitting in). Almost all respondents had strategies for dealing with their children's expectations. In the majority of cases, the goal was to lower the children's expectations if they were felt to be pitched at too high a level (generally interpreted in terms of the affordability of what they asked for and not being spoiled). However, it should also be pointed out that a minority of respondents tried to procure the desired good or activity for the child even if this meant debt and privation in other areas. Most often, this was a phone, computer or other technology-based item, expenditure on which could also be justified through its educational and development potential.

It was far more common, however, for respondents to try to temper their children's expectations. Some took a blunt approach. Leah, a mother two young children, who had recently been made redundant, said: "I just had to tell them, there's no job now … and Santa's been made redundant as well, so there'll not be as much for Christmas." Another mother also told her children that this was a bad year for Santa, just like it was for the family. Yet another respondent, Sandra, a lone mother of two young children, said that she explained to them in the following way:

> 'I told them that Mammy gave Santa the money. Mammy has to give Santa the money and there's only so much money you can give Santa…. And they were saying, "Mammy, thank you for giving Santa the money." I don't know if that's wrong to tell them, but they have to understand that there's a limit.'

DeVault (1999) highlights this type of activity as a form of work. For her, the management of emotions in this way – whether among children or other family members – is a form of emotion work.

In general, respondents veered between protecting their children and being honest with them. But protecting them could mean different things. Sheila worried about the balance between not buying into the materialist culture with which children are surrounded and yet having to try to make them "comfortable in their world too". She described this kind of balance elsewhere in the interview as enabling her daughter, who is 14, "to be able to hold her own". The quote below is an example of how another mother – Sandra – tried to turn the family's circumstances into a lesson for her daughter:

> 'If I tell Julie, "Your Mammy hasn't got any money today," she goes, "Well, just go to the bank machine and just get your card and put it in," and I'm, like, "Yeah, but you have to work hard to get money into that bank." I'm trying to pump it into them that you need to get your education; you need to work hard and get a good job. You just keep pumping them so they don't go down the same road that I went down.'

This raises questions about the nature of childhood in these families. While we did not investigate this specifically, and, of course, have no first-hand evidence from children, the research does reveal some insights about what it is like to be a child in these families.

Being a child in a low-income family

According to Ridge (2002), children, too, sacrifice their own needs to help their parents in situations of low income.

Quite a significant minority of the children represented in the study population appeared to take responsibility and seemed to know the family's situation even when their parents did not explicitly tell them. Moreover, it seems that the parents are aware that the children know. Here is Emma, a married mother of three children, telling how her first child (a son aged nine) behaved in a particular instance:

> 'Me and my husband say we will cut down on Christmas and not let the wee ones know that we're worrying about money because sometimes the older boy would understand. He would say, "Is that too dear, Mammy?" And one day his aunt was taking him to school and they were going to post the Santa letters and he said, "No, we will leave it until some day that you're taking us, Mammy, because I don't want her to have to pay for the stamps."'

This is a young boy acting like an adult. He and some of the other children in these families were at once young and old, as in Helen's family where the children congratulate her for reaching the end of the week while at the same time being all too aware of the realities of the situation:

> 'I say to the kids, "This is all I have left to do me 'til Friday, 'til I get paid again."… Sometimes if I have a bit extra over after the week the kids will say, "You've done well this week, Mammy," and I will say, "I know, I have to make it stretch." Some of them would say to me, "Ach, we know you've no money, Mammy," … which makes me feel bad but deep down they must be feeling it as well, you know.'

These quotes give a strong sense of mother and children as comrades in a strategy for survival.

There is evidence of children self-censoring in other ways also. Emma, who suffered from crippling arthritis, told of her eight-year-old boy:

'His wish for Santa was for me to get better. That broke my heart because I thought any normal child would have wished for a new bike. And that was his wish. He's an emotional wee boy.'

Other examples of self-censoring – whereby the child either does not ask for something or chooses not to tell the parent of a trip being organised by the school or some other event that requires money – also emerged during the interviews. This suggests that protection is a two-way process and that some of the children in these families actively tried to protect their parents. The gap between adult and child seemed smaller in these families than in society at large.

There is another sense also in which, under conditions of poverty and low income, childhood loses its lustre as a period of protection and play. Some of the children were active contributors to their families. At least one child was a carer, including Molly's daughter, aged 13, whom Molly describes as caring for her grandparents in the following way:

'She goes to my Mammy's at the weekend. She goes down and does their house and does the shopping for the week and looks after them and sorts out their tablets and all, puts them into wee boxes for the week. She's a wee mini carer. But she loves it. She doesn't feel stressed by it. She likes going.'

The distinction in the literature between priceless and useless children – which has been used to chart the changing nature of childhood whereby children have gone from being essential to the family's survival strategy, as potential breadwinners, for example, to being valued and regarded as precious for who they are and hence 'useless' from a utilitarian perspective – has no place here (Zelizer, 1985; Miller, 2005). The children in these families were both priceless and useful.

There were a number of instances given where older children (from 16 years up) helped by getting part-time work or, when they were older still, full-time jobs. In a number of cases the part-time job was in a local supermarket, which had the double virtue of providing income but also enabling the family to avail of the staff discount. While it was not clear whether the young people had deliberately chosen the line of work for this reason, there was no doubt that they were actively involved in enabling their family to avail of the discount and that, according to their parents anyway, they derived a sense of family solidarity through this. This is an interview excerpt from a married mother of four children, the eldest of whom – Owen – was aged 17 years and worked in a local shop. In this family, the income was low, even though the father was employed on a full-time basis. The respondent herself was on sickness benefit and told how she suffered from depression. Her seven-year-old girl had just been diagnosed with a serious illness at the time of interview.

> 'Owen, my oldest wee boy, he's very good to them now he gets full wages. He would go up and buy them wee things, he's great that way. Or say one of them wanted a football top, he would come in and say, "If I buy Robert, will you buy Mark?" He's great that way. I think because he knows … before when I was working full time there was always money but there isn't with me not working at the minute and they know that and he's great that way, I didn't think he would be … I thought, "This is going to be a nightmare," but he is great.'

While we did not investigate specifically what happened when children got older and left the family home, any spontaneous references to this indicated that they remained quite active as family members, although the degree of contact and nature of their role obviously varied. Helen, a lone mother of five, spoke of how her eldest son, who had moved out but lived close by, regularly came by, "bringing wee treats for us and entering with the words, 'Is everything all right here?'" She explained this in terms of his having been "the man of the house for years", as the parents split up when he was young. In another case, reference was made to a son who had emigrated to Australia as a source of help.

Note that the older children were sometimes called on to be altruistic so that the 'childhood' of the younger children could be protected. Here is an example recounted in a very matter-of-fact way by Lizzie (lone mother of four children). Patrick, the son to whom she refers, was 17.

> 'Yeah that's Patrick, he's 18 next month, he's very good, he would help me an awful lot, because I'm on my own now and he was 15 when I had Rebecca … it felt like because he was minding her, well not minding her, interacting with me with her. I've looked at the side where he's took on a role, not a role of a daddy but this big brotherly thing with her. People say to me, "It's a pity your oldest isn't a girl," and I go, "No, he's a boy, but he's very maternal." And I think he's just took on that role himself, it hasn't been

pushed on him, because I've always given him the choice. Because I'm on my own and he's seen that, he's sort of just wrapped his arms around Becky as if it's his own wee one, you know, because he's had to help me.'

In their study of low-income families in Canada, Gazso and McDaniel (2013, p 15) use the term 'generationing' – usually understood as people of different generations interacting in normative ways. However, they found that the enactment of relationships among generations in their respondent families was flexible and the relationships between generations were often flipped over. This is visible in the current study also – where children 'parent their parents'. One example is the daughter, mentioned in an earlier quote, who chastises her mother for buying treats for the younger children. There were other examples, too, including teenage boys playing the father (and in some cases father/provider) role in lone-mother families. That said, while there may be some overturning of generational relations and roles, the responsibilities in this regard remain highly gendered: the girls mother and the boys father.

Overview

As parents, the respondents in this study negotiate a narrower path than is likely to be the case in families where there is no scarcity of money. They have less freedom of action and a very constraining set of boundaries. Perhaps because of this, much of their energy is taken up with working out what is good parenting in their situation. This means trying to protect their children by, for example, instilling in them the need to conform (or 'be good'), trying to ensure that they are not too different from or deprived relative to other children in terms of social and leisure participation, not 'spoiling' them (which has a sense of not allowing them to have unrealistic expectations of what they can have, given the family's circumstances), and being fair to all of the children.

Respondents work hard at raising their children and they have strong values that they continually strive to adhere to. Keeping the family going means not just surviving as a financial entity, but keeping it functioning as a meaningful system of altruistic relations between parents and children. Parents applied different standards to their children's consumption than they did to their own (a finding also noted in a Belgian study by Kochuyt [2004]) and were readily prepared to forego fulfilling their own needs to try to ensure that their children did not go without.

Throughout, the evidence indicates how meaningful the role of parent is to respondents, as well as how they attempt to construct a meaningful role for themselves through their parenting. Respondents' identities and ontological security are invested in their children more than any other family member, relationship or activity.

This sense of an active and highly moral family life is in stark contrast to the image of families living in economic hardship and deprivation portrayed in recent media coverage and in policy.[1] In particular, it contradicts the representation of poverty as being primarily linked to cultural or behavioural deficits, a depiction that is widely prevalent at the current time. These findings also raise questions about the recent government emphasis on love and affection in a committed family setting as one of the greatest influences on a child's life chances, more so than any socioeconomic structural factor (Field, 2010). An influential report on child poverty (Centre for Social Justice, 2012) reiterated the Field review findings, referring to lack of support and love as 'real poverty' (2012, p 6). Against this backdrop, it is worth emphasising that there was no shortage of love in the families taking part in this study and that lack of money explains their situation far better than lack of love, affection and caring.

---

[1]   See Levitas (2012; 2014) for a critique of the recent government Troubled Families Strategy.

FIVE

Wider family relationships and support

This chapter investigates the meaning and significance of family relationships in terms of supportive relationships among adults and especially those outside the immediate or nuclear family. This is examined mainly through the prism of whether and how people's familial relationships involve the giving or receiving of resources and support, including money, other forms of material support, and emotional support. This chapter is essentially focused on the ebb and flow of instrumental and affective forms of support within families and establishing what is of most importance to people in regard to maintaining the exchanges that are understood to constitute family life and family relationships under conditions where the supply of resources is limited. Among the topics that will be investigated are the nature of the support received (if any) and the relational context within which it takes place. Much of this chapter turns on questions about the chains of family relationships that people are involved in, how these figure as part of a support network and the extent of reliance on relatives. As well as looking at the congregation of resource exchange and usage, the chapter is especially interested in investigating the understandings that people have of receiving and giving help from and to relatives and the particular norms that govern exchanges among family members.

Family relationships tend to be entwined with social obligations in a way that other relationships are not. Such social obligations are changing, however. Familial networks of support cannot be assumed to operate today, unlike the past when extended kinship networks of support were seen, as Allan (1996, p 29) notes, as 'an unremarkable, largely taken-for-granted feature of people's routine activities'. As discussed earlier, the degree of change in this and other regards is such that the category of family itself is destabilised, becoming the source of a vibrant body of research around the question of what is family (Gubrium and Holstein, 1990; Weeks et al, 2001; Morgan, 2010). Playing a causal role here are general societal trends towards individualisation and pluralisation. Both tend to weaken family bonds, the former in emphasising and placing value on autonomous functioning and an individualised identity, the latter in rendering traditional family values and practices somewhat out-moded in the face of autonomy. However, there is also evidence to suggest the continued relevance of family – especially the fact that substantial transfers between adult generations in the family beyond the nuclear household still exist (Kohli, 1999). This goes somewhat against the assumption that the nuclear family form and increasing individualisation of social life make for independence between the generations. In fact, the indications are that transfers from parents to their adult children – so-called '*inter vivos* transfers' – as well as other forms of intergenerational support are becoming more rather than less important (Hills et al, 2010).

It is not clear how any of this plays out in situations of poverty and low income. Existing research indicates that the contribution of family, friends and neighbours can be vital in helping to mitigate the harsh realities of life on a low income. It is also known that support can take many forms, but that the most common forms are financial – such as gifts and loans of money – and emotional support, which is usually realised through a willingness to listen, to give advice and adopt a sympathetic attitude towards the person's situation (Gosling, 2008; Green and Hickman, 2010). Let us hear respondents' experiences.

Degree of support from family

Interviewees were asked in a relatively open-ended way about where (if anywhere) they got support from. In reply, relatives emerged spontaneously as far and away the overriding source of support. These were most often close kin (defined either by family of origin or marriage). Parents, siblings and in-laws were to the fore but even cousins and aunts were mentioned by some respondents as among their significant sources of support.

Of the total sample, only three respondents said they got no help or support from their families. This was almost exclusively because of issues around accessibility: the respondents in question did not have close relatives living in Northern Ireland. This gives an immediate cue to proximity as one of the factors affecting patterns of support and exchange. A further five respondents (in addition to the three who received no support from close family) could be said to receive relatively little familial support. This was for a mixture of reasons: in some cases a lack of physical proximity, in others emotional distance, and in still others a wish to be independent of family of origin or marriage. The remaining 43 respondents were more or less evenly divided between those who were by their own accounts receiving either a high or medium level of support from their close family (the differentiation being mainly based on the frequency of support and the degree of expressed reliance on it). Overall then, only a minority of respondents were without support from at least one family member.

Parents, primarily the respondents' own but in a few cases the parents of their partner, were far and away the main sources of support (38 out of the 43 cases). Mothers figured prominently – it seems to be almost an automatic response to turn to one's mother: "We all run to our Mummies", is how one respondent put it. Mothers-in-law were less commonly approached but figured sufficiently prominently to suggest that they, too, play an important support role. Notably, fathers (or fathers-in-law) were specifically mentioned by nine respondents as a source of medium or high support. Apart from parents, sisters were the next most common source of support, followed by brothers or another female relative such as aunt or cousin. If respondents had adult children, they too were mentioned as a source of help and support.

The fact that only a minority of people listed just one supportive family member suggests that respondents had access to a network of family support, at least in the sense that they could call on more than one family member. To the extent that this was the case, there are grounds to suggest that support occurs within a network rather than being a property of relations between two individuals. It is important not to overplay this point, though, because in reality people tended to prefer to turn to one or two people (with parents sometimes discussed as one source). This patterning picks up on a theme mentioned earlier (in Chapter Three) when there was a reference to 'tiers' of family. The idea of family within family seems apposite.

No one was casual about asking for help and people were very conscious of what could be asked of different relatives. The nature of the bond and the degree of intimacy emerge as very important factors in this regard. The consideration that seems to make the greatest difference is what Pahl and Spencer (2004) in earlier research called the 'intrinsic quality of the relationship'. This refers to the strength of the tie, the degree of dependability of the link, the level of trust and confiding involved, and the sense of being known and accepted 'as oneself'. The results here confirm that there was a strong 'relational' underpinning to respondents' requests for help from their family.

A second point to note is that, while members of the respondent's family of origin were more important in terms of support, one-third of the relevant respondents identified in-laws as a significant source of support. This indicates a degree of interchangeability in terms of whether they would receive help from their family of origin or their family of marriage/partnership. In a significant minority of families then, having access to support from a partner's family acts as an additional buffer against adversity. A third point to note is the highly female character of the support. Support tended to flow between women (actually mothers) rather than men and the exchange was more commonly precipitated by women. This may reflect the gender (im) balance of the sample, but it is also in line with the results of other research. For example, Mitchell and Green (2002, p 19) concluded the following from their study of young mothers:

> For many of the young mothers in Townville (both lone mothers and those living with partners), kinship networks, especially female kinship between mothers and adult daughters (with children), played a pivotal role, practically, socially and emotionally in their everyday lives. Indeed, female kinship was closely interwoven with one's self-identity as a caring and capable mother.

The specificity of the Northern Irish context must be acknowledged as playing a role. There are two main points to note in this regard. The first is cultural. Research has established that there is a very high frequency of contact between parents and their adult children in Northern Ireland – data collected in 2000 and 2001 indicated that 41% of people see or visit a non-resident adult child every day and that almost a quarter see their mother on a similarly frequent basis (Daly, 2004). This and other evidence indicates that family and kin relationships are a very important part of social life in Northern Ireland. Second, there is the matter of propinquity. People in Northern Ireland tend to live close to their families. This is true for the respondents in the present study as well, in that about two-thirds (38) lived no more than a 15-minute walk from their own parents or siblings or in-laws. And many in fact had family on the same street or in the locality (as discussed in the next chapter).

As one would expect, there is a relationship between the receipt of support and the propinquity of relatives. People were more likely to receive support from relatives living close by. There is a double causality at work here: people choose to live near the relative(s) they feel closest to and physical proximity means greater contact, and hence greater visibility of one's situation, and perhaps openness about need.

Types of support received

Interviewees' accounts suggest that there are different types of family support. These can be arrayed along a continuum. Material support – which is conceived here to include both financial support and support with tasks and activities – dominated, closely followed by emotional and psychological support. Since these types of support are rather different in character, they need to be discussed separately.

To start with material support, both financial assistance and help with tasks and activities from family members were widely received by respondents. In fact, material exchanges were relatively routine. The financial assistance mainly took the form of micro credit. Only in one case where amounts of money were specified did loans from close family exceed £20. These small financial transactions were described in terms that indicate their importance in keeping the household ticking over until the next income day: 'my lifeline', 'my safety net', 'my breathing space'. But they were also typically short-term in nature. In fact, such transactions functioned to some extent as a short-term borrowing facility in that the money borrowed would usually be paid back within a short period (typically when the respondent received their pay or benefit). It is to this that most people turned on those days of the week when they had no money (provided it was available, of course).

But there was also a significant minority of cases where the financial assistance was a one-off occurrence with little or no expectation that the money borrowed would be paid back. This could be for routine functioning or for more occasional expenses, like those associated with a family rite of passage such as starting school, or a christening, confirmation or Holy Communion. Such help was also given at birthdays or Christmas. Here is an account from Fiona, lone mother of one son, about how the costs of her son's First Communion were met:

> 'He made his First Communion in June and I didn't have to buy him nothing, my family all bought him. My mother and father paid for his clothes, my sister got him his shoes. Everybody was buying him and I didn't have to pay for nothing. At Christmas time I'll not have to buy him nothing because they buy him his clothes and somebody will buy him his shoes.'

By and large, the sums of money passing between relatives were small and routine, but there were also cases where people were lent or given significant sums of money. This was usually for a large expense – among the examples given were buying oil for the central heating, paying large bills and, in one case, a deposit for a house rental. Here is Carmel's (a partnered mother with four children) account of how the latter situation transpired:

> 'It is quite hard … but then I do have a good family but none of them has money but what they have got they would share.… I was moving house and I needed a rent deposit for the house. I was telling my auntie I needed it for Friday and she said, "If you can't get it by Friday I have the boys' Christmas money there, I could lend you that for a couple of weeks." That would be their type. I was, like, "No, it's alright." In the end, Mummy ended up coming up with it. That's the way we would be but we would be the same back.'

It was quite common for people to receive food as a gift. Other 'gifts' included household items and/or clothing. Along with food, children's items figured prominently among gifts, with one grandmother even giving her grandchildren pocket money every week in lieu of parental pocket money. Here is how Jenny talked about the help she received from her mother:

> 'I'm saying I help her but she would help me in that she would buy me bread and milk every day. Them wee things … and you don't realise how much they add up. She would buy maybe a chicken now and again or a wee bit of ham now and again. And she buys the kiddies sweets. She would buy them so that they don't go without. So she is quite good in that respect. It's not an awful lot, but when you start to count that up over the weeks it is.'

The implication here is that chicken and ham are foods that the respondent herself could not afford and hence constituted appropriate gifts from her mother. There is a subtext here about the appropriateness of receiving help as evidenced by the respondent's noting of the cumulation of help from her mother over time.

It was equally common for respondents to receive practical help from members of their family. Child minding was the most common form of material help. It included short-term babysitting, but also quite extensive child minding on a regular basis (most typically to assist respondents with a job, for example, or in cases where the child had a physical or mental disability to give the parent time to attend to other things). The 'giver' was most commonly the respondent's parents or a sibling. This echoes the findings of other studies showing the importance of support from grandparents. For example, investigating how lone mothers and their children adapt to employment over time, Ridge and Millar (2008) found that childcare support provided by grandparents played a vital role in many lone mothers' work and care strategies. The extent of the gift of care in this study is remarkable. For over half of the respondents, the childcare support allowed them to go to work or, if they were not in employment, provided a breathing space from other pressures, like coping with a young child's behavioural problems or learning difficulties. Relatives also assisted by providing transport (most often for the school run, shopping, lifts to and from work and on occasions to attend an appointment). All of these types of help were commonly cited by respondents. Less common was help with cleaning, DIY or decorating but this, too, was present as a form of support from family.

Family members were also a vital source of affective support for respondents. What was 'given' here was most commonly advice about family and financial decision making, as well as more generic support (in the words of one respondent, "comfort and closeness"). A number of respondents expressed the latter type of support in terms of "just knowing they're there". Many respondents identified having someone to talk to among family members as helping to stave off or ameliorate situations when they felt down or depressed.

For the majority of respondents, help from family – whether practical or emotional in nature – was routine. While it might not occur on an everyday basis, it was part and parcel of everyday living. People counted on it – a few even took it for granted. The interviews convey a strong impression that a significant minority of families (about a fifth) could hardly function without this assistance. This is confirmed by other research on Northern Ireland (Hickman et al, 2014). In the current study, interviewees were asked what they thought would happen if such support was not available. The responses were almost all in the same vein: people either could not or would not imagine such a scenario. In fact, this was one of the questions that respondents found most difficult to answer. The following reply from Lily is typical of what people said in response:

> 'Oh, I don't know. That's the God's honest truth, I don't know.'

It would be wrong to assume that there was a perfect correspondence between the level of support and its perceived significance. A common theme was that people valued highly the feeling that their family was there for them should they need them. This seemed to be independent of levels of support, since it was as commonly expressed by those receiving little material or other forms of help as by those who were heavily reliant on practical and emotional assistance.

As mentioned, there was considerable support from in-laws, which accounted for one of the main differences between couple families and lone-parent families. An example of such significant support from in-laws is demonstrated by the case of one family with three young children of primary school age where the respondent had no siblings and sole responsibility for her own mother, who lived alone and had multiple physical and mental health problems. In this case, the respondent (Susan) provided her own mother with all the physical help and emotional support she needed. Her mother was unable to reciprocate, but Susan's husband's mother provided extensive support to the family in the form of child minding, financial assistance and emotional support. For Susan, this helped to compensate for the absence of support from her own family and even allowed her to continue looking after her own mother. This is how Susan described her mother–in–law:

> 'She's a brilliant help with everything, with the wee ones, if I needed to talk, I would go to her, financially I could go to her, everything I could go to her. If she wasn't there, I don't know what I would do – we don't always get on, but I always like to know she's there.'

This illustrates the value of being able to call on what might be thought of as a partner's resources to counterbalance a support deficit. However, the fact that Susan revealed that she did not always get on with her mother-in-law implies the relationship is not without difficulty, suggesting that calling on kin may generate ambivalence.

In two cases, family support went beyond the material or the emotional. Two lone-mother respondents (Rachel and Isabel) had moved back into the parental home because of their financial circumstances. The situation in both cases not only provoked ambivalence but also created friction and arguments with other family members still living at home who resented the situation because of overcrowding and scarcity of resources. Things were further complicated for Rachel because her parents were on benefits and, if it were known she was living at home, her parents' benefit income would be reduced. This also meant that she could not register on the social housing waiting list because she could not declare she was there. This was a major source of friction between her and her parents. She discussed it in terms of the biggest struggle she faced at the time.

Sometimes there was what was akin to an invisible fence between the respondent's own family and family of origin, and there were also boundaries within families also. Here is Molly talking first about her husband and then her dad.

> 'We support each other, we are each other's support. And he is very good, very, very good. They think he might have cancer of the mouth at the minute and he's going next week for that ... and there'd be a wee bit of support from my Dad around that. He says, "I'll go with him to get his results." But me and John, we're used to it just being me and him and it's, like, "No, this is it, this is what we do." And then I suppose I don't tell them half the things so they don't know because they don't need my problems on top of theirs.'

Overall, the findings are unequivocal that relatives were a major form of assistance and actively provided a range of different types of support on a relatively regular basis. About a fifth of families would be unable to subsist without the support of family members. The fact that respondents valued the support that comes from knowing family members are "there for you" resonates with other qualitative research on family relationships and responsibilities. For example, Finch and Mason (1993, p 33) describe moral support from family members as being 'the essence of family life'.

Looking at patterns overall, people's requests for assistance from family were generally relationship-centred. It was more complicated than this, though, with requests for and receipt of support filtered through an 'appropriateness lens' in terms of the degree of closeness and quality of the relationship; norms around what one asks of, say, one's mother as against an aunt or cousin and so forth; whether the potential giver is likely to be able to help without incurring hardship for themselves; and the history of receiving help and reciprocating. Receipt of family support is shaped and influenced by a number of factors and circumstances along with the quality of the relationship and physical propinquity. Considering these provides a window on prevailing norms and values.

One such factor is respondents' age. Younger respondents were more likely to be receiving assistance from family than older respondents. This was especially the case with material assistance (both financial and practical). In some respects, age is a proxy for need and stage of family formation, but there is a set of normative elements around generation operating here also. The younger the respondents are, the younger are their children, and also the more likely are their relatives to be in a situation to offer help. Health was another major factor in conditioning need – as mentioned elsewhere, quite a number of respondent families had children with special needs. Hence, these families' need of assistance was greater than that of other families. A third factor that tended to precipitate help was the recent occurrence of a financial crisis – most typically through a loss of a job, an accident or indebtedness. Across the sample the crucial underpinning factor influencing whether people got help from family or not was the strength or quality of family relationships.

Ambivalence surrounding family support

It would be wrong to view family-based assistance either as automatic – sometimes it was asked for, at other times it was proffered – or easy to accept. People were generally very conscious of what was involved and often desisted from asking. One reason for self-censorship was because in a lot of cases the family members were in a similar financial situation. Some people explained that they did not like having to borrow from their family because they too had their "good weeks and bad weeks". This also, however, meant that people might prefer to ask a family member who was not in straitened circumstances (should they have one). One respondent (Mary) mentioned her "rich sister" and another (Beth) her "rich uncle". Exactly how rich they were was not clear, but what this kind of finding indicates is that people were very conscious of the relative income situation of different family members and this was taken into account when they were considering a request for support. They may not end up asking the 'rich' relative, but it was a consideration (and may also have been something of an interview construction to convey an alternative impression of themselves and their family to that of poverty and low income).

People were quite reflexive about the help received from their family and the conditions attached. Such reflexivity was usually morally grounded. The complexities involved were manifold. One reason for not wishing to borrow from a close relative may be because the giver may not want it paid back. Here is Margaret, mother of four whose husband was employed:

> 'I hate borrowing off my Mammy because she never wants you to pay her it back. She'll say, "No, buy something with that or buy the kids something." So that's why I really only would ask her if I had no other option. But I do pay her back, but she'll say, "No, keep it, keep it, I don't want it."'

The sense of a moral struggle is palpable.

Sometimes the help is surreptitiously given; or, viewed through another lens, 'forced on' people. Here is Susan, mother to three young children, speaking of her mother-in-law:

> 'She's a big support ... just like last week, we had to go and do Santa shopping and she said to me, "Have you got everything in for Christmas?", and I said, "Yeah, we only have to get three things." But these three things were coming to £400. That night she was up in my house and she left and she phoned me and said to me, "Do you see the picture of you and Josh? There's an envelope behind it." And when I looked in the envelope there was £300 and she said, "It will help with the Christmas shopping." Just things like that there. She knew if she had given it to me personally, I wouldn't have took it. Just wee things like that there, she's brilliant.'

This kind of 'surreptitious giving' was evident in at least a fifth of cases. The above respondent recounted this in very positive terms, but inherent in her account also is a struggle between neediness and independence, and around boundaries. This had an echo in other interviews also.

Ambivalence not just about requesting but also about receiving help was in fact quite common, although it must be said that there was only one case in the entire sample where a respondent refused to ask for help. This was out of a sense of, or desire for, independence. However, there were cases where people expressed great difficulty in asking for support and went out of their way to pretend they did not need help. The excerpt below is from Joanne, who had one dependent child and who had recently been made redundant. She was confident her parents-in-law would provide financial help if she asked, but the thought of asking was too much for her to contemplate:

'My husband's Mum and Dad would offer, but I go, "No, no everything's grand, everything's grand, don't be worrying about it," because I don't want to be a burden on anybody else. I don't want anybody else to be responsible for me. Like, they're pensioners and I'm, like, "No, this is wrong." If it was like the end of the world, my husband would go and say to his Mum, "You couldn't help us out?" and they would gladly do it. But I don't want to do that.'

The question is why? It seems that a sense of being 'independent' is at the root of this. The two quotes that follow, in response to a question about how they cope when there is too little money, are from Sheila, a 48-year-old, and Ruth, a 25-year-old, respectively:

'Being able to fall back on my Mammy, which is almost shameful at my age. You shouldn't even have to think that but that absolutely would be the case.'

'My Mammy and Daddy. I don't know what I'd do without them. They're the other ones in my life that are ... the main people in my life are my Mammy and Daddy. More so my Daddy, he helps me out as much as he can 'cause they're on a low income themselves so.... But, you know, my Daddy would do anything to help me to make sure the children are fed and to make sure that I'm fed. I'm, like, 25 and don't even live at home and he's, like, "Have you ate anything today, have you eaten?" You know, things like that [laughs] ... he's on the phone and I feel about 12 answering these questions [laughs].'

Here is another account from Lily, a 28-year-old partnered mother of a three-year-old, who was expecting another baby and who worked part time. All of the following was said in a self-deprecating manner:

'Yeah, so I'd go down to my Mammy's about 3 in the afternoon and then we'd sit and have a wee cup of tea and a wee chat and then she'd be, "Do you want to stay for dinner?" and I'd be, "Yeah, sure [starts to laugh and puts on a funny voice], that's what I'm here for, I'm not going to tell you that's what I'm here for but it is. You think I'm here to see you but I'm not at all, I'm down to raid your fridge" [laughs again].'

Independence and struggles to achieve it are the sub-text in these and many other cases. Independence as an age-related norm underpins many of these struggles – by the time people become parents themselves, they are expected and expect themselves to be independent (financially, anyway) of their own parents. It did not happen like that for the present respondents, however. Mitchell and Green (2002, p 19) drew the following conclusion about the tension between the young mothers they studied who were at one and the same time forging new lives and yet being drawn into traditional relationships in a working-class community in the north east of England: 'Female kinship in Townville thus holds a complex and dual edged potential, practically and emotionally providing vital support and security in an increasingly insecure world, whilst simultaneously engaging young mothers in discourses, which can foster Foucauldian style self-surveillance and control'.

The following account from Sheila, a part-time employed mother of two in her late 40s, shows what it is like to be at the receiving end of parental benevolence:

> 'I do know no matter how much you're trying to pretend ... every now and again my Mammy would give you a card that everybody publicly sees and then maybe she'd have a wee envelope for you later and there'd be a note in it, "For God's sake, do something with that hair," [laughs] or "For the love of God, buy a jumper."'

Giving (back) to family

In his classic work *The gift* (1966), Marcel Mauss argued that a gift is never 'free', but is part of a complex system of relationship building in which gifts incur obligations around exchange and reciprocity. He also outlined how being able to give enhances one's status, whereas receiving without giving back reduces it. In the current study, it is not only receiving that connects these people to their families, but also giving back.

In general, respondents were givers as well as receivers. In only six cases did people who were in receipt of significant help from their families not reciprocate (at all or to a roughly similar degree). In most of these cases, this was either because of an incapacity to reciprocate (either due to an illness, financial shortage or other lack of resources) or because respondents felt their families did not need anything from them at the present time.

If money was one of the main forms of support that these respondents received from their families, what they gave back was mainly in kind or practical in nature. The main practical forms of support that flowed between respondents and their families were meals, care (either of children or ill or elderly adults), home-related services such as cleaning, DIY or gardening, and driving. Some of this support or help was given to elderly relatives – most commonly shopping, providing cooked meals, visiting, dispensing medication, helping with official forms, and arranging doctors' visits and hospital appointments. The return support, however, was also given to people closer to their own age, mainly because of illness or disability. Respondents were also by their own accounts relatively heavy providers of emotional support to close family members.

But it must be said that there was no necessary quid pro quo in terms of what was received and what was given back. The form of reciprocity was asymmetric. These were loose exchanges, mediated by a number of factors. The first was people's capacity to give back. The second was relative need, which implicitly brings in a sense of time. There was an implicit norm that the giver be reciprocated as and when they need it. Hence, there seemed to be an openness – although it was not necessarily always a 'settled' matter among all involved – to exchanges taking place over time and in a context of greatest relative need. The idea of delayed reciprocity, which Fine and Glendinning (2005, p 612) talk about in relation to care-related needs and exigencies later in life, serves to convey the meaning involved here. There is a further layer of complexity to this, though, in that relative need is a communal concept and so extends beyond the giver and receiver. Hence, someone in receipt of a 'gift' from a family member – especially their mother – may not necessarily give back to the giver but rather to another family member who was seen to be in greater need. Nina, a young lone mother with two children, gave one such example. She received substantial help from her mother and in return supported her sister by having her sister's son to stay sometimes at weekends. Her nephew has ADHD, and she wanted to give her sister a break. Respondents used terms like "we sort of lean on each other" and "we just try and work together so that it does run smoothly and everything's getting done what needs to be done". Giving back, therefore, may not be in an equivalent degree, form or time period. It may not even be offered to the giver.

All of this means that there may be a circularity in exchanges within families. Lily, whose partner had heavy debt due to negative equity, described borrowing from family and giving back like a domino effect.

'If partner is stuck, I hit my Mammy, partner gets it off me and I pay my Mammy back.'

Money or services can, then, circulate among more than one person – as mentioned earlier, there were many cases of small amounts of money regularly being transferred between parents and siblings. The phrases "the floating £20" and "the rubber piece of money" convey the extent to which money bounces back and forth:

'Me and my sister have this thing – the floating £20 – nobody knows who actually owns the £20, but it's back and forth "Can I borrow it?", "Can I borrow it?" and we don't even know where it is now, it's in the air somewhere.' (Rachel)

'There's almost money that's on this bit of elastic because if I haven't got it my younger sister has it, if she hasn't got it. It just seems to be this rubber piece of money that doesn't really belong to my Mammy at all, it just seems to bounce between us all.' (Sheila)

The lack of clear ownership in these two separate cases is quite striking and indicates a sense of collective exchange. There is also the fact that the giver and receiver cannot always be easily identified. But one of the most important points to note is that there can be no float if one member does not pay it back, so it depends on acceptance of mutual responsibility.

While the details are blurred and constituent elements not always dyadic, there was no ambivalence about the need to give back. If they could not give back in their present circumstances, people constructed scenarios where they would be very generous. Here is Beth – a married mother of three young children, who, like her husband, was employed, but who was heavily in debt – on how she envisaged giving back:

'People laugh at me. I had an Excel spreadsheet done for the Lotto, for how to win the Lotto. I had it all done, all formulated, all my columns of families and all rationed out so that when I win the Lotto they don't have to wait for me coming back from Spain to get their cheque. It will be written straight away so they don't have to wait, so I don't forget to give anybody because you could imagine in that madness you could forget somebody and that's terrible.'

Support received from family was generally reciprocated, then, but the term 'give and take' better captures the nature of the reciprocation in these families than 'paying back'. 'Giving back', the term used by people themselves, while a widespread norm had no singular metric attached. It may be helpful therefore to speak of 'asymmetrical reciprocity' – in regard to the form, timing and identity of the recipient.

The concept of negotiation is prominent in scholarship on family, kinship, personal relationships and friendship. The belief is widespread, following Finch and Mason's (1993) influential study, that family responsibilities are negotiated rather than prescribed through norms and values. According to Mason (2008, p 36), 'negotiations involve and construct not just what support passes between whom, but also the moral identities and reputations of the participants and a sense of the morally appropriate course of action. But they do not *determine* the kinship 'outcomes' or the shape and nature of affinities, because these are achieved in cumulative, situated interactions and negotiations between specific people, over time' (emphasis in original).

Against this general backdrop, one of the interesting findings from this study is of very little overt negotiation in family exchanges. It seems that many of the conventions are silent, taken for granted, on the part of both the giver and receiver. Here is Emma, a mother of three young children, who was unemployed along with her husband. She was very close to her mother and her siblings and felt she had received a lot of help from them.

> 'I've been saying to everybody, "Thank you very much for helping," and they're all saying, "I know you would do it for me if it was the other way about." So I'm thinking, well, thank God they know that.'

People found it embarrassing and even demeaning to mention their need of help and to be explicitly asked was to invite a denial or refusal. Here is Sheila again:

> 'I know my Mammy and Daddy do things like that so that they're doing it in their own way. They would do silly things, like if a taxi came to the door, my Daddy would be away down to pay the taxi man or you'd go home some days and I'd open my glasses case and, like, maybe there's £20 and you'll phone and say, "Did you put money?" and they'll say, "No" and you're thinking, "Do I look simple or something?" And you know they're trying so very hard.

Like – "I just happened to be out with your sister and I seen your favourite thing." It could be four tins of tuna and she'll have got you two packs of them, "Ach, they were only such and such a price." You know, they're doing things because they know if they were to come and say, "Do you need money?", you would always say, "No, I don't.'"

This can be read in several ways: that Sheila was forced into a situation of accepting her parents' help or that she constructed the situation wherein the parents took the initiative to give because they knew she would not ask for help.

There is also the 'burden' of not knowing how to respond to or acknowledge the help. Lily's family had had their house repossessed. She explained how she felt about the situation wherein she and her partner were struggling to pay rent in private accommodation and were dependent on help from both sets of parents who lived nearby:

'I'm not a very emotional person, I can't really show my emotions that well, so you know, in my head I'm going, "Get up and give her a hug" but I'm going, "Ach, thanks very much, that's great, thank you" – when I really want to jump up and go, "Oh my God, thank you".… Without John's Mammy and my Mammy I would genuinely, and I mean this, I'd be screwed, they're amazing – two amazing women.'

It was not uncommon for older respondents (aged 45 to 64 years) to be providing practical and emotional help to their 'non-dependent' children at the same time as giving help to elderly relatives. Three of the respondents were grandparents and in one case the respondent talked about providing support to her mother, a dependent child at home, a non-dependent daughter who lived close by and her grandchildren. In a small number of cases – which were exceptional to the main pattern – respondents were giving older parents more intense help, most commonly where a parent had a disability or suffered ill health. Existing research confirms that such support does not stop when children leave the parental home (McKendrick et al, 2003, Horgan, 2007; Ridge and Millar, 2008).

What was clear from the narratives of the small group of respondents providing very large amounts of support was the increased risk of negative mental and physical health associated with this situation. Being relied on too much, feeling smothered, wanting a bit of space for oneself and needing a break for a while were the most common feelings expressed by people in this situation. However, not everyone was comfortable admitting to such feelings and in the interviews some felt the need to quickly qualify their views by saying that they did not always feel like this or that they would not let the other person know they felt like this.

The following two quotes reflect this ambivalence. The first is from Sarah, a mother of two, whose husband had been unemployed for at least five years and whose father-in-law, who had heart problems, resided close by and lived a life that was very intertwined with that of the respondent's family. The second is from Ciara, a married mother of two children, who worked part time but who provided a lot of care to her own mother, who was an alcoholic:

> 'I would feel stressed a lot, not because of the lifestyle – it's just everyday general things like my father-in-law's health and depending on me too much … days I feel smothered. I just want left alone. Do you know what I'm saying?… Not that I don't mind, but there's just days I feel like I just want to be left alone myself, I just think you want that bit of freedom, nobody torturing you or nobody annoying you.'

> 'Yeah, I hate to complain about it, I really do and you feel bad for saying it's a pressure, but it does be. I would never let her know that it was but….'

The stress of providing high levels of support caused a few of these respondents to develop serious conditions such as depression, mental breakdown, anaemia and hair loss. While there were no reports from respondents of the support coming to an end, two (of the seven people in this situation) indicated that they were at breaking point.

Overall, the evidence suggests that kin relationships are characterised by a moral commitment to give help if it is needed and if it is possible to do so, and to make up for any help received in whatever way possible. Given this, it would be very hard to describe respondents as independent of their family of origin. These are people in a state of 'semi-dependence' (like the young mothers in Schofield's [1994] study). One should be careful, however, about the use of 'independence' as a frame to understand what is going on. One of the underlying characteristics of this kind of framework is the construction of a binary between dependence and independence, and their juxtaposition as opposing states or conditions. A second underlying assumption is about power – those on whom we depend are said to have control over us. Looking closely at what is going on in the families in this study, however, leads us to question the degree to which those who receive are dependent and whether they are subject to power relations. In the latter regard especially, it could be argued that because their families were or felt they were generally in a similar situation, the scope for the exercise of power or control was delimited. In other words, relative dependence was a condition of all. This is not to say that power was not exercised in these families. It was. But it was not necessarily economic power, and being in receipt of assistance did not necessarily entail dependence or being controlled by others. Third, both dependence and independence are contested concepts and could be argued to be normative constructs rather than states or conditions that obtain in real life (Fine and Glendinning, 2005). For the respondents and their families in the current study, interdependence would seem to better describe their situation than either of the other two concepts.

Overview

This chapter has examined the 'chains of relationships' characterising respondents and how these are at once strengthened and weakened by needing aid, receiving support or having to give it. As well as revealing the support received, the information presented has a broader set of references: showing the extent to which the wider family acts as a resource pool to protect against scarcity and the conditions attaching to support received.

The evidence makes clear that wider family was a vibrant and multi-dimensional source of private transfers for the majority of respondents. A large volume of practical, emotional and small-scale financial support passed between members of the family network. Family support took a number of forms, including regular childcare but also food, clothes for children and small household items such as washing powder. Micro money lending to help with immediate bills and costs was a very important form of support, especially for younger parents. The amounts involved tended to be rather small, but in a number of families of younger parents, respondents spoke about receiving one-off gifts of money from their parents to help with the additional cost of children's toys and clothes for special occasions like Christmas. On the whole, for the majority of people, family support was crucial in dealing with the worst effects of poverty, from getting a meal provided by parents to the more ephemeral 'knowing there is someone in my corner'.

One of the insights of this chapter is that one cannot and should not work with a singular understanding of support from relatives. 'Support' is contextualised, in terms of form, degree and meaning. It is located within relationships and is set in a normative context specific to that relationship, family or group. 'Family' is therefore too broad and undifferentiated a category to serve well in revealing the nature of support. The idea of 'family within family' is a better way of representing the processes whereby people select particular family members to seek support from and give support to. This has some affinity with the 'families of choice' idea (Weeks et al, 2001), but it is different in that families of choice is a concept used to depict the sense in which people choose to make family-like relationships outside of their kin group. People in this study stayed very much within their kin group and exercised agency by usually turning to a small number of relatives. Hence, while their support was vibrant, the idea of a wide supportive family network is inaccurate.

Support was not costless, however. People who were heavily relied on to provide support gave an account of the resultant personal costs to their own health and well-being. These included psychological costs. In addition, very few in the sample wanted to rely on their relatives for help and, for a small number, receiving support brought with it costs to self-esteem, as well as feelings of embarrassment and lack of independence. In general, interdependence is a more accurate characterisation of people's relationships than independence or dependence. There is little evidence of a calculative orientation – or that people had worked-out strategies, either in giving or receiving. While sometimes loans from family members were repaid straight away or the terms were agreed at the outset, most usually 'giving back' was a drawn-out process with no clear or worked-out agreement or timetable. This had the downside of placing a psychological burden on people who had to figure out how to give back.

SIX

Social networks and local engagement

This chapter examines both the local lives and engagements of respondents and the 'localness' of their lives. It first looks at people's sense of the locality in which they live. Particular questions were asked about this and it also came up spontaneously at different points in the interviews. One of the questions running through the chapter is the extent to which people are socially isolated or locally engaged. Hence, the second part of the chapter looks at friendship networks and also involvement with neighbours. The chapter then goes on to piece together other elements of life locally, looking at people's use of a range of local services and considering how they see their own involvement in the local community. Finally, the chapter discusses respondents' evaluations of how they and their family compare with others in terms of various aspects of standard of living. The chapter as a whole seeks to reveal the meaning of locality and neighbourhood in people's understandings of their situation and how they view themselves vis-à-vis others in a similar situation. Underlying this and the next chapter are questions about what is acceptable behaviour from people in this income situation and how they are faced with particular expectations. The respondents' accounts can be taken therefore as a mirror in which are reflected societal patterns and expectations.

The locality and family life

A number of striking points emerged in regard to local life. The first was the localness of family life (and of life in general). Most people's lives were encompassed by a geographical area no larger than a mile or two (especially if they lived in urban areas). Their spatial (and arguably also social and cultural) spaces of interest and interaction were miniaturised (Savage, 2010, p 27). This was for two main reasons. The first was money – and in particular the high costs of transport. Whether people had their own car (which was a minority situation and the case mainly for rural dwellers) or needed to use public transport, the cost of travelling outside the area made journeys strikingly rare. People saw themselves as making only essential journeys (mainly interpreted as taking children to school, for shopping, for medical and other official appointments or to visit family). Those who lived in the suburbs of Belfast, for example, might travel into the city no more than once a month at best, especially if the trips were for leisure. This tended to render 'going into town' an unusual occasion and perhaps even a treat. The interviews were full of references to the costs of travel and how high costs – of bus fares, taxies and petrol – made trips outside the local area into outings.

The impact of shortages of money on people's mobility was not just about costs, though. It also curtailed the capacity to socialise. Here is the viewpoint of Lily, who, conscious of how much she talked about money, said she did not socialise because:

> 'People turn the other way when they see you coming ...
> it's alright if you're talking about it on Monday but if you
> are still talking about it on Friday nobody wants to listen
> and you are left sitting on your own.'

The second reason for the local nature of many respondents' lives was that most had family close by. In fact, 15 had relatives living on the same street or within a few streets (or a short distance if they were rural residents). It is important to note, therefore, that family was in some respects a place-based attribute among the current sample (and indeed maybe in low-income areas of Northern Ireland more widely [Hickman et al, 2014]). The local proximity of family in general was considered in a positive light (and in some cases had been specifically planned). This in some ways helps to explain how closely intertwined respondents' lives were with those of their family of origin. It was also implicated in their view of the locality.

Present in people's narratives was a sense of the 'mean streets' in which their children were being reared. Frequent references were made to the presence of bullying or the fact that on their way to and from school their children might be confronted by scenes associated with alcohol or drug taking or even gang-related behaviour. This sets a context for the efforts we saw parents making to bind the children to the family as well as create a strong sense of internal family life for children. The view of life in the locality through the lens of children's well-being also provides a justification for some of the retreating behaviour seen in families. In fact, such a sense of retreat – through creating the family (home) as a place apart from the harsh outside world – was quite extensive among respondents. Retreat often involved distancing the family from the larger world and was effected through an inside/outside binary: "inside these four walls, this wee family, we're a team, we're a tight unit". There was a sense of intimacy and of creating family as a group – even a space – bound together by bonds that were not only close but different to what happened 'out there'. The external world was sometimes used a foil against which to create a virtual reality of the closeness of 'this family'.

One possible consequence of this is social isolation. Another is that with life lived so locally and so home-based, housing becomes an even more important determinant of quality of life than it might otherwise be. At least a third of the sample mentioned problems with their housing (apart from the cost). Problems pertaining to the 'inside' included poor décor and furnishings, very old appliances and overcrowding.

Overall, there was some ambivalence in people's portrayals of their locality. While they worried about what their children were being exposed to, only a relatively small minority spoke negatively about their local area. The key to understanding this ambivalence is that respondents viewed their situation from different perspectives. When people considered the local area in terms of their children's safety and well-being, they were more negative, but when they thought of it from an adult perspective they were less likely to be negative. Those who highlighted negative aspects of local life primarily spoke of anti-social behaviour and the lack of local opportunities, from both a leisure and employment perspective. But there was in most cases a distancing of anti-social behaviour from their own immediate area – it happened in other streets. Children's future (as well as their present) also featured strongly in respondents' deliberations about their local area. Respondents wondered if their children had a future in the area. This was important, especially given the localness of family life. There was little or no mention of experiences of sectarianism. Most respondents tended to view the locality not so much as a place but as a 'local community'. 'Community' was not necessarily inflected with the usual positive meaning – its use was meant to indicate that respondents viewed their local area in terms of the people who lived there rather than as a place.

Quite a number of respondents were actively involved in the local community, however. This reflects to some extent the methods used to recruit some respondents, especially in the Belfast area. This notwithstanding, the capacity to volunteer, to undertake short courses at local centres or to get mentoring support was hugely significant for those who could do so. The respondents involved spoke of this as a turning point in their lives. The fact that some of the training was in basic skills underlines the significance of such involvement. The narratives of those with an involvement in the local community centre – especially the women's centres – underline the significance of such a service such a facility. Localness matters. Here is a lone mother with four children aged between two and 17 years:

> 'I think the resources within your community helps you a lot because you open up more, because they're part of you, you feel you're not alone, that's the only way I can explain it. They make you realise you're not alone and that you are worthy of these courses and things that you want to do.'

And here is a quote from Katy, who had had a long involvement with the local women's centre, so much so that she felt she had done almost every course on offer there:

> 'I know there are a lot of people who haven't got access to that community stuff and I don't know how they're surviving. It's no wonder there is so much suicide and depression because there is no light at the end of the tunnel. I know if I come down here and say, "Look, I've a problem with this", somebody listens to you … if you didn't have that you couldn't sit with it in your head … you couldn't sit with that worry in your head all the time.'

For other people, involvement in the local community – typically on a volunteer basis – was an opportunity to gain self-esteem and purpose in life through 'giving back'. This was the case for six respondents in the study.

Another possible route of involvement in the local community was through faith-based activities. This, perhaps surprisingly for such an outwardly religious society as Northern Ireland, was rather insignificant in respondents' accounts, either as a source of comfort or local engagement. Only 11 of the respondents indicated that religion was important to them and none of these seemed to have an attachment to the community through this medium (although they did attend church services).

Friendship networks

Given the local nature of their lives and the fact that the majority of respondents continued to live in the areas in which they were reared, friendships too had a strong local character. They are therefore another lens through which to view aspects of local life as well as respondents' social networks and engagements more broadly.

The vast majority of people interviewed felt they had at least one person whom they considered a close friend. Typically, people had either one or a very small number of non-family members whom they thought of as close friends. In all, nine respondents were without friends (and therefore the potential support of friends), almost all because they said they just did not have close friends. The extent to which low income tests friendships was not specifically investigated, but there is some evidence of this being the case. Sheila put it rather evocatively: "You kind of lost people along the way."

It is also important to be mindful of how people's circumstances constrain their chances of building and maintaining friendships. Here is Katy, an unemployed lone mother of four, describing the situation in an earlier period of her life overshadowed by domestic violence and its many consequences:

'I think because of the lifestyle I don't have friends. Because of domestic violence I was isolated quite a lot by someone else [husband] and I actually moved away from everybody and everything that I knew to get away from that. I moved across town to get away from that so that isolated me also for a lot of years. It also broke down trust about people. I could see prejudice because sometimes you just ... you don't actually hear them say it, but you could nearly feel it from them – like, well, "She must have done something." So there's an awful lot goes with the domestic violence, you see. You're not very trusting of people. But also I wasn't allowed friends, that was part of the control, I wasn't allowed friends by my husband.'

At the other extreme, a small number of people reported having a lot of close friends in their social circle. But even in these cases there was a differentiation made in terms of degrees of closeness. A typical clarification here is: "I would have very close friends and then I would have friends." Respondents went on to describe very close friends as those they "would talk to about anything". Generally, very close friends were distinguished by one of two hallmark features. The first is a personal or relationship characteristic – trust – and the second pertains to what one does with friends – in particular, activities around socialising or leisure.

Overall, nearly two-thirds of respondents considered that they received a high level of support from their friends. The frequency with which people said they knew their friends understood them because they were "in the same boat" was striking. Walker (1995) has suggested that friendship functions differently for working- and middle-class respondents. Friendships among those from working-class backgrounds have a strong instrumental element (unlike middle-class friendships, which are marked by a high degree of material independence). One function of friendship for the former is to provide those who are friends with needed goods and services. In the present study, too, instrumentalism is found in close friendship bonds and is indeed expressive and constitutive of such bonds. It is difficult to say with certainty whether friendships were stronger because many of the friends were in a similar situation, but this was a view widely held by the respondents and so may play a causal role.

One other matter concerning friends is also relevant, especially in view of the evidence from other studies to suggest some interchangeability between friends and family in certain instances. Pahl and Spencer (2004) made a distinction between relationships that involve high and low commitment and speak of the phenomenon of family members specifically recognised as friends (they describe this as a 'chosen high commitment relationship'). In general, in the current study, friends occupied a rather different place and role from family and there was little interchangeability, except in those (few) cases where respondents had no family available to them locally. Moreover, the fact that when people had family members among their neighbours and that they identified them as such rather than as neighbours suggests limited or no interchangeability.

Differences between friends and family are especially visible when it comes to the type and degree of support offered. For those who received support from friends, it was almost always emotional or psychological in nature. The classic reply here is: "Knowing people would be there for you if you needed to talk things over." Only a small minority of respondents received practical help from their friends. Most of these had no family living in Northern Ireland, in which cases it seems that friends substituted for family. Childcare was far and away the main type of help provided by friends (and even then not very frequently). For those respondents receiving it, the help was highly significant. For example, during one interview a lone-parent respondent (Clare) explained how she had come to Northern Ireland from a different country. She had met her partner locally and had had a baby. The relationship became violent and she had to leave with her child. She had no contact with her previous partner or any member of his family, and no family of her own living in the region. The help she received from her friend meant the difference between having a job and not having a job:

> 'I have a friend here, her daughter is in the same class as my daughter, and she brings her to the after-schools because when my daughter finishes I'm still at work so I can't just leave work and go to pick her up. So she does that every day for me, which is a brilliant help. I mean, if she stopped doing that, I'd have to leave work.'

Financial support was not a typical currency of friendship. In fact, economic support from or to friends was almost non-existent. This is in contrast to other research that has reported financial support among friends in addition to family members (Crisp and Robinson, 2010). There were two main reasons why people in the current study did not seek financial support from friends. One is normative – the belief that the exchange of money is not proper to friendship relations. The second reason was that people's friends tended to be more or less in the same situation as they were. In one instance a respondent's close friend had helped her to pay fees for a university course, but this help had been offered without being requested. In another case, a female respondent said she herself would not borrow from her friend, but that her husband sometimes borrowed money from his friend to pay for electricity.

The accounts of the remaining nine people who said they received little if any support from friends indicated that they regarded this as a source of loss in their lives and that the circumstances were not of their own making. The causal factors here related one way or another to people's family situation. One such factor is domestic violence. The quote given earlier by Katy, who had suffered domestic violence, shows how this type of situation tends to remove one, both physically and psychologically, from one's friends. A second factor leading to relative isolation from friends is disability or the health-related needs of a family member. Respondents spoke of other people's lack of understanding of disability and their experience of others' apprehension about being in the company of disabled people. This comes across very clearly in the following account of Roisin, a married parent of a severely disabled child, who herself suffered from rheumatoid arthritis and fibromyalgia:

'I wouldn't say I've any close friends. I've acquaintances, a lot of people know me and I'm very friendly with them and all but I don't let... I have no good friend that I would go, "I've known her from I've been ...." That's just the way it is. I think having our daughter has isolated us as well because my husband has no friends either. We sound really 'Billy no mates' there, but it definitely has without a doubt ... you can see the shock on their face if she happens to kick off or do something that she shouldn't be doing. It's like, "Right, I'm away here now." It definitely does, it stops people coming up to the house.'

There are other types of family situation that deter people from inviting friends in or having them visit. This could be, for example, because respondents do not want others to find out about their private or family lives, or see the state of their house.

Examining norms around giving back to friends helps to reveal the moralities involved for the respondents (just as it did about family relationships in the last chapter). In fact, reciprocity is almost universally perceived as a component element of friendship. It turns out, however, that there was a much greater degree of reciprocity in respondents' friendships than in their relationships with their families when it came to giving and receiving support. While in a few cases respondents recounted experiences where elements of their friendship were not reciprocated, in general they were very conscious that being a good friend meant 'being there' in return. Core to this was a willingness to give back. In comparison with family relationships, there was a much greater sense of equality in friendships; it was not considered acceptable to be 'dependent' in a friendship. A corollary of this is that reciprocity is non-elective in these relationships, whereas in family – especially close family – there is a greater degree of voluntarism.

The findings give little evidence of what Pahl and Spencer (2004) referred to as a process of 'suffusion', meaning the merging or blurring of kin and non-kin within networks. Their exploratory findings, based on qualitative research in the UK, show that the exercise of personal choice in determining who are significant family members seems to be conditional on the level of commitment in relationships. This explains why some friends are considered as family and provide support as such, whereas some relatives are not considered as supportive family. The degree to which this is specific to social class or income group is not clear from Pahl and Spencer (2004), but that may be a factor in the divergence between their research and this study.

Contact with, and support from, neighbours

In contrast to the significance of family and friendship networks, respondents generally attributed a lower level of importance to contact with, and support from, neighbours. Respondents' depictions of their level of neighbour contact and exchange is shown in Table 6.1.

Table 6.1: Characterisations of contacts with neighbours

Level of support/ contact	Description
No close contact	People preferred to keep themselves to themselves. They did not salute or greet their neighbours or interact with them in any way. The family's privacy was paramount.
Polite greeting	Respondents knew their neighbours, always said 'Hello' and were polite to each other. People preferred not to get too involved, but did help out with such tasks as taking in deliveries.
High level of support	Behaviours included keeping a watchful eye on elderly neighbours by dropping in regularly to see if they were OK and doing some shopping for them. Also included was being able to ask a neighbour for assistance if someone was sick and needed a lift to hospital. Other mentioned behaviours included watching over other people's property if they were away and doing gardening for neighbours.

Approximately half of families reported having no close contact with their neighbours. This should not be interpreted as a reflection of the neighbourhood, however, because sometimes respondents who said that they did not interact much with their neighbours went on to talk about a good sense of community in the area. In many cases, remaining aloof or distant from neighbours was out of a desire for privacy – people preferring to keep to themselves. There was a strong sense in some of these cases of people not wanting their neighbours to know of their difficulties around income or problems relating to the functioning of the family – as one male respondent (Conor) put it, "We sort of keep most things in-house." Maintaining family privacy in the locality or neighbourhood may be paramount in situations of difficulty.

The desire for privacy was not universal, though. The other half of respondents fell in almost equal numbers between those with high levels of neighbourhood connectedness – where neighbours looked out for one another – and those who would no more than say 'Hello' to their neighbours and leave it at that. The latter group, who tried to manage their neighbourly relations to be civil but uninvolved, sometimes tended to ignore and take for granted what could be called 'neighbourly acts', such as taking in mail or deliveries or watching out for each other (in a sense of safety and security especially).

Then there were the high-intensity neighbours. These people could be said to be engaged in 'neighbouring'. It should be noted, however, that among this group of families, about a third had close relatives living in the same street. In a few cases, there were several families of close relatives living nearby. In general, support from and by neighbours tended to take a practical form. Almost no references were made to giving or receiving economic or affective forms of support among neighbours. However, there was one exception – a respondent who received financial help and childcare from a neighbour. This was a person with no close family members living locally. In this case, neighbours provided a lifeline in terms of childcare at short notice and small amounts of cash (typically £10) when the gas or electricity meter was about to run out. This person considered his neighbours to be good friends as well, so the dividing line between friend and neighbour was somewhat blurred here.

Among the supportive behaviours mentioned by respondents were dropping in on elderly neighbours to check on them, doing some shopping and performing chores such as gardening. A few respondents also mentioned being able to ask a neighbour for assistance if someone were sick and needed a lift to hospital. Other neighbourly behaviours mentioned were watching over other people's property if they were away or taking delivery of mail for them. It is notable that neighbour support was almost exclusively behavioural and practical in nature.

Relatively clear lines were drawn around what was considered appropriate contact with neighbours. There was certainly a wish not to be dependent on neighbours and a sense that it was not appropriate to actually ask support from neighbours, as expressed in the following quotes from Heather and Connie, respectively:

'We would say "hello", and they're nice neighbours, but they wouldn't be anything in my life. I wouldn't depend on them for anything. If there was anything wrong, I'm sure I would know their door and I'm sure they would help but I don't ask.'

'Like, if I needed something, I wouldn't go in and ask my neighbour for it. But I'd rather ring and ask my Mammy for it because I think they'd look as if "Go get it yourself," you know, going in and asking to borrow something. You don't do that now.'

The suggestion in the latter quote of a change in the norms around neighbour relations as compared with the past was echoed by many other respondents.

In general, there was a universe of difference between the intensity of support people received from family and what someone who saw themselves as getting high support from neighbours received. The latter was both less substantial and frequent.

It should be noted, however, that there were two general registers to people's replies here, in that people tended to differentiate between support from neighbours as individuals and the state or condition of social and other relationships in the neighbourhood or locality in general. When evaluated positively (which was true of the majority of cases), the latter was often framed in terms of "people look out for each other here". Nor are the relationships and feelings synonymous, in that some respondents who said they did not bother with their neighbours still felt that there was a good sense of community in the area.

Similar to support from friends, help from neighbours was viewed as needing to be reciprocated. It had a strong degree of mutuality, perhaps because it is 'public' in a way that support from family or friends is not:

> 'If John was making stew or soup or anything I would send
> her a wee bowl of it over and then she would send the kids
> a selection box at Christmas and all.' (Margaret)

There was a lack of precision in the replies around how neighbour support was precipitated – it is not clear from the interviews whether it was initiated through a particular occurrence (like a crisis of some kind) or whether it was a process embedded in an everyday set of relationships. The strongest sense from the narratives was of respondents feeling they had to be prepared to respond to the need for neighbour support. This was not always out of need, but from a sense of what is right and proper in these kinds of relationships. For example, the following quote from Sarah, a married mother of two teenagers whose husband was unemployed, is revealing of the norms involved:

> '... if you were ever in distress just knock on the door and
> they come to you and help you. If it's a death or an accident
> or something like that, they would definitely come to help
> you ... the neighbours don't really bother unless you have
> to bother them. So if you want them, they're there for you,
> so that's what I like about the neighbours.'

The use of the word 'bother' here is significant.

As mentioned, there was a subset of respondents who were quite involved with their neighbours, especially in the sense of offering them help. These people appeared to give more to their neighbours than they received back. And some of them seemed to go out of their way to create opportunities to give to their neighbours, like Leah, who consciously engaged in a neighbourly act, even though she did not know whether it was of value to or used by the recipient.

> 'Well, I would bring Jill there over a couple of buns on a Friday or maybe if there was something in the fridge that wasn't going to be used and I wasn't going to use it that day, I would send it over to her just to see if she wants it, like meat or something. She never refuses, she takes everything. I don't know if she uses it – she might throw it in the bin. I don't know. But no matter what I send over, she takes it.'

It is not clear exactly why Leah sent food to her neighbour when it had almost reached its sell-by date. It did not seem to matter to her whether it would be used or not; what mattered was that the neighbour took it. She seemed to be enriched by feeling that she was acting in the role of generous, altruistic neighbour. This can be taken as an example of 'neighbourhood work' or neighbour making in the sense of engaging in behaviours that have their most significant meaning in building the relationship and confirming a status/reputation as a good neighbour.

Local services

Let us turn now to another way of conceiving of local involvement: people's recourse to local services (apart from those community centre and women's group services mentioned earlier). It is possible to map the services used on the basis of the evidence obtained on people's use of the following services and what their level of satisfaction with each was: general practitioner (GP), dentist, school-related services, social services, citizens' advice, faith-based services, credit union and any other services they availed of. A service tree with generally two or three services emerged.

The GP service was the most widely-used service of all – it was also the service with which people said they were most satisfied, although it should be noted that a significant minority of respondents mentioned the difficulty of getting an appointment to see their GP. The second most widely used service was free school meals. In fact, the significance of the local school as a service provider emerged rather strongly from this study – schools were regarded as the single most important local service provider. This was not just because of the free school meals service (available in Northern Ireland to parents in receipt of income-related benefits or earning very low income), but also for the after- and before-school services (for example, breakfast clubs and homework clubs). The following two quotes give an indication of the kind of need that free school meals meet. The first is from Heather, whose two young children were aged four and six respectively; the second is from Ruth, whose two children were roughly the same age as those of Heather.

> 'The dinners in school, it takes a weight off your shoulder because you know he's getting a healthy … well, you know they're going to give him as healthy as the government thinks it should be giving him. It's not going to be junk food, whereas sometimes when you're making them a dinner or making a lunch they're maybe not eating it, you don't even know where it's going. Whereas at school, they're sitting down and there's people watching them and they're with their friends.'

> 'I couldn't provide a lunch. Like I say, I can barely put food on the table, let alone provide a lunch for him to go to school with. And he wants packed lunches but I'm, "You know Mummy was a wee girl and I was never allowed to go to lunches like you." So he's like, "OK." And then he asks his Granda and I'm, like, "Daddy, just say yeah that I wasn't allowed to go."'

The next most widely used service was the credit union. About half of the respondents were personal members (or 'banked' through a family member). This service was viewed in a very positive light. In fact, after free school meals, it was the most highly evaluated service. Not only did people indicate that they would turn to the credit union to deal with the unexpected expenses, but it was also referred to on occasions when larger sums of money were required, such as for holidays and Christmas. The regularity with which people spoke of the credit union and their familiarity with its procedures indicate some reliance:

> 'I'm a member of the credit union, so if there was no credit union, there would be no Santa.'

However, there is evidence of a perceived change in the purpose served by a credit union loan for people. Whereas it used to be for special occasions, like a holiday or a wedding or Christmas, it is now being used for more basic needs. The following account conveys a shift in emphasis from credit union loans being part of a back-up plan to cover large occasional expenses to being a fundamental bridge for maintaining necessities. This is how Leah, mother to two children who had recently lost her job (although her partner was working full-time), explained it to us:

> 'I used to just use it for holidays, for spending money 'cause you always knew you didn't have to save up for spending money because you had it there in the credit union. But now I can't use that money for that any more. I have to use it for emergencies if I'm short. I don't know if one month I'll be really, really skint and maybe don't have the mortgage money and maybe have to go up and lift if out of the credit union and put it in my account to pay the mortgage that month.'

Citizens' advice was the next most widely-used service. Like the credit union, the fifth of people who used this service found it extremely useful. People used it especially to get help with establishing and claiming entitlements, especially cash benefits. They saw the citizens' advice service as an essential intermediary service. They did not personalise or individualise this, but viewed their own difficulties in navigating the benefit system as generic. The need for such a service is a reflection of how difficult it is for 'people like us' to access benefits and public services. However, given that citizens' advice is usually based in a town or city centre, this was a service that most people had to travel to use.

The extent to which people made use of social services – understood to include social work services as well as specific services associated with child development needs – was quite limited. In fact, people were at their most critical when talking about the latter type of service. They bemoaned an inadequate support of speech therapy, for example, or the relative inflexibility or inability of educational and other services to respond to children with special needs (such as Asperger's Syndrome).

The dole office services were reserved for much negative criticism (and were in the eyes of the respondents who used the citizens' advice services a big reason why such services had to exist). Here is an account from Joanne, a married 47-year-old mother of three children, who had worked more or less continuously since she was 16 until she was made redundant last year.

> 'The benefit offices are awful. I mean they're nice places to go into; they're pleasant environments and lovely offices. I remember when I signed on when I was 16, my God it was like going into some kind of utilitarian prison or something. They were awful scary, horrible, dirty, concrete, smelly, horrible places and now they're all these gorgeous carpeted offices, all very pleasant with the radio on. But they're crap. They don't give advice, they don't help you, they don't support you, there's no humanising sort of policy. It's all very impersonal – they don't relate.'

Suffice to say that there was little evidence of a feeling of quality services from the perspective of receivers, and the disconnect between the quality of the building and the lack of quality in the service was notable.

In regard to specific assistance with money shortages – such as crisis loans or the Social Fund – the strong impression conveyed was that this form of loan would be sought only in dire need. The following account from May, a 41-year-old lone mother with three children, conveys this interpretation:

> 'Yeah, there's times I've had to go to the dole to put in for a crisis loan and then they turn you down and you're walking out and your face is purple because everybody knows you got turned down.'

Sheila recounted the following experience of being turned down also; she felt she should never have tried:

> 'Unfortunately for us, my husband had been the victim of a sectarian attack and that meant he wasn't working so we found ourselves ... oh God, even thinking about it ... I had to go down to the bru[1] and actually sign on and sat and cried my eyes out because I had tried so hard that you were going to make a different sort of life and then you found yourself in a situation that I may as well never have tried. But there you go....'

---

[1]   A colloquialism for benefit receipt in Northern Ireland.

On the other hand, assistance from the Social Fund by way of a budgeting loan was a current and ongoing form of help for a small number of people in the study. For these respondents, budgeting loans provided a helpful way of covering large household expenses that were difficult to budget for on a restricted income. This is the view of Marie, who had a budgeting loan at the time of interview and was planning to apply for another one once her existing loan was repaid, as she said it was the only way she could cover large expenses:

> 'Yes … because I'm on Income Support you can get a social fund loan for big items which I have. It's paid out this January coming, a £1,000, and I used it for decorating the bedrooms and putting new carpet on the bedrooms, the stairs and just other bits and bobs. They take that out of my money at £11 a week, which – interest free … I mean that's fantastic. So what I'm going to do is, because I only have another year left on Income Support, when this one's paid out in January I will get it again and that will allow me to do a bit of decorating in the kitchen because I know after that I won't be able to afford it so that's another way of sort of getting big items.'

Looking at services overall, two points are notable. First, people's agency was generally that of recipient. There was no respondent involved in a planning or management capacity in any of the services. Second, the extent to which people accessed local, place-based resources to mediate the impact of stressors was relatively limited (as noted by other research on low-income areas also – Batty and Cole, 2010; Platts-Fowler and Robinson, 2013).

The last section of this chapter turns to look at how people compared themselves and their families with others. The actual questions asked people to rate their family on standard of living and quality of life in comparison with other families.

Comparisons with others

Throughout the research, it was obvious that much of people's discussions was relative, in that they readily compared themselves with others and when they did so they were consoled by knowing others were in a similar situation. The impression was almost of a normalisation of poverty and low income, with the recession being seen as helping to lessen negative feelings because it had brought others into the realm of the low-income experience, hence also diffusing fault. Paula, lone mother to a young son, expressed it as follows:

> 'I think that the recession has kind of helped because it's put a lot of people in the same boat and they can see the struggle that it is, so it's embarrassing but not mortifying. You'll find someone in the same position.'

According to Runciman (1966), there is a connection between relative deprivation and social change. For example, favourable economic conditions can lead to an increase in relative deprivation whereby people come to expect more, with demands for greater advancement and opportunity more likely. Conversely, during adverse situations as in a recession, people can feel less aggrieved because they have lowered their aspirations and expectations. That said, though, it is important to point out that the recent period of recession has seen a hardening of attitudes towards those who are poor (National Centre for Social Research, 2012).

Regarding quality of life, the majority of respondents felt that they enjoyed a high or very high quality of life, scoring it a 4 or 5. If this appears at odds with all that has been presented up to now, it should be noted that most people evaluated their situation through the lens of the quality of their personal relationships with or among family members and these were seen as generally good. The following are typical replies:

> 'Because I know that the two of us love each other and we're really, really good together and I wouldn't be without him and like any family we have our odd argument, but it's nothing more than that.' (Rachel, lone mother, talking about the relationship between her and her young son)

> 'I'd say a 5, mostly a 5 90% of the time. Ten per cent it's a 4 because there can be that hiccup if there's one or two not getting on, but it always sorts itself out.' (Maureen discussing the relationship between her, her partner and their five children)

For the minority of respondents who reported having a poorer quality of life (scoring it as 1 or 2), there were two main reasons – high indebtedness caused by sudden or unexpected unemployment, and the burden of long-term caring responsibilities. The stories of Leah and Joanne serve as an example of the former. Both had recently lost their jobs in the service sector. Both had been in full-time employment since leaving school, had been used to a good income and had used credit cards as a normal way of managing their money. Repayments only became problematic when they were made redundant. Neither woman had any previous experience of unemployment and spoke about the difficulty of trying to manage 'debt' that had never been viewed as debt because heretofore it had been credit and a normal part of life. The negative implications for the quality of these respondents' life are evident in the quote from Joanne below:

> 'I'd say it is about a 2 at the minute, to be honest, with everything that's going on and the lack of financial stability.... If they [the CAB[2]] help me with the credit cards, I can face the world because that is a big deal at the minute. That is really starting to make me panic because I've never been in trouble in my life for anything and I really don't want to be in trouble for not being able to pay somebody something because it was me spent the money on them and it's my responsibility. You know, it's not as if I can walk away with it and just ignore it, but if they help me cope with that, I can sit in the house with no bloody heating because that's real and I can deal with it. But all that hanging over my head in the background is killing me.'

The vulnerability of people engaged in providing care on a long-term basis was also made evident through the interviews. Sheila framed it in terms of the added pressure of trying to make family life appear as 'normal' as possible for the sake of her children. However, it was evident during the interview that this extra pressure was intensifying the existing situation, as the following extract reveals:

> 'It would probably be 1 because I'm trying so hard to keep it all ticking over. It isn't a normal situation and I would like to think that my children would be thinking it's 4 or 5, but sometimes the effort going in to make it all seem as if it's normal is exhausting. So, for me, I would say it's poor. But I'd like to think that the efforts I'm making that the children would think it was good, if you know what I mean.'

---

[2] Citizens Advice Bureau.

Generally, when it came to standard of living as distinct from quality of life, most people described themselves as being in 'the middle'. Again, here, the reference group was very important. The response from May below is indicative of the average replies:

> 'Right … well we're not 'poor poor' and we're not really rich, about two and a half, I would say.'

As one might expect, people's evaluation of their current situation was closely related to their past circumstances. If respondents' current situation compared relatively well with a previous set of circumstances, the sense of deprivation was diminished, as was the case for Maura:

> 'I wouldn't put myself at 1 because I was at 1 so I would say 2 because I can't afford to do certain things that I would like to do in my standard of living, but I'm better than 1.'

Only a minority of people saw themselves as having a very high standard of living. One respondent, Marie (lone mother to two children, one of whom required full-time care), who reported a quite high standard, did so because she said she did not know who to compare her situation with:

> 'I suppose a 4 again because I really don't know who to compare it to because I don't really bother with people. Yeah, I think we're quite lucky, the house is clean, comfortable, warm, there's always food. Yeah, I think our standard of living is quite good at the minute.'

Overview

This chapter has looked at people's local life, both in the sense of the location or place in which people's lives are set and also in terms of how they interact and engage with life locally. One of the most striking findings presented here – but also of the research in general – was the highly local character of people's lives. Respondents did not leave the area much and the services and resources that they most used tended to be locally based (with some exceptions). Two main factors acted to localise life: money and the propinquity of family. The lack of money had many implications, not least the cost of travelling out of the local area and limiting one's capacity to socialise (either at home or outside it). The second factor – the proximity of family – was in many respects a positive aspect of the localness of life. It enabled people to feel a tie to the area and generally (although not universally) gave them a source of support locally. But there was also a sense of retreating from the outside world on the part of some respondents and their families.

It is clear from respondents' descriptions that the areas or localities in which people lived were not uniform. Nor were they necessarily depicted negatively. In fact, a majority of people viewed their local area positively, seeing a sense of community there. A small number of respondents did speak negatively about the area in which they lived, but this occurred mainly when they were thinking about their children. Anti-social behaviour and the general lack of services and opportunities – especially for children and young people – were the most commonly mentioned locality-related shortcomings.

Respondents were not necessarily socially isolated – indeed, most were well connected. About half had good relationships with their neighbours and the vast majority also had friends who lived locally. Friends were far more important in people's lives than neighbours, and the type of support received from friends tended to be emotional in nature, whereas relationships with neighbours were mostly practical and functional. While neither group was as vigorous a source of social support as family, they did tend to add another layer to people's local embeddedness. Taking the information on community and local life together, one could say that, against the general rhetoric of broken communities, there is evidence of 'small society' in operation. People live in areas they know well, they tend to have family close by, they view their local area in generally positive terms and many feel they have support there (albeit that much of this comes from family living locally).

The degree of involvement in the local community was mixed. About a fifth of people were active as volunteers or as recipients of services at their local community centre or women's groups. For those involved, such involvement was extremely important and valued for the skills learned or contributed and the sense of personal affirmation obtained. It was seen to enable personal and cultural growth (as well as providing support for some). People also, of course, used other local services. Of these, the most important in order of frequency of use were GP services, free school meals and other school-based services, credit union and citizens' advice. Notably, the social services and those of the benefit office were used sparingly and were the subject of a lot of negative comment.

Nor did respondents voice a strong sense of relative deprivation. Most commonly, people evaluated their lives as comparing generally quite well with those of others, although there was a general sense that their situation was getting worse. The majority of people believed their standard of living to be around average. However, there was something of a disconnection between people's evaluations of their objective standard of living and the family's subjective circumstances. The extent to which respondents reported high quality of life was very striking, given their straightened financial circumstances and health and other problems. This seemed to be due mainly to the belief that quality of life was evaluated positively if relationships among family members were seen as good. And since most respondents portrayed their immediate family relationships in positive terms, this tended to elevate their evaluations of their quality of life.

SEVEN

Representing self and family

This chapter adds another dimension to the socio-locational aspects of life by investigating how respondents interpreted and engaged outside the home, especially in situations involving perceived negative constructions and expectations. The chapter is especially interested in public encounters, viewing these as arenas of moral scrutiny. The discussion identifies respondents' experiences of situations in which they have to represent themselves and their families, and investigates the cognitive and social processes and activities that they engage in to counter negative depictions of themselves and family members. We hear especially people's accounts of key interactions in public settings – ranging from casual encounters in supermarkets and so forth to more 'formal' encounters at schools and benefit offices. To what extent and why are such encounters associated with embarrassment and/or shame and does this affect people's sense of empowerment, identity, well-being and resource use? This set of questions is considered in the first two parts of the chapter. The third looks at if and how people engage in 'othering', that is, distancing themselves from others through negative depictions, especially of those who appear to be in relatively similar situations. The emphasis throughout is on how people on low income view social interactions and how they seek to convey particular images or impressions of themselves and/or their family.

The chapter is guided by a number of theoretical touchstones: in particular shame, embarrassment and othering. Over 50 years ago, Helen Lynd (1958) expressed the view that shame was so pervasive that it was like water to fish. Scheff (2000) has suggested that shame is increasing in modern societies, while at the same time awareness of shame as a general feature of social life is decreasing. It is so taken for granted that it is part and parcel of everyday life. In the contemporary context, Peacock and colleagues (2013, p 394) suggest that neoliberalism has opened up additional spaces where the working class can be shamed and at the same time has undermined what might have been sources of resistance. The existing literature tends to confirm this, identifying shame and humiliation as part of the experience of being on a low income (Sen, 1983; Narayan et al, 2000; Lister, 2004; Hooper et al, 2007; Chase and Walker, 2013). Embarrassment, too – a somewhat different phenomenon from shame in that it is a less profound emotion relating more to what somebody does rather than who they are – is widely reported as associated with poverty and low income.

One of the processes that contributes to negative depictions of, and attitudes towards, poor people is what Lister (2004, p 100) calls 'othering'. She uses this term to denote a dual process of differentiation and demarcation. In the first instance, 'the poor' are distanced and represented as different to 'the rest of us' and, in the second, negative value judgments are applied to label and stereotype and often stigmatise people who are poor (Jones and Novak, 1999). 'Strangers' in our midst is how Katz has put it (1989, p 7). Language and image are both cause and consequence here. There is a vast repertoire of negative depictions of labels for poor people: 'feckless', 'dependent', 'scroungers', 'untrustworthy', 'of low intelligence', 'threatening'. In a more positive vein, but a rendering that still distances, people who are poor may be represented as to be pitied, pathetic, passive, hopeless or victims (Lister, 2004, p 116). It is clear that sections of the media regularly use both types of image to represent the poorer sections of society, but so, also, are government agencies engaged in processes of distancing those who live in poverty from the rest of the population by making a distinction between those who are 'undeserving' and those who are 'deserving'. While it may not be the intention, 'othering' serves to blame those who are poor and justify existing distinctions and inequalities (Lister, 2004, p 102). It also acts to affirm the identities and power of those who do the labelling while denying those labelled an opportunity to create or retain an identity worthy of respect – how are they to think of themselves other than as failures? According to Lister, 'othering' draws from a profound history of morally censoring poor people (2004, pp 103-4). It is also another important reason why we need to hear what people who are poor have to say – in the absence of their voice, they tend to be depicted as 'others'.

Embarrassment

It turns out that respondents are very accustomed to being categorised by others. Embarrassment was a common experience. Three-quarters of respondents said they had experienced feelings of embarrassment directly relating to their lack of income. As outlined by them, embarrassment was mainly about losing face – the fear that others know or will come to know that they have too little income or are poor, and will judge them for it.

Who did people feel embarrassment with or towards? There were very few instances of people feeling embarrassment with intimates.

For example, only one respondent voiced feelings of embarrassment with her children – when she had to explain that something the child wanted could not be afforded because it was too dear. However, people did feel embarrassment for their children. Some of the precipitating circumstances have been mentioned already – being unable to afford school trips, for example, or their child looking 'out of place' or not being able to participate in the same way as other children. While respondents recounted experiences where their child felt embarrassment – most widely at school – it was far more common for people to anticipate embarrassment on the part of their child and to wish to prevent it. No respondent voiced particular feelings of embarrassment in relation to their partner, siblings or parents, although one respondent did feel that her former partner's mother took every opportunity to embarrass her because she suspected she was on benefits (which she was).

Two main types of situation or setting precipitated feelings of embarrassment. One was in the company of friends and/or acquaintances; the second was when people's financial situation became obvious in some kind of public setting. In both cases, the fear was of exposure of their circumstances, although the nature of that exposure varied with the setting. Embarrassment was especially associated with what might be called 'a generalised public' – that is, where strangers were present and could see the encounter. Let us briefly outline each type of situation in turn.

Embarrassment with friends and/acquaintances occurred mainly when respondents were placed in situations where they were unable to afford something. The most common example given was not being able to accept an invitation from friends for a night out or a trip to town because of inadequate income. Being unable to afford to go on holiday like the families of friends and acquaintances (and in some cases relatives) was also frequently voiced as a source of embarrassment. Typically, situations of embarrassment or potential embarrassment provoked attempts by people to prevent or limit the loss of face. Most widely, people tried to manage this situation by withdrawing from it and making up an excuse rather than admitting to a lack of income. This is a response from Conor, parent to one child and unemployed; his partner worked part time for a low family income:

> 'It's demeaning ... all my friends are working and they're going here and there and they're ringing on Saturday night saying, "Are you going out this week?", "Are you going out next weekend? There's this on, there's that on, we're

going to go here, do you want to go?" ... Sometimes you have to make up excuses. Instead of saying you don't have the money. "Ach, I can't get a babysitter," or "I couldn't be bothered." Do you know what I mean? You never say, "No, I don't have the money."'

In regard to public and more generalised scenes of embarrassment, two general types of encounter were mentioned most frequently. The first was in supermarkets or shops. For some respondents, the 'public other' here was very generalised – it was fear of embarrassment in front of a group of strangers. This could come from either being seen with their basket full of the cheapest brands and imagining the reaction – "Oh look at her with her cheap soap powder and her cheap stuff" - or being seen to count and tot up the cost of the items in the trolley or basket as they go along. But actual experiences of embarrassment were also recounted. A source of profound chagrin mentioned was when people miscalculated the price of what was in their shopping trolley as they were shopping and had insufficient money to pay once they got to the checkout. Jenny (a working mother of three children) gave this account:

'I was in Tescos and I'd obviously lifted a bit more. I was trying to count it in my head and when I got to the checkout I was £6 short. And I actually think I asked the girl to take things off, which has never happened in all my life. And I was mortified, mortified. It was cereals and that ... it wasn't ... everything was a necessity that was in it. And I thought I had counted in it in my head, but I hadn't.'

At least part of the story here is of validation – she tries to reduce her embarrassment by pointing out that her basket was full of essentials like cereals, rather than luxuries.

People felt embarrassment in other public settings as well. Being identified as being in receipt of benefits or other needs-oriented services was quite widely referred to as a source of public embarrassment. Here is an example of Marie (lone mother to two, and full-time carer of a son suffering from Asperger's and ADHD) being embarrassed about receipt of a concession on bus fares that is tied to benefit receipt. Having secured a form that would enable her to get a reduction on her bus fares – which was a process she found very difficult to undertake and negotiate – she did not use it so as to save herself embarrassment:

'I didn't use it on the Metro bus because some of the drivers can be real sort of iffy and I thought, "I'll just buy a ticket" … I didn't use it in case one of the drivers said something to me. I thought, "I'll just not bother." You know, they can be a bit funny. I thought one of them's bound to ask me for a [Income Support] form and I go, "I don't have it" and I'd be more embarrassed and I thought, "It's not worth it."'

Or consider the case of Leah, a mother of two whose husband was employed, on her experience with paying for her children's costs at school. She uses the word 'scundered', which is a Northern Irish colloquialism for a mixture of being caught off guard and embarrassment:

'At the start of the month, you have to pay £5 for his milk and £3 for his fruit money and £3 for Sarah's fruit money. And because it's Christmas, they did calendars as well and I felt I had to buy two calendars at £8. So the day I went in, I was paying £19 and the teacher said to me, "Are you sure you can afford it?" I was scundered, so I was, because his teachers know I don't have a job. They're being supportive… saying, "I hope you do get a job," and "I hope you've told mister there [son] that Santa can't bring him as much now."'

There are many emotions in this quote: the need to save face, and yet the ambivalence about the financial cost of doing so, the sense of intrusion by the teacher, and the respondent's embarrassment that the teacher knew her situation and that of her son.

One mother – Lizzie, a lone parent of four – highlighted how she used to feel about her children getting free school meals:

'You just feel, "Free dinners – oh my God no! Oh my goodness my child is going up with a dinner ticket." You just felt that way, but I don't know why you feel that way, but you just do and it's a horrible thing. But now that I am in that position, I don't feel like that no more. I go, "No, I worked for 11 years, I'm entitled to this at the minute." And I do want to go back to work, but it's good that people have the resources if they do come out of work.'

Note the mixture of current and past tense and the assurance that she did want to go back to work. Her resistance to feelings of embarrassment is also notable. Acceptance of some sense of entitlement (albeit qualified in nature, given that she saw it as temporary) was, she said later in the interview, how she coped with feelings of shame.

Embarrassment does not just happen. An important part of the context is the degree to which people (are made to) feel stigmatised for being poor or on a low income. There is some evidence of stigma in Leah's quote, for example. People were not asked specifically for occasions on which they experienced stigma, but some such occasions came up spontaneously, of which the following, from Lizzie again, is an example:

> 'The stigma of a single mother is, like, "She's on the bru" and "She's on benefits." That's the way you feel, like scroungers, scrounging off the bru. "Why don't you get off your ass and go work?" Well, I did work for 11 years and I had a baby and I am on the bru now.'[1]

This kind of generic sense of categorisation was widespread. What also came strongly through the interviews was people's sensitivity in regard to their situation and how it might be perceived.

Respondents were not by any means passive in response, though. Three different types of response were evident: accommodation, resistance and rejection. These were not necessarily fixed, but varied depending on the situation.

In the cases where the response or posture could be said to be one of accommodation, people seemed very vulnerable to possible public opprobrium. The following quote from Rachel, a lone mother of one young child, gives evidence of both:

> 'You do, you feel ashamed, like ... So many people say if you're on a benefits that they're rearing your child. I don't think I really feel ashamed, just angry that people say, "I'm paying," but their tax goes everywhere to everything.'

In some cases, people's very identity was rendered vulnerable. The extract below is from an interview with Marie, who had been out of the labour market for a long time. She was receiving Carer's Allowance in respect of her disabled son at the time of interview. Here she discusses

---

[1] A colloquialism for benefit receipt in Northern Ireland.

the embarrassment she feels when she meets people socially and they ask her what she does for a living:

> 'It does make me feel embarrassed, you know, when someone asks. Unless they ask I'm not going to tell them, but when you meet someone it is one of the questions, "Well, what do you do?" I suppose I should just say I'm a housewife or whatever, but for some reason I always go, "Lady of leisure." They laugh at it and then they don't ask any more questions after that, you know.'

In this quote Marie makes no mention of her role as a full-time carer. Her embarrassment was associated with having no links to the labour market. The value of her caring role was completely underestimated by her. An important point to note – and this is evident in the two quotes above – is that these feelings of embarrassment signal that the respondents accept personal responsibility for their situation; their modes of understanding their situation tend to be individualistic rather than to see their situation in more structural terms (Reay, 2012).

If there were situations where people lost face, there were also situations where they tried to 'create face'. This constitutes the second type of response: resistance. Here, actions tend to be pre-emptive, like the woman who says that she is the first parent in her children's class to pay lunch and breakfast club money. Equally, there are the cases, some of which are recounted elsewhere in the book, where people go out of their way to be generous. An example is the woman who gives the food to her neighbour without knowing if it is needed or used. In these cases, people are not necessarily critical of the negative depictions, but are, rather, trying to prove that they are undeserved or to pre-empt such judgements. Below is a very specific situation of a family taking the opportunity to be givers rather than receivers, which in many ways is an effort to salvage pride and to resist depictions of themselves as 'needy'. The background is that Sarah's family – consisting of herself and her husband, both of whom were unemployed, and two teenagers – received a 'box' from the charity St Vincent de Paul Society at Christmas some years ago. The donation was completely unexpected and had been hand-delivered by a neighbour, which made Sarah feel very 'exposed':

> 'They did give us a few years back a wee box, but we were sort of knocked back because I would have preferred it if a stranger had brought it, but because it was somebody that

knew me you felt like…. And we said, "No, take it back, please, take it back and give it to somebody else who might need it more." But they said, "No, the group have decided it's coming to this family and that's the end of that." So what we done then is we gave one back the following year for them to donate to another family. We gave back as they gave to us and then we would put a pound or two into the wee box and that helps them to have the wee Christmas party for the pensioners and maybe have a hamper and a raffle. You feel good giving them something back that they gave to you, but we never thought that we would be one of the families that they would want to visit – we get on great with them because we know them. They are our neighbours. It's just that we never thought they would pick us. We were thinking, "Why would you want to give it to us? There's bound to be people who was in the same boat as us." But we were just thinking of our pride and saying, "Look, we don't need it," but they thought we needed it. It's just their kindness, but my husband said, "Bring that back," and I said, "If they're offering it, you can't refuse, but we can repay them back and return the favour back to them." So that's what we done. It was anonymous, nobody knew we done it. We just gave it to the chairman and he distributed it out to whatever house he decided.'

This long quote has been reproduced because it is so revealing. The mixture of emotions is notable: the puzzlement and 'surprise', if not shock, at being selected for a donation by a well-known charity for the poor; the chagrin at the very public and local way in which it was done; the authoritarian and paternalistic lack of option to refuse; the difference of opinion if not discord between Sarah and her husband; the deliberateness, resolve and number of actions engaged in to give back. In addition, the anonymous nature of the giving back indicates that reclaiming honour for self was key to the entire exercise. Also noticeable is the frequent identification of others who were more needy and the many references to giving or paying back. In fact, in the quote above, the word 'back' is used 10 times.

There were other instances in the interviews of people resisting by generating a benefactor role for themselves. Anne, a 46-year-old full-time mother of three children aged between 18 and 11 years, who, along with her husband worked part time, was prepared to engage in a behaviour that risked being considered as 'wrong' for someone in her situation in order to give to others, although she had major reservations about doing this, given her own family's straitened circumstances. Here she is on what she might cut back on:

'This sounds really bad, but, I mean, I pay monthly to cancer research and for a wee boy that lives in Kenya, no, not Kenya, ach, I can't remember where he lives. I've been sponsoring him for years and years and years and he's about 16 now or 17. So I think I would look at that as well for cutting back, just for a wee while like, and then maybe do it again. But I still haven't done that because I just can't get around to it, I would feel really guilty. Same with the cancer research, I know it's only £10 but I've been doing that for years and years, so I have.'

Giving to others also helps people attain a positive perspective on their own situation. Here is Sheila, a part-time working mother of one dependent child whose husband is disabled, talking about how she helps her sister's charity efforts for Romanian orphans.

'I was in one of the shops and they had wee Christmas stockings and bath balls, all reduced to 20p, and you're kind of thinking, "For the sake of a couple of pound, you could be buying all those wee bits and pieces for putting in." At Christmas time, our kids put on their Santa hats and sit there and paper the shoe boxes and they make up all the boxes. And in Primark, two pairs of gloves were reduced to 50p and then reduced to 25p and I bought loads of gloves and you're thinking, "Well, we divide each pair up and that meant each box had a set of gloves." And there's still always that bit where much as things are tight here, you do have a roof over your head. Poverty's relative when you look at people in India or whatever else and you realise even if it's hard and you're struggling, you're still more fortunate than other people. I want my children to understand they are lucky and you always have to remember that there's other people out there that need more assistance. There's the shoe-box people ... and no matter how little you have, you've still an awful lot more than some other people have. And I think it's important if you took support, and I have absolutely needed it this past few months, that you give it because what goes round comes round, I sort of think.'

A quarter of the sample said they never or almost never felt embarrassed by their constrained financial situation; in other words, they rejected feelings of embarrassment. The situation of others in their immediate environment was the major rationale for this. These people did not view their situation in individualistic terms, but rather saw what was happening to them as part of a broader economic and social process. The term 'all in the same boat' was a common phrase here. This is what Paul, who was on a government back-to-work programme, said when asked if he had ever felt embarrassed because of his financial situation:

> 'No, not really. If you can't do nothing about it, embarrassment is not going to help. If I was the only person in the whole country, maybe, but there are thousands of other people that are in the same boat, so it's something you live with and get on with.'

This type of sentiment was voiced frequently, especially in people's conversations about shame.

Shame

The responses to the questions asking people whether they had ever felt ashamed of having a low income are more difficult to interpret. This is so for a number of reasons. First, this was a difficult question to ask and it provoked quite a strong reaction in many respondents. Some bristled at the question, while others seemed to feel belittled by it. Second, people's understandings of what constitutes shame as against embarrassment were not very clear (even though the questions were put at different points in the interview) and both emotions were not always seen as different from each other or from other negative emotions (such as annoyance or frustration). It was evident that people were trying to work out the difference as they replied; a few changed their mind mid-sentence, first saying 'Yes', then changing to 'No'; some said 'Yes' and 'No' to the question about shame. Many respondents spoke about embarrassment and shame interchangeably. Often people would start off talking about shame and then change to embarrassment. The coded nature of shame has been found by other research as well (Chase and Walker, 2013).

Most widely, though, respondents seemed to understand and interpret shame as a negative emotion "deep within yourself". Shame, then, is not about what one does, but about what one is. This conforms with the definition of shame offered by Chase and Walker (2013, pp

739-40): 'It entails a negative assessment of the self with reference to one's own aspirations and the perceived expectations of others, and is manifested as a sense of powerlessness and feeling small'. The processes involved include an internal judgement of worth and ability, an anticipated assessment of how one will be judged by others, and, in some cases, a sense of inferiority inferred through others' words, gestures or actions (Chase and Walker, 2013). These feelings may be exacerbated by the sense of disempowerment induced by shame, generating feelings of inability and lack of agency and culminating in a sense of being controlled or dehumanised.

Some respondents couched their responses in terms of being seen as inherently inferior. Alice (mother to one dependent child and working full time) put it in terms of "being looked down on":

> 'I feel it. Maybe it's not … and it's just my persona but I just feel that they are looking at you and saying, like, "You're nothing, you're from low income … you can't afford to give your family what we can give." Maybe it's just me, but, no, I think I feel it sometimes.'

This sense of felt inferiority, inadequacy and self-doubt was echoed in at least a fifth of interviews. The question on shame for some respondents also brought up references to long-standing inadequacies, making some people reach for perceived failures in their past life. In this context, people referred to regret that they had not taken their education as seriously as they now felt they should have, for example, or their failure to pursue a career.

In a context where shame might be present, it is extremely difficult for people to 'expose' themselves and their private circumstances. And yet they are frequently called on to do so. People made express mention of the local benefits office and other public or private offices in this context, seeing them not just as settings in which they were required to reveal details of their financial situation, but as encounters in which shame was engendered. Reference was made to probing and ultimately judgemental encounters with officials who decided whether they deserved assistance or not. Stigma is a potentially important component of these environments also. Hooper and colleagues (2007, p 32) describe the experience of stigma as one of feeling that one's identity is spoiled or discredited. One should add reputation here. In response, it is reasonable to expect people to try to control or manage the information they give out about themselves and the impression they create.

An important thread differentiating respondents in all of this was the extent to which they accepted that their situation was their own fault. Were they breaking their own expectations or those of society at large? There emerges a very complex interplay here between 'me' and 'society'. For some, shame was induced by the feeling that they were contravening a set of core norms. Dependence – lack of independence – was commonly mentioned as a source of shame. Recourse to family – which was interpreted in some cases as dependence – was also highlighted in this regard. Shame and guilt were closely associated. The general feeling expressed by a number of respondents was that, while grateful for help, they felt bad or "crap" taking help from people who were themselves struggling to manage on a low income and were often in bad health. Sheila described it as "shameful" at her age (late 40s) to be still reliant on her mother. One young lone mother (Cathy) expressed shame and embarrassment when she talked about getting help from her sister. This is how she explained it:

> 'My child wanted to go to Funderland on Monday and I had no money ... but then my sister paid for him and took him. Then I felt ashamed, embarrassed about it, you know what I mean, because I hadn't got the money there and then – no money.'

On the other hand, more than half of the respondents said they had never experienced shame. This again was a form of conscious rejection: why they should feel shame? However, these respondents tended to be emphatic in their reactions – their posture was often defensive and it was as if they were rejecting the very idea outright that they should feel shame rather than thinking the question through.

There are two main reasons why people did not feel ashamed. One is that shame implies moral failure and these people did not necessarily feel that they had failed. They rejected culpability. The cognitive exercise that people engaged in here was to generalise their situation, which in turn enabled them not to feel responsible as individuals for it – how could they be responsible if there are large groups of people in a similar situation? But there is a risk in such generalisation in that it may make people feel disempowered (which, as was shown earlier, could be said to be true of about a quarter of respondents). A second reason is that feelings of shame were considered inappropriate when people thought of what they had achieved in the circumstances in which they found themselves. Here they are not generalising, but rather particularising. The following is a telling reply to the question about shame from Helen, a lone mother of five children:

> 'I'm not ashamed. I'd be embarrassed, because I don't go nowhere, the kids don't go anywhere, really. But I'm not ashamed, because still inside my four walls we are all happy. Do you know what I mean? We're happy with ourselves.... And we are not starving, you know.'

As well as showing a certain degree of resentment at the question, her reply indicates that she tried to distance herself and her family from 'out there' as well as pointing out that appearances may be deceptive. Other respondents also reacted to potentially negative imagery by differentiating between how the family might appear to outsiders and what life was really like inside the family. One woman (who was employed part time and had a disabled husband) said: "We may look dysfunctional, but we are actually quite a tight unit."

In a similar attempt to construct a positive narrative, some respondents replied to the question about shame by making reference to something they were proud of. The following such response is from Paula, a lone mother of one young child who was studying at university:

> 'Sometimes, not overly. As I said before, I think because there's so many people now in the same boat, even people that were earning big money a while ago and then the recession hits and suddenly they're not. I think they probably feel a bit more embarrassed, but sometimes you do. I'm proud of the fact that I'm trying to do something about it and it's not through any bad decisions or bad lifestyle that I am on a low income, so in that respect I'm not ashamed.'

The quote mirrors the sentiments of others in rejecting culpability but at the same time demonstrating considerable ambivalence. Her main point, though, was that embarrassment is a more accurate word for what she feels. She went on to outline how she used to feel ashamed, but not anymore because she believed she was moving on. A number of other people also gave replies in the same vein – essentially that they were in the process of changing their situation and so should not be expected to feel shame.

But the complexity of emotions was continuously demonstrated. Here is Lizzie (lone mother to four children), answering the question about whether she feels shame by reference to her children's receipt of school dinners.

> 'Of course. Of course you do. Of course you are ashamed that your kids have free dinners … yet it's good. I feel ashamed within myself, but that's for me to deal with, but in a different scenario, if you know what I mean, it's pulled me out of a lot of holes. It's meant my kids get free meals and it means I don't have to pay £19 per week. They get a good hot meal. But of course it does. But it's learning to not feel ashamed and it's only there as a resource until you get on your feet and get back to work and get the youngest one up.'

Although Lizzie felt shame about her children receiving free school meals, she was in a sense trapped because she needed and readily acknowledged the value of the provision to her children. For this she was prepared to suffer personal shame. She had a way to deal with it, though – through cultivating a sense of temporary entitlement, as is obvious from the second section of the quote.

Othering

One way of coping with negative feelings and evaluations of self is for people to locate themselves vis-à-vis others who are seen to be (or are represented as) lower down a hierarchy or in some way more worthy of opprobrium than they. This is a process whereby 'we' are distinguished from 'they', and barriers are erected for the purposes of distancing the speaker from the imagined or depicted other (Lister, 2004; Krumer-Nevo and Benjamin, 2010). While the interviews sought to explore people's feelings of being 'othered', in fact there was more evidence of respondents themselves engaging in 'othering.' This essentially took the form of people trying to represent the social categories they belonged to – they did so by differentiating themselves from those who were seen as less worthy and of lower status, even if their formal status or living conditions were similar to their own (to the outsider anyway). Such instances were not that widespread, however.

When 'othering' occurred, it was especially likely to be on the part of those who were in employment. They saw their own employment as a major source of both status and differentiation. Those who were in employment – or who had a recent history of employment – tended to construct an edifice of themselves as 'hard working' as against others who were lazy or idle. Here are the accounts of two women – Molly and Lily, respectively – both of whom worked on a part-time basis:

'You're working. You should be able to afford nice things and then you're looking around and you're seeing the people who are on benefits having lovely things, going away on holidays. I mean, I know a girl on benefits and she goes to Turkey three times a year. And we're sitting going, "Where am I going wrong? Where am I going wrong in this life?" You know, my sister can afford to go out every weekend on benefits and you do sort of think to yourself … I mean they know that from Monday to Friday their kid's getting a lunch in school. If I send mine to lunches, it costs me £33 a week for school dinners, £2.20 a day for each … so I make them take packed lunches.'

'And then what sickens me is that you have other people who aren't working and who are sitting with their rent paid and getting the dole and getting crisis loans and things like that to cover their bills. And you're sitting and going, "Hold on a second, you're not working, you're not struggling the way I'm struggling to try and make ends meet." It's frustrating, very frustrating.'

Later in the interview, Lily said:

'I believe the government should sit down and recognise what families actually need help and what families don't. Like, obviously, if you're on the bru you get your rent paid for, plus you get your bru every week. You can't rationalise that. You can't give money and give money for doing nothing. Them people are doing nothing all day long, nothing. They're not working. Do you know what I mean? There's John [husband] knocking his pan in doing 50 and 60 hours a week and we're going nowhere, we're staying in the same spot. We're still in debt, we're no further ahead and will not be further ahead in the next few years.'

Consider what it is like to be at the receiving end of such views. The voice below is that of Katy, lone mother of one dependent child who had done many courses over the years at local centres to try to make herself feel better and gain some employment-related skill:

'Well, I don't have many friends who work because I would feel inadequate being with them. I couldn't be with those people because I would have that shame of they're working and they're able to pay for themselves and if a conversation comes up about money or benefits I am going to feel like shit … You feel worthless and it's like you're taking money off them or it just feels bad so I tend not to be about people who work.'

And here is the voice of Peter, father to two young children, whose wife worked but who himself had been out of work for nearly two years after at least a decade in the building industry. In this quote, he also makes a strongly moral case about his own virtues and values vis-à-vis those of others:

'I'm annoyed with the government, the dole and all that. They don't care. An honest man, we're honest, wife would be more honest than me. But they treat you like rubbish, whereas somebody who has never worked a day in their life is treated better – people where husband and wife don't work. People in this estate are better off than us. I know that for a fact. But that won't stop us going on the way we are. I'm not going to rely on the dole. That's just not the way I am. I'm always active even if it's out working in the garden or something.'

References to 'them' also help to generate feelings of being hard done by or the victim of injustice as that quote plus the following one illustrate. Here, as in the following quote from Molly, references to 'them' also help to generate feelings of being hard done by or being the victim of injustice:

'You know it's a double-edged sword. He's not on great money, he's not quite on the minimum wage, but he's not on great money.… We don't qualify to get free dental care because we earn over £15,300, my husband's only on £18,000 a year. We've four kids, so somebody with one kid on £15,000 gets all their free dental … we get nothing and you're sort of thinking, "That doesn't really work out, they still have more money for two people than what we have for six."… And the likes of school selections now with free school meals being one of the criteria for grammar schools.

Again, my kids miss out because they're not entitled to free
school meals because their daddy works. And Amy, for
example, didn't get a free nursery place because they went
to people on benefits first. So you know they do miss out
because he works.'

Behaviouralist references were a second currency used by respondents
to differentiate themselves from others of a similar status, but who were
to be depicted as less deserving. People tended to represent themselves
as different from those whose behaviour was seen as bringing 'poverty
to their door'. The subtext here is of culpability – projecting others as
deliberately engaging in poverty-inducing behaviours enables people
to see themselves as relatively upstanding. It introduces another level to
the differentiation underlying 'othering' – behaviour rather than status.

Some people clearly had internalised the negative depictions of
people in similar situations to their own. But yet they were able to
distance themselves from the archetypal benefit claimant (Lister, 2004;
Chase and Walker, 2013). So while the 'us' may not always be clear, the
object of the negative depictions – the 'them' – usually is. Irresponsible
benefit recipients were almost exclusively the 'others' in this study.
Sheila, who had been off sick for the first time in her working life,
bemoaned the situation, saying:

'I didn't want my kids growing up in a house where you
were seen as "bru hoppers", where there wasn't an example
of having a bit of pride or a bit of self-respect.'

Sometimes the negative depictions of benefit recipients came up in
the most casual of conversations.

'As I say, the last thing I would class myself as would be
lazy or a scrounger, you know, on the dole or whatever.'
(Conor, unemployed father of one child, whose partner
worked one day a week)

'Even people that's on the dole, maybe if they stopped
their smoking and their drinking with the money.' (Anne,
46-year-old full-time mother of three children, whose
husband worked part time)

'I know that just so many people think they're hard done
by in a Housing Executive rental, but what do they want

for? Nothing....' (Beth, married mother of three young children, two-earner family)

Such casual references underline how widespread are negative depictions of people receiving benefits.

There are a number of things going on here. One is an attempt by respondents to construct an image of themselves as virtuous (mainly by reference to their values). A second is people trying to protect themselves from invidious comparisons (and in the process accepting the cultural stereotypes of people like themselves) by drawing boundaries between themselves and 'undeserving' others.

Overview

A recurring theme to emerge from the interviews is the negative emotions caused by the inability to afford items and activities that other families are seen as taking for granted. This kind of feeling is compounded by the frequency with which people see themselves as being the object of negative categorisation by others. Embarrassment about their situation was widely reported by respondents. Two main types of situation tended to provoke embarrassment. The first was when people had to turn down or opt out of a social occasion with friends. The second was more public in nature. Here the object of embarrassment was not an intimate but a generalised other who is felt to be judging one negatively. Examples given of this kind of embarrassment included not having enough money to pay for shopping at the checkout or for services for children in school. Fewer people said they experienced shame; for those who did, such an emotion was generally precipitated by similar types of situation as feelings of embarrassment. People made a differentiation between embarrassment and shame, though, with the latter seen as a more profound experience.

The respondents generally tended to describe experiences relating to being on low income as embarrassing rather than shameful. Whether these are more akin to what Sayer (2005) calls 'low grade shame' is difficult to tell. But they do appear to indicate everyday exposure to numerous minor and major incidences of disrespect and misrecognition. These were so commonplace that respondents regarded them as normal (almost). But it is also important to say that people resisted being made to feel shame. Shame can be differentiated from embarrassment by reference to people's orientation to their situation. Those whose understanding was individualised were far more likely to see themselves as somehow responsible for their situation, and they were therefore more likely to experience both embarrassment and shame. They had internalised the stereotypes in popular discourse. But those who had a more structural understanding of why they were in the situation they were in were more likely to resist the feelings induced by negative categorisations. Core to their reasoning was that they did not necessarily view themselves as being to blame for their situation. They tended to utilise the numbers of people in a similar situation as validation of a more general structural problem.

The regularity of references to people being 'in the same boat' gives support to the existence of subjective relative deprivation, in that people evaluated their situation not just in terms of their own circumstances but in how they compared with those around them. Rather than the common cause or collective consciousness implied by the boat metaphor, though, there is evidence that some people tended to distance themselves from 'others' who, although in a roughly equivalent situation, were depicted negatively. With the focus usually on benefit recipients, 'othering' occurred in two main ways. Those who were working or were unemployed but felt they were actively looking for work depicted themselves as industrious and deserving vis-à-vis others who seemed willing to remain on benefits and not search for work. Second, people identified their own moral traits and behaviour as superior to the classic 'scrounger'. 'Othering' served two main functions. It enabled people to give a positive representation of themselves and to feel better about themselves. People try to protect themselves and preserve their sense of self-worth by invidious comparisons and depicting 'undeserving' others was a mode of self-protection. Second, othering allowed people to construct a sense of injustice or resentment about their situation and in this and other ways to assert their own values as different (by making negative reference to those who are seen to violate such values).

EIGHT

The policy context and the implications of the findings

The wider political context within which this study is set is one of radical reform of the welfare state in the UK. This chapter discusses and highlights key elements of the current policy context, especially the welfare reforms, and reflects on these in light of some of the key findings. It also uses the circumstances reported to reflect on the type of policy approach that is necessary to respond to the complex individual and family circumstances that are revealed by the research.

At the outset, it is helpful to set the broader context by highlighting, following Horgan and Monteith (2009) and McCormick (2013), some of Northern Ireland's distinctive features relevant to poverty and policy reform:

- persistent child poverty is double the rate for Great Britain and is especially high among lone-parent families;
- there is a serious lack of affordable childcare, especially in poorer areas;
- there is, compared with Great Britain, a very high rate of worklessness and long-term unemployment, lower wages and a greater share of jobs in the public sector;
- there are significantly higher claims for Disability Living Allowance due to mental health problems than in Great Britain;
- disadvantage is underpinned by 'deep social distress' if not 'community trauma' in the aftermath of conflict;
- child poverty is substantially concentrated in areas most affected by conflict.

Welfare and family policy reform

Almost from the moment it took office in 2010, the Conservative/Liberal Democrat coalition government started to reform the benefit system, largely undoing the relatively generous, family-focused provisions of the preceding Labour governments (Churchill, 2013). This was for the purpose of cutting back on public expenditure, but it was motivated also by a desire to simplify and streamline the

UK's benefit system. A whole host of reforms has been introduced. Tax Credits – which emerged as so important to the families in this study – were reduced in number and generosity. In 2011, the Child Tax Credit was withdrawn from families with annual incomes over £40,000 (but increased slightly for those on less than £15,000). The extra payments to families for infants were withdrawn completely. In regard to the Working Tax Credit, the rates for lone and couple parents were frozen and all payments were to be uprated in line with the consumer price index. In addition, the conditions attached to receiving the Working Tax Credit were tied more closely to longer engagement in employment: couples have to work in excess of 24 hours a week (rather than 16) to qualify. The maximum cost covered by the Childcare Tax Credit was reduced from 80% to 70%. Child Benefit was also subjected to major reform – in a move away from universalism, a net income threshold of £60,000 for the highest earners was set for qualification purposes. It is estimated that more than a million UK families are affected by this. The value of the benefit was also frozen – at 2010-11 rates from 2011 to 2014 – and then uprated by 1% from April 2014 for two years. Of all the benefit reforms (including those under Universal Credit, which will be outlined below), this is the one estimated to affect the largest number of families in Northern Ireland – more than 240,000 (Beatty and Fothergill, 2013, p 12).

All of these changes were in many ways the lead-up to the major overhaul of the benefit system being undertaken through the introduction of Universal Credit, the coalition government's flagship social policy reform project. The Welfare Reform Act gained Royal Assent in Great Britain in March 2012, allowing the government to introduce Universal Credit in England, Scotland and Wales. Social security is a devolved matter in Northern Ireland and so changes there go through the local parliament. However, in practice, retaining 'parity' with Great Britain is an attractive option for the Northern Ireland Executive, as the UK government has agreed to meet the costs of benefits in full only if parity is maintained (Browne and Roantree, 2013). The Northern Ireland Executive therefore proposed that Universal Credit also be introduced in Northern Ireland, and the Welfare Reform Bill was introduced in the Northern Ireland Assembly on 1 October 2012 for this purpose.

The aims of the reform are to integrate and simplify a very complex benefit and tax system and reduce disincentives around earning. In addition, the government hopes that the reform will make it easier for claimants to claim benefits, render the gains to paid work more transparent, and reduce the amount spent on administration and lost in fraud and error. Implementation, which is planned to be in three phases up to 2017, has already started in England, Scotland and Wales. However, the introduction in the UK has been significantly slower than previously planned, dogged by critical technology failures and major delays (National Audit Office, 2013). Consequently, Universal Credit was 'reset' in June 2014 as a new project. Officially in Northern Ireland, Universal Credit was due to be implemented in April 2014. However, final passage of the Welfare Reform Bill is required before Universal Credit can be implemented. To date, disagreement between the two main political parties (Democratic Unionist Party and Sinn Féin) on welfare reform per se, including the workings of Universal Credit, means that the Bill at the time of writing had yet to reach the Assembly for full debate. Meanwhile, the UK Treasury grows impatient and has set financial penalties (said to be £5 million per month) to be applied to the Northern Ireland Block Grant for failure to implement welfare reform.

Universal Credit is for working-age adults. While it will have its main impact in the low-income sectors, the government estimates that up to 8 million households will be affected across the UK. The new payment (which replaces six different existing benefits)[1] is organised in terms of a basic allowance (like a negative income tax) with additions that recognise the presence/costs of children, disability, housing and caring. The credit will be paid only once a month and to one person in the family. A core element of the credit is a benefit cap, which is set at £350 a week for a single person and £500 for a couple or lone parent regardless of the number of children. The absolute cap is £26,000 annually (a threshold calculated in relation to the average earnings of UK households). This cap will apply to a wide range of benefits combined (including Child Benefit, Child Tax Credit, Housing Benefit, Carer's Allowance, Maternity Allowance and Widow's Allowance). The childcare element is exempt from the cap, as are households where someone is claiming a disability-related benefit and/or Carer's Allowance. The Department for Social Development has estimated that 13,000 households in Northern Ireland will be affected by the cap. However, the vast majority will be exempt, given that someone in the household receives Disability Living Allowance. Approximately 600 households will be capped. These households contain 3,120 children. An average of five children live in capped households and approximately two-thirds of these households are

---

[1]   Income Support, Jobseeker's Allowance, Employment and Support Allowance, Housing Benefit, Child Tax Credit and Working Tax Credit.

lone-parent families. It is estimated that 61% of capped households will lose up to £50 per week (Department for Social Development, 2013a).

Another signature change involved in Universal Credit is that conditionality is extended to some people in employment – around 1.2 million workers are expected to be affected across the UK. These are mainly people on low pay who require Income Support or claim benefits related to housing or other needs. These people are expected to meet a new higher conditionality earnings threshold equivalent to a 35-hour week (through a combination of additional employment, higher hourly wages or increased hours).

Third, in an associated change, a space/bedroom threshold has been set for receipt of Housing Benefit, the so-called 'bedroom tax'. Families living in council or housing association accommodation whose property is deemed to be larger than they need will have their benefit cut. These changes tie people's housing subsidies to their usage of bedroom space. In calculating entitlement, the rules allow one bedroom per couple or parent(s), up to two children aged under 16 years have to share a bedroom if they are the same sex and children under 10 are expected to share regardless of their sex. Some 660,000 claimants are expected to be affected, with an average loss of £14 a week per claimant unit. Families with severely disabled children, foster carers and families of armed services personnel are exempt.

There are likely to be some regional variations in how the reform template will be implemented. But, as mentioned, while matters relating to social security are devolved to the Northern Ireland Assembly (and Northern Ireland has more welfare-related powers than either Scotland or Wales), the 'parity principle' limits the power of the Executive to make major changes to the Welfare Reform Bill. However, the Northern Ireland Executive has negotiated flexibility in the operation of Universal Credit to reflect the circumstances of the region. The following changes can apply 'in special circumstances, where necessary' (McCausland, 2012):

- the housing cost element of Universal Credit will be paid direct to landlords rather than tenants;
- payment of Universal Credit 'may' be split between two parties in a household;
- payment of Universal Credit 'may' be made twice each month rather than monthly.

Likely impact of welfare reform

The changes involved, which will mainly affect people of working age, have huge implications for family organisation and well-being. All the indications are that they will have a more severe negative impact in Northern Ireland than anywhere else in the UK. It has been estimated that when the welfare reforms come into full effect, they will take £750 million a year out of the Northern Ireland economy (Beatty and Fothergill, 2013). This is equivalent to £650 a year for every adult of working age; the equivalent figure for Scotland is £480, for Wales £550, and £560 for the two hardest-hit English regions, the North West and North East (Beatty and Fothergill, 2013, p 17). In fact, Northern Ireland, with 3% of the UK population, faces 4% of the overall financial loss arising from welfare reform. This is because of comparatively high reliance on benefits and comparatively lower incomes in Northern Ireland.

These reductions will affect different sectors of the population, but they will arguably have their greatest impact on families with children, affecting not just income levels but also incentives around labour market engagement and the way that family life is lived. Internally in all regions there will be 'winners' and 'losers' (Beatty and Fothergill, 2013).

Among the predicted likely 'winners' in Northern Ireland are couples with children – especially single-earner couples with children. Moreover, this group will gain proportionately more from the introduction of Universal Credit in Northern Ireland as compared with the UK as a whole, mainly again because of the greater prevalence and particular distribution of low incomes in Northern Ireland. Lone parents are among the estimated main losers. Beatty and Fothergill (2013) suggest that around a third of lone parents will lose from the reform whereas only a fifth will gain. Losses for lone parents are driven by those for non-working lone parents who either have significant amounts of unearned income or are entitled to the severe disability premium, which will be abolished under Universal Credit. It should be noted that lone parents are consistently in this study among the most disadvantaged sectors.

Apart from income levels, how might these changes affect everyday life in light of evidence from the study?

There is, first, the issue of household budgeting patterns and arrangements. One very important feature characterising the familial economy revealed by this study is the very short-term budgeting cycle, usually weekly, whereby certain activities are designated to particular days of the week and are paid from particular income sources. For example, gas and electricity cards tend to be purchased on the day Child Benefit is received, and items for children are also bought through this money ('child money'). Rent and other outgoings are paid through the 'big money' when it comes. The government has contributed to this pattern by labelling elements of the benefit package for particular needs, and paying them to a particular person in the family (for example, child elements to the 'main carer'). The main point here is that people's lives are lived and managed on a particular daily and weekly budgeting cycle in which spending is closely calibrated with the receipt of different income sources and all income is accounted for. Once the reforms come into effect, while Child Benefit remains separate from Universal Credit, and will still be paid to the mother, other means-tested benefits (including for housing costs) will be made in just one payment a month with no labelling or targeting to particular people. This will be a huge disruption to family budgeting and money management patterns, and will require major relearning and adaptation. And, since it is women who tend to manage the budget in low-income households, monthly payment of Universal Credit in one undifferentiated lump sum will be likely to make their lives harder (Bennett and Daly, 2014, p 86). People have become accustomed to – and in many ways have been socialised by government practices into – using the current differentiated cycle of benefit payment as a vital set of links in a chain of money management – each payment because it comes on different days and is paid in different time cycles acts like a form of bridging. All the evidence obtained through this study suggests not a gap but a chasm between the patterns of money management practised in the families studied and the planned reforms. And it may not just be true of these families – there is historically a social class basis to how people get paid. Wage earners were typically paid on a weekly or fortnightly basis, while a salary – which is a component of white-collar employment – was a monthly payment. Entire lifestyles as well as family and community histories are based around these differences.

Further concerns about Universal Credit relate to the reliance on an online claiming system. Although specific support will be available for claimants who may need help with online access, it is not clear what back-up plans there are for technology failures and such like. The evidence from the current research underlines that the consequences of income failure can be detrimental. There is little or no margin for error in most families' budgets and when unexpected charges or delays in income happen, they throw budgeting plans askew and may also force people into borrowing from moneylenders and other high-interest credit sources (given that their existing sources of informal support can mainly make available only small sums). What seem like small loans outside low-income families loom very large within them. It may take families years rather than weeks to recover and get back on their feet, and indebtedness brings a heavy weight of anxiety around repayment.

As mentioned, Universal Credit will replace a number of income-related benefits that are currently used as a passport to other benefits. The provision of free school meals is one such benefit, the value of which has been established in a wealth of research evidence (Department for Work and Pensions, 2012). The study confirms this, with free school meals emerging as one of the most important forms of provision and those receiving this benefit evaluating it as the most beneficial of any service received. It provides an invaluable contribution to children's nutritional intake as well as being a major help to highly constrained family spending on food. The existing entitlement criteria for free school meals are actually more favourable in Northern Ireland as compared with other jurisdictions, with eligibility extended to very low-income families for nursery and primary pupils and on a time-limited (two-year) basis.[2] In addition, from September 2014, the Working Tax Credit eligibility criteria will be extended so that children at post-primary school in Northern Ireland will be eligible for free school meals in the same way as those at primary school or nursery. This will enable more low-income families to benefit from this service – like Ciara, the young mother of two whose child at primary school was able to receive free school meals (which she described as 'brilliant') but whose older child at post-primary school could not.

The changes to be made in Housing Benefit for working-age claimants in social housing are also likely to be of huge significance. Known as the 'bedroom tax', people will have their Housing Benefit reduced if they are deemed to have a 'spare' bedroom. The cut will be a fixed percentage of the Housing Benefit eligible rent and will be set at 14% for one 'extra' bedroom and 25% for two or more 'extra' bedrooms. This means that low-income people living in social or rented housing that is deemed larger than required will have to either make up the shortfall of the difference between rent and Housing Benefit received or move to smaller accommodation.

Much of the focus on Housing Benefit reform has been on the 'bedroom tax'. Often going unnoticed is the 'non-dependent

---

[2] In December 2013, the Liberal Democratic leader Nick Clegg announced a free school meals policy for all five- to seven-year-olds in England from September 2014. However, media reports of disagreement over issues of affordability indicate that cross-party support is not guaranteed.

deduction' element. Currently, a non-dependent deduction is made from the amount of Housing Benefit awarded if a non-dependent child is living at home (regardless of whether they make a financial contribution to the household). Deductions are calculated, on a sliding scale, according to the income of the non-dependant. These deductions have almost doubled over the past three years as the deduction has been brought up to the level it would have been had it been increased in line with inflation since 2001. The largest deductions affect low-income households receiving Housing Benefit where the non-dependant is in paid work. This means that having a non-dependant living at home can substantially reduce household income. It also heightens anxiety, as we saw in the tension between Rachel and her mother, described in Chapter Five. Under Universal Credit, non-dependent deductions will be replaced by the more regressive system of Housing Cost Contributions. Instead of deductions imposed on a sliding scale, a flat-rate deduction of £68 per month will be made. For the first time, it will apply to unemployed 21- to 24-year-olds. From a housing support perspective, then, the 'bedroom tax' and Housing Cost Contributions are a 'double jeopardy' – Housing Benefit is reduced if a non-dependant lives at home and, if they leave the family home, Housing Benefit is reduced by the spare bedroom penalty.

The results of this study suggest that those who are required to find alternative housing will suffer significant hardship. People live in a place rather than just a house, and a vital place-based attribute is the support of family and friends, who often live locally (Hickman et al, 2014). Chapters Five and Six demonstrated both the localness of family and other networks and the extent to which such networks (especially those associated with family) are relied on for financial, emotional and practical support. Given the strength of respondents' views on social support systems, it is difficult to overestimate the damage that could be caused by the separation of families from existing support networks. In many cases, families are an additional tier to the welfare system. Young parents in particular emerge from this study as being most reliant on support from their own parents in terms of informal childcare, small cash advances, food and gifts for children such as clothes and pocket money. Apart from the hardship and disruption involved, there is a structural problem in regard to the Northern Ireland housing stock, which involves an under-supply of properties with fewer than three bedrooms, particularly in rural areas. And of course there is the highly segregated nature of housing in Northern Ireland, which places additional barriers on people's sense of a capability to relocate.

From a policy perspective, assumptions made about family responsibilities do not translate neatly into real life. Moves to develop social policies based on an intensified version of the level of family responsibility risk placing on them more responsibility than families can bear, thus threatening what already exists. It also seems contradictory to be considering legislation that will impose more responsibility on families at the same time as introducing legislation that could result in splitting family networks through policy measures such as restricting Housing Benefit, cuts to mortgage support and reducing Local Housing Allowance.

Illness and disability

Welfare reform also embraces disability payments and in fact it is these – rather than Universal Credit – that will involve the biggest cut-backs in spending in Northern Ireland (Beatty and Fothergill, 2013). The reassessment of all Incapacity Benefit claimants for transfer on to Employment and Support Allowance began in February 2011. To date, the process has resulted in fewer people qualifying for help as assessment and eligibility criteria have become more restrictive, with advice organisations reporting huge increases in the number of people seeking help to challenge adverse decisions. The high numbers of successful appeals have brought into question the soundness of the assessment process – up to March 2014, of those appealing decisions, 38% had been successful (Law Centre, 2014). Furthermore, Budget 2014 announced a seven-day waiting period to apply to new claims for contributory benefits and income-related Employment and Support Allowance from October 2014. As our respondents have demonstrated, the budgeting routine of low-income families is ill equipped to cope with breaks in the income cycle.

The replacement of Disability Living Allowance with Personal Independence Payment was initially planned for April 2013. However, the final passage of the Welfare Reform Bill (NI) is required to trigger the introduction of Personal Independence Payment. As with Employment and Support Allowance, fewer people will qualify for it. It was estimated in November 2012 that 118,010 claimants would be affected by the introduction of Personal Independence Payment (Department for Social Development, 2013b). An essential element of the background is the significance of these benefits in Northern Ireland. The overall incapacity-related claimant rate in Northern Ireland in November 2012 was 10.1% – one in 10 of all adults between the ages of 16 and 64 years (Department for Social Development 2013b, p 22). This puts Northern Ireland well ahead of the British average of 6.5%. Likewise, Northern Ireland has the highest Disability Living Allowance claimant rate among adults of working age – also 10.1% in May 2012 (compared with 6.2% in Scotland, 6.8% in Wales and an average of 4.9% across Great Britain as a whole). One of the reasons why Northern Ireland has relatively higher incapacity and disability claimant rates may be the long-term impact of the 'Troubles'. There is evidence to suggest that the Troubles were associated with significant mental health problems (O'Reilly and Stevenson, 2003).

A recent report suggests that sickness and disability claimants can expect to be hit hard by the changes (Browne and Roantree, 2013). It is likely that those affected will include the families in the current study. Twelve percent of families said their primary source of income came from disability-related benefits, including Employment and Support Allowance and Disability Living Allowance. Other families in the study may be affected also given the high levels of ill health and disability. It is known from other research that children living in persistent and severe poverty are more likely than other children to live in a family where there is someone with a disability (Monteith et al, 2008).

Childcare provision

There is a strong story to be told about the inadequacy of childcare in Northern Ireland. The region has the lowest level of childcare provision in the UK. Recent officially reported data indicate that, in 2011/12, there were only 5,320 registered childcare providers in Northern Ireland (Northern Ireland Executive, 2014). Childminders accounted for more than three-quarters of this total (77%); playgroups, 9%; and day nursery and out-of-school providers, 6% and 5% respectively. Between them, these providers offered nearly 56,000 childcare places. With some 355,000 children under the age of 15, this makes for around one registered childcare place for every six children. This under-supply of provision deprives children of developmental opportunities and makes paid employment difficult for parents, especially mothers. Moreover, the longer school summer holidays (nine weeks as opposed to five or six in the UK) mean that parents often have to take unpaid leave to meet caring commitments during this time.

Lagging behind other regions in the UK, Northern Ireland has introduced the first stage in the implementation of a childcare strategy only in recent months (Northern Ireland Executive, 2014).[3] Known as Bright Start, the new Strategic Framework and Key First Actions make provision for some 7,000 childcare places. All but 2,000 of these are to be created by social enterprises or individual enterprise (as through a childminder incentive scheme in rural areas, for example). Around 40% of provision is to be targeted on children in need – with provision largely organised through social enterprises in the 25% most deprived areas of Northern Ireland. The framework document states that childcare places will be offered at a tariff based on the ability of the parent to pay. Maximum tariffs will be put in place to ensure affordability for all, with a reduced scale based on ability to pay. However, it is planned also to maximise childcare vouchers and Child Tax Credit. The Office of the First Minister and Deputy First Minister has taken the lead on the development of this strategy and the publication of a substantive childcare strategy with more details is planned for 2014. While this is a welcome start, it is a small response in light of the gaps in provision and the scale of the need for childcare provision in low-income areas. The absence of provision for 0- to three-year-olds in the Key First Actions is a major concern.

Income (in)adequacy and employment

Employment is now the main focus of anti-poverty policy in the UK and elsewhere, so much so that protection against poverty depends on the quality of and rewards from employment, as well as the costs of engagement (Bennett and Daly, 2014, p 10).

Nearly half of the families in severe financial hardship in this study had some attachment to the labour market – indeed, in two cases, both partners were working full time. Hence, employment per se does not offer a defence against financial need. Recent government policies have focused on a supply-side approach to the labour market, emphasising especially so-called 'activation' in the form of preparing people to take up work through such measures as training and job placement assistance. This kind of measure is important, but it is insightful to look at it through the circumstances of the families in the present study.

Respondents' narratives and life stories indicate a real shortage of adequately paid employment. The precariousness of insecure employment coupled with the uncertainty of working hours make it hard for family members to gain an adequate income from employment.

---

[3]   Following a consultation – see Office of the First Minister and Deputy First Minister (2012).

It is important to bear in mind also that the planned benefit cuts will take money out of these localities and will most affect the poorest neighbourhoods. The current broader employment/labour market situation has given rise to what some are calling a new class of people, 'the precariat', whose lives are characterised by working in a series of short-term jobs with no progression and scant social protection (Standing, 2011). This idea has some resonance for respondents in the present study, many of whom have great difficulty finding an established place in the labour market. This underlines how fundamental it is that policy decisions regarding benefit entitlement regulations take into consideration macro conditions such as structural labour market characteristics. The latter should be the subject of policy in their own right. Researchers reviewing the causes of poverty stress the importance of the demand side of the economy, in terms of jobs being available (Harkness et al, 2012). A recent study by the Trades Union Congress (2012) reported that the number of people in involuntary part-time work (part-time workers seeking full-time jobs) in the UK has almost doubled since 2008. There has also been an increase in the number of people who want to work additional hours in their current job (although they may not want to work full time, and may not be in part-time employment). This situation of being under-employed is more likely to affect young people, women and those in low-paid jobs. Moreover, Northern Ireland has seen the greatest rise in the number of people in under-employment – an increase of 85% since 2008. Two main points emerge from the Trades Union Congress analysis that are confirmed by the current study: under-employment is not accurately reflected in labour market statistics and headline unemployment rates fail to reveal many of the weaknesses of the current labour market and the ways in which these are affecting people's ability to 'make ends meet'.

A further relevant point to emerge from the study is that most of those outside the labour market (as well as many within it) are carers and have heavy responsibilities in this regard, with little or no support other than informally through family members. There is ample evidence that caring restricts both paid work opportunities and rates of pay (Pickard, 2011; Paull and Patel, 2012; Shildrick et al, 2012). Lone parents face a particularly sharp trade-off between employment and family. Earlier research in the UK found that about half are unable, no matter how hard they work, to rise above the poverty line and still meet their basic obligations, including caring for their children (Burchardt, 2008). Moreover, lone parents' risk of living below the minimum income standard has increased sharply in the UK (Padley and Hirsch, 2014).

Education and training are important for all, but especially for women who have focused their energies on caring and men whose skills are outdated or too low-level for today's labour market. Dorsett and colleagues (2011), using evidence from the British Household Panel Study, suggest that lifelong learning has a substantial return for women, in terms of wage effects and especially their employment prospects, in particular for those who were initially least qualified.

Fuel poverty

One of the most significant themes to emerge from this research is the ubiquity of fuel poverty as a feature of family life on a low income. This affects children in particular, although it has been seen that parents endeavour to protect children from the worst aspects of inadequate heating by sacrificing heating and utility usage on themselves. Research on the impact of fuel poverty on children documents how living in fuel-poor homes is associated with significantly greater risk of health problems for children, especially respiratory problems as well as poorer weight gain and lower levels of adequate nutritional intake (Liddell, 2008). Existing studies also detail how adolescents living in fuel-poor homes are at significantly greater risk of multiple mental health problems when other contributory factors have been accounted for (Barnes et al, 2008).

To set the general backdrop for the Northern Ireland region, recent fuel poverty statistics show that, of the four UK nations in 2011, Northern Ireland had the greatest proportion of fuel-poor households (followed by Wales, then Scotland and finally England). Some 42% of the population was estimated to be in fuel poverty compared with 15% in England (and 25% and 29% in Scotland and Wales respectively) (Department of Energy and Climate Change, 2013). More detailed information produced in Northern Ireland reveals that 32% of households containing children were living in fuel poverty, with lone-parent households accounting for more than half (63%) of households with children that are fuel poor (Northern Ireland Housing Executive, 2011).

The higher fuel poverty rates in Northern Ireland are attributed to a high percentage of off-gas-grid households (which therefore use alternative, more expensive fuels to heat their homes) (Committee for Social Development, 2012; Department of Energy and Climate Change, 2013). An independent review into energy policy in Northern Ireland, commissioned by the Consumer Council (Whitty, 2012), underlined the complexities of the regional energy market and policy framework. The peculiarities highlighted included: the high dependence on oil for home heating, particularly in rural areas; the substantially higher electricity and gas prices compared with the UK and the EU averages; and an underdeveloped gas network serving only 15% of households. In addition, the remit of the Utility Regulator does not extend to the heating oil sector on which the majority of households rely for their heating, and despite Northern Ireland being such a small market, eight government departments are involved in energy policy formulation. All these complexities and more were manifest in respondents' accounts of covering energy costs. The entire sample reported high increases in the cost of fuel and electricity in the past years, in some cases a doubling of this expenditure. A substantial number of people relied on oil for their heating and in rural areas respondents said they were unable to access gas.

From a policy perspective, currently there are two main initiatives for tackling fuel poverty through income maintenance: the Winter Fuel Payment, which is an automatic payment of £200-£300 for anyone over the age of 60 years, and the Cold Weather Payment, which is an automatic payment of £25 per cold weather period to those who are disabled, pensioners or families with children and on a low income.[4] This is the only additional support with fuel costs that people with disabilities or families with very low incomes receive. And yet, 'householders with children under the age of 16' are identified in Northern Ireland's Fuel Poverty Strategy as being among the most vulnerable groups affected by fuel poverty (Department for Social Development, 2011b).

What is clear from this study is the lengths to which families are already going so as to restrict their use of energy (see Chapters Two and Three). It is difficult to imagine how more energy efficient they could be, given the limited level of control they had over their circumstances and the costs of fuel. Moreover, a high number of families in the sample was renting from a private landlord in properties reliant on oil for their home heating. In the general population, lone-parent households are highly represented in the private-rented sector, with 37% of all lone-parent households renting privately. The profile of renters in this sector is also characterised by an over-representation of unemployed tenants (Northern Ireland Housing Executive, 2011). These are the people most vulnerable to fuel poverty but with the most restricted choice in regard to housing.

---

[4]   A 'cold weather period' is any seven-day period with a mean daily temperate at or below freezing.

Welfare reform will undoubtedly see a rise in the number of households in fuel poverty. Nationwide, poorer households pay more for goods and services such as oil, electricity and gas. For instance, current pricing structures mean the unit cost of electricity is higher for lower users than it is for higher users – the more you use, the less you pay per unit. This study confirms a restricted energy use on the part of low-income households as part of a survival strategy, but tariff structures mean they end up paying more per unit – a situation that is 'both socially regressive and environmentally counterproductive' (Whitty, 2012, p 74).

Place, locality and an integrated set of services

Locality emerges as very important to the people in this study. The respondents lived very local lives. In many regards, poverty and low income give people no other choice but to live locally and confine their main interactions to an area in which they can move about without incurring significant transport costs. The very local basis to life is also explained by the propinquity of family living locally. The services people use also tend to be local.

The importance of services to low-income people and their families should never be underestimated. Facing a cumulative set of challenges, the service needs of these families are more wide-ranging than those discussed already. Many families have need of additional support services for children, for example, especially in the context of challenges relating to children's health and development, and it seems like many also live in areas that are characterised by inadequate service provision. In this and other ways, their communities are 'poor' communities. There is a constellation of factors involved. Along with income, these span the domains of health, education and the local environment.

One major difficulty is health. We saw earlier that only about a fifth of all the families represented in the study had no major health-related problems. The latest research results on poverty trends nationally indicate that the risk of poverty for households headed by people who are ill or disabled has risen sharply (MacInnes et al, 2013). They now appear to be one of the most vulnerable groups of all. In the present study, the income that many people had available to them made a healthy diet and lifestyle difficult, if not impossible. A related matter was intergenerational transmission of ill health and disability, especially in terms of health-related practices and behaviour. Underlying all of this is access to services. While people did appear to make frequent use of health and some other services, their generally poor state of health spoke volumes about the inadequacy of health service provision.

In relation to education, the main issue was very low levels of human capital and basic skills. Many people in the sample had low educational achievement, including some with no educational achievement. This had left some people with literacy and numeracy problems. Nor did the respondents have the opportunity to acquire skills through employment. If they were involved in paid work, it was mainly unskilled and provided few if any training or developmental opportunities. It is pessimistic but nevertheless true to observe that many parents' negative experience of school and the education system was being repeated in the lives of their children. There were other, more severe barriers to children's educational progress, however. The costs involved, both direct and indirect (in terms of foregone earnings), can be high for families living on low income and young people may have nowhere to do their homework and may know no one who can demonstrate at first hand the benefits of staying on in school.

Finally, in relation to the local area, the question for policy is two-fold: how is life in low-income areas to be improved and how can low-income areas be helped to function in a way that is positive for all residents? There is a whole series of policy issues involved here, some of which are already being addressed. The measures being taken include moves towards integrated services and community or area regeneration. In regard to services, the new Northern Irish government framework, Delivering Social Change, seeks to provide a coordinated departmental approach to take forward key work in the reduction of poverty, promote equality and improve the health, well-being and life opportunities of children and young people. The idea of funding a small number of concentrated initiatives is central to it.[5] In October 2012, six 'signature projects' were announced to combat area-based disadvantage. The projects focus on support for families in areas of multiple deprivation; extra literacy/numeracy support for under-achieving pupils; and targeted support to improve skills/enterprise. Northern Ireland's approach has a clear element of targeting disadvantaged households and places (McCormick, 2013). A seventh project was announced in October 2013 to enhance play and leisure opportunities for children and young people.

The objectives of the signature projects may be commendable, and the framework still in the early stages, but the limited and short-term

---

[5]   See www.ofmdfmni.gov.uk/index/delivering-social-change/delivering-social-change-introduction.htm

nature of existing projects calls into question their ability to adequately address poverty across all ages. For example, in January 2014 the Office of the First Minister and Deputy First Minister published a consultation document, *Delivering social change for children and young people*. The draft strategy proposes the integration of three major policies and strategies that deal with improving children's lives: the Child Poverty Strategy; the Northern Ireland Executive's Ten-Year Strategy for Children and Young People 2006-2016; and the fulfilment of the executive's obligations under the United Nations Convention on the Rights of the Child. At the time of writing, a full report on the consultation has not been published. However, publicly available responses record major concerns. These include, but are not limited to, the omission of the needs of vulnerable groups of children such as those with disabilities and Traveller children, an over-emphasis on paid employment and failure to take into consideration the likely impact of welfare reform on children, young people and their families – all of which are claimed to undermine existing policies and strategies.[6]

The results of this study shed light on what an integrated perspective would look like. They suggest that 'integrated' might have three references. The first is that an adequate response must aim to improve families' access to a combination of services, income and other resources. Action on one front alone is inappropriate; policy has to think in terms of the resource capacities of low-income households as a whole (with capacities conceived of in a broad way). The second meaning of 'integrated' is that there is a need for policy to respond or act with regard to four levels simultaneously: households/families, individual adults, children, and the local areas in which people live. A third meaning of 'integrated' is in the sense of a 'package approach', by which we refer to a tailored response to the needs of particular families in particular situations. In this regard, the diversity of people's situations and their preferences for voluntary as well as statutory services is to be noted. A range of groups/supports is needed – catering to the needs of women, young people and women and men as parents, as well as to local area development, to name just some among many.

---

[6]   See www.improvingchildrenslives.org/filestore/Filetoupload,442354,en.pdf

NINE

Conclusion

The discussion in this short chapter, meant as an overview of both the findings and the theoretical framework, is organised mainly around the four elements of the book's theoretical framework. To begin, the chapter outlines the main findings on the incidence of poverty and low income among the study population and sets out the predictions for poverty in Northern Ireland in the near future. Following this, it sets out the main findings on the relationship between family and poverty/low income and discusses the insights yielded for the reconceptualisation of family in a context of poverty and low income.

Facing the future

The majority (53%) of participants had incomes in or around the poverty threshold for the Northern Irish population as a whole in 2009-10. One-third of the families in the study could be said to be in severe financial hardship. Nearly half of these families had some attachment to the labour market – indeed, in two cases, both partners were working. Hence, employment per se does not offer a defence against financial need. While inadequate income was the overarching facet of deprivation and social exclusion, the situation of families was exacerbated by a high prevalence of health-related difficulties that not only made demands on people's time and other resources but also created problems in accessing well-paid work. Lone parents' situation was generally worse than that of two-parent families; contributory factors here included the level of income available to them outside of the labour market (which as mothers many cannot enter either because their children are young or because of the unavailability or unaffordability of childcare) and lone parents' relatively greater propensity to report ill health.

How are these families (and those like them) likely to fare in the future?

The latest evidence (Browne et al, 2014) predicts a sharp increase in income poverty among children and their families in Northern Ireland. While the projections of rising poverty also apply to the UK as a whole, the rate at which child poverty in particular is projected to increase in the country as a whole is significantly slower as compared with Northern Ireland. Measured before housing costs, relative child poverty in Northern Ireland is projected to be 9.2 percentage points higher in 2020-21 than 2011-12. The projections for the UK as a whole are for a 5.0 percentage point increase over the same period. As a result, a child poverty rate of 30.9% (measured on the basis of 60% of the median income before housing costs are taken into account) is predicted for Northern Ireland in 2020-21, compared with 21.6% in 2011-12. Poverty among parents is also projected to increase – from 20.7% in 2011-12 to 26.8% in 2020-21 (based on the same relative poverty measure as above) (Browne et al, 2014, p 28). The benefit reforms are estimated to play a major role in increasing child poverty. According to Browne and colleagues (2014, p 11), by 2015-16, reforms introduced since April 2010 are projected to increase child poverty in Northern Ireland by between 5.4 and 7.0 percentage points (depending on the way that poverty is measured). Universal Credit is not the main culprit here – its long-run effect (to 2017-18) is estimated to be a reduction of 2.4 percentage points in relative child poverty, compared with 2.0 percentage points in the UK as a whole (Browne et al, 2014, pp 16-17). In terms of causal factors, the effect of Universal Credit is outweighed by the impact of other tax and benefit reforms being introduced. There is also the likely impact of a weakening in previously forecast employment growth in Northern Ireland. Furthermore, UK job creation in the next decade is expected to be concentrated in sectors that are under-represented in Northern Ireland.

All the indications are, then, that things will either stay the same or get worse for the families in this study as for many other families.

Overview of results in the light of theoretical framework

The view of poverty and low income that has informed this book is one that focuses on resource accrual and resource expenditure in a context of family and the conditions that affect them. While financial resources dominate, other resources are seen to be important also, such as time and energy and relational and cultural resources. But resources per se are insufficient to understand poverty and low income. Rather, one must look also at the processes affecting resource accrual and resource use. A signature aim of this of this book has been to elucidate how family considerations are implicated in these processes. Family brings and family also consumes resources. This complex of processes, relationships and patterns has been theorised to inhere in four elements:

- family as structure, composition and mode of organisation;
- family as locus of cultural specificity, meaning and identity;
- family as a set of relationships, activities and processes;
- family as an object of public representation.

It is insightful to consider how each works in practice.

The structural and organisational factors relate to family composition, the characteristics of individuals and the general circumstances characterising the family unit as a whole. These directly and indirectly affect the resources available. However, composition effects are not adequately captured by size and age of family members. They also relate to people's health (as well as that of their close family) and functioning, educational level and labour market-related resources (including employment history and skills). Lone parents' situation especially illustrates the impact of structural factors; they were generally in a worse situation than two-parent families, partly due to the absence of a second adult income but also given that in this study such families had comparatively greater health difficulties and fewer human capital resources.

The trajectories that led people to their current situation also revealed structural elements at play. While these varied, the circumstances characterising respondents and their families not only displayed significant underlying commonalities but also confirmed that there are pathways that lead to poverty and low income. For some people, it was a failed marriage or partner relationship that was the initial trigger for low income and/or poverty; for others, it was disability, illness or an accident or a combination of these; for still others, it was bearing and rearing one or more children without a partner. All of these affected people's capacity to earn a decent income through employment. While one factor may be the initial trigger, problems and difficulties mount over time and it is quite common to find families with a combination of disabling conditions that lock into each other over time. No outcome is foretold, but finding oneself and one's family in one or more of the situations listed above profoundly limits the courses of action available.

The presence and significance of structural factors reveals some of the limits of a pure agency approach to understanding poverty – the people in this study exercised agency all the time, but their choices were constrained by structural givens, elements outside of their control. Negative structural factors have a double impact: first, they limit the resources available, and second, dealing with them in turn eats up further resources. Think of dependency, illness or disability in a family, for example. As well as involving extra financial costs, caring for a sick or disabled child or other family member may preclude the mother or father from employment. Caring also consumes other resources that may be scarce – time and energy. Furthermore, the psychological and emotional impacts of ill health and/or disability may further deplete resources. In this context, two particular characteristics of the situation of low-income families should be noted. First, whereas better-off families are able to reduce the time and other resources required for care by paying for it, this is hardly possible for low-income families. Second, people in low-income families are more likely to experience ill health and disability, so the volume of care required is greater as compared with other sectors of the population. The costs fall heavily on mothers especially.

The cultural and cognitive was the second lens through which the relationship between family and poverty was viewed. Northern Ireland is a good (although particular) place to examine these issues, given the strength of family as an element of collective ideology and social life there (McLaughlin, 1993).

People's cultural resources and their dispositions and orientations were very clearly highlighted by the research. The respondents value getting by and surviving the many challenges facing them. They value also the skills and capabilities that they find within themselves to do so. There is no alternative value system or culture here. We see in these families the values that Savage (2012, p 156) views as prevailing among the British working classes (or popular classes, as he calls them): endurance, graft and getting by. What is clear also – and further research is needed to know whether this is particular to Northern Ireland or whether it is a widespread feature of culture among low-income and poor families in the UK more widely – that these values are inflected with a strong sense of family.

One such value is around family solidarity and family togetherness. The language and concerns of family were ubiquitous. In a situation where money shortages create instability and insecurity, the construction of an image and ideal of 'our family' can be very important. The first major finding in this regard was that family, generally thought of in the first instance to refer to children, evoked a strong and powerful set of references for people. Moreover, these were often positive references. But such references did not connote an undifferentiated sense of family as positive. People had bad family experiences and struggled in many ways around existing and past family relations, but they still invested – cognitively, emotionally and even materially – in creating an ideal set of family relations. So they may cut themselves off from bad experiences and family members with whom they have had difficulties but there was always some group or set of family relations that held positive orientations and expectations for them. Most widely this was their children. These respondents' identities and ontological security are invested in their children more than in any other family member or relationship. It was rarely only children, though, because most people had at least one other family member with whom they were close.

Second, it was clear that family togetherness did not just happen but was consciously aimed at. While 'a sense of family' may sound vague, it is an ideal that was evident both in people's dispositions and in the way they managed their activities and interpreted their various courses of action. Their attitudes towards money – and also the way they used it – were shaped by their views of family life. Considerations around children dominated. Parents apply different standards to the children's consumption than they do to their own and are readily prepared to forego fulfilling their own needs to ensure their children's needs are met. Some examples here include people's decision to celebrate family occasions (such as children's birthdays and Christmas) – even if this resulted in considerable privation – and the many ways in which they sought to create family as an 'oasis', protecting children as much as they could from the family's ongoing struggles and distancing life inside the home from the world outside.

Evidence of the normative reproduction of family inheres, *inter alia*, in the fact that people's conversations were full of both rules relating to family life and moral prescriptions in this and other regards. For example, respondents represented their systems of child rearing as being quite rule-bound and the information on wider family support also revealed a strong set of normative orientations and responsibilities toward family. People know what is expected of them and they try to live up to expectations. Ethical parenting was very important in all of this, but was largely interpreted in the context of the situation people found themselves in. Against a backdrop of increasingly tightly scripted roles for parents in society generally, these parents negotiate a narrower track than is the case in families where there is no scarcity of money (Gillies, 2012). They have less freedom of action and a very constraining set of boundaries. Perhaps because of this, much of their energy is taken up with working out what is good parenting in their situation. They interpreted this mainly in terms of trying to protect their children by, for example, instilling in them the need to conform (or 'be good'), trying to ensure that they are not too different from or deprived relative to other children in terms of social and leisure participation and material goods, not 'spoiling' them (which had a sense of not allowing them to have unrealistic expectations of what they can have), and being fair to all of the children.

The extent to which people actively engaged in constructing a sense of family was striking, as was the effect of this on the activities engaged in and the way resources were used. 'Kinkeeping' – a term used to denote the activities engaged in to keep family members in touch with each other (Rosenthal, 1985) – captures some of what is involved here. However, the scale and intensity of people's perceptual schemas and activities in the present study suggest that keeping in touch is too vague a term. While keeping in touch in Rosenthal's work is about letter writing and visiting as well as economic aid, it lacks a sense of the significance of concerns around children and family on an everyday basis that this study uncovers. 'Family making' is actually a better term, in that it is close family members who are the focus, and there is a strong cognitive element involved. The latter may be described as 'thinking family', whereby familial considerations are consciously interwoven into resource-related decisions and activities.

The third dimension through which the relationship between family and poverty was theorised was the processes and relationships engaged in to 'keeping the family going' and how this was implicated in the use of resources. The relevant chapters (especially Chapters Four and Five) outlined the way family is interwoven into the myriad processes of managing family life on a constrained income.

The familial and the financial are very closely intertwined. One can see this in a number of ways. One is in the existence of a familial economy, that is, the family is the unit of budgeting, essential items for the family as a whole are prioritised, there is a low level of individual resource holding, and there is a strong sense of resources being seen and treated as collective. A second way of seeing how closely family considerations are stitched into activities and patterns is by recognising that alongside a rational economy there is a moral economy. The difference between the two rests mainly on how need and exigency are understood and acted on. In the rational economy, money is very tightly organised around three main types of expenditure: rent/mortgage, utilities and food. In the moral economy, decisions around spending are inflected with personal and relational considerations and spending decisions are less tightly rule-bound. There are three defining features of the moral economy. The first is a hierarchy, mainly along generational lines. This sees children and their expenditure prioritised over that of adults. In fact, prioritising children and minimising their social deprivation was the most widespread child-related norm found. The presence or absence of children was the key determinant of how people used heating and other utilities, for example, and children's needs also influenced how people viewed the costs and benefits of television and internet connections. Second, the moral economy sees a lot of 'leakage' between what is an absolute need and a relative need, especially when it comes to children. Hence, parents struggle to try to make leisure opportunities available to their children and to give them 'treats' and buy them luxury items, even if these have to compete with more essential spending and open up parents to opprobrium from the outside world, where attitudes about what 'poor parents' should and should not do become increasingly judgemental. Third, the moral economy is characterised by selfless giving of parents to children – parents' own needs are suspended for later, perhaps for ever.

A further relevant finding is that family relationships are central to both resource use and resource accrual. In fact, for the current group of respondents, family life in conditions of poverty is sustained by 'chains of relationships'. Wider family – especially parents and siblings – is a vibrant source of private transfers for the majority of respondents. A large volume of practical, emotional and small-scale financial support passes between members in what could be called a 'family network'. Besides money, family support takes a number of forms, including regular childcare as well as food, clothes for children and small household items such as washing powder. Micro lending of money to help with immediate bills and costs is arguably the most important form of support, especially for younger parents. The amounts involved tend to be rather small, although this does not make them any less important. In fact, they are so regular as to be routine (in a temporal sense, but not in a relational or emotional sense). All the indications are that, for this group of respondents anyway, life without wider family would be very different, and generally much harder.

There is a strong sense of a supportive family network at play. This differs from people's ideal, though, and the associated relationships, responsibilities and obligations are complicated. While support is often proffered, it cannot be taken for granted. In addition, there is a general expectation that support will be reciprocated, although no single metric governs how and when and indeed to whom it should be paid back. Reciprocation is sometimes discussed between people and made an overt part of the 'deal' or contract – the process is similar to what Finch and Mason (1993) term 'negotiation'. But actually support is more likely to be implicit, based on perceived need, trust and generalised understandings about appropriate behaviours in the context of the particular relationship or wider family practices and family culture. While in some ways this avoids a situation in which people's need is made overt, in other ways it could act to increase anxiety, since the recipient has to figure out how and when to reciprocate. It may also act to heighten people's ambivalence about needing help from family members (which was quite widespread). In this sense again, we see the double-sided nature of resources, in that family relationships may confer resources but also use up resources (including psychological and emotional resources as well as time). One clear insight of this study is that one cannot and should not work with a single understanding of support from relatives. Family support is differentiated and 'family' is too broad a category to serve well in revealing the nature of support. We suggest that the idea of 'family within family' is a better way of representing the processes whereby people select out particular family members to seek support from and give support to. People in this study exercised agency by turning to a small number of people within their close family. Hence, while the support network was relatively vibrant, the idea of a wide supportive family network is somewhat inaccurate.

The final dimension to the conceptual framework is self/family as an object of representation. This opens up considerations of how people relate to their local area and their 'official' and unofficial encounters with others. This too has a number of different elements and was instantiated in various ways.

One such example is of self and family 'going public', that is, being called on to present themselves and their families in both routine and non-routine settings. In the case of people on low income, these are more likely to be 'representations' than presentations. This is true for two reasons. First, the generally negative climate that surrounds those who are poor and on a low income means that they have to continually demonstrate their good character and deservingness. The second reason is because some encounters are crucial for such people (especially official encounters such as the application for and receipt of certain public services and benefits). The extent to which respondents were subjected to or felt a series of indignities associated with their financial situation was very striking. Such indignities were especially likely to occur in situations involving encounters with public officials (including in school settings but most often in benefits offices). In their routine forms, they are equivalent to what Pierre Bourdieu (2001, pp 1-2) called 'a gentle violence, imperceptible and invisible, even to its victims, exerted for the most part through the purely invisible channels of communication and cognition (more precisely misrecognition), recognition or even feeling'.

While indignities and misrecognition exist in people's environment, they are not external. People internalise dominant classifications and meanings as legitimate (Reay, 2012, p 36). Our study uncovered three general ways in which this was the case.

First, the feelings of embarrassment widely reported by respondents suggest that people accept some sense of their own situation as negatively deviating from the norm. Two main types of situation tended to provoke embarrassment. The first was when people had to turn down or opt out of a social occasion with friends. The second was more public still. Here the source of embarrassment was not an intimate but a generalised other who was felt to be severely judgemental.

The second indicator of respondents' internalisation of negative depictions of themselves concerned their feelings of shame. This was a less common experience than embarrassment and there was no clear dividing line between embarrassment and shame. That said, experience of shame – especially low-grade shame – was still significant and when experienced was more profound than embarrassment (which can more easily be shrugged off). Respondents' accounts suggest that shame is more often associated with implied moral failings. It should also be said, though, that the concept of shame might plumb the limits of people's internalisation of negative depictions in that many people resisted feelings of shame. This is because they did not necessarily see themselves as being to blame for their situation.

A third type of evidence suggesting some internalisation of negative depictions relates to instances of 'othering'. This occurs when people affix a negative label to others and distance themselves from this negative depiction, thereby attempting to place themselves within rather than outside the social norm. Work/employment and general behaviour/value systems were the two main criteria used by respondents in this study to construct 'others'. The fact that some people distanced themselves from such others indicates not only their attempts to represent themselves in a positive light but also that they had internalised hegemonic discourses around poor and low-income people as being personally responsible for their situation. This should not be overstated, though, because 'othering' was a minority practice and people did have a sensibility that their situation was structurally conditioned. But they constantly felt guilty and evaluated themselves sometimes as failing to live up to their own and others' expectations.

When one is poor or on a low income, the representation of self and family is not only a continuous process but it is also consuming of scarce resources. For this and other reasons, there was a highly local character to our study respondents' lives. People did not leave the area much (and a few hardly left their homes) and the services and resources that they most used tended to be locally based (with some exceptions), as were their informal networks of support. Two main factors acted to localise life: lack of money and the propinquity of family. Lack of money had many implications, not least the cost of travelling out of the local area and limiting the capacity to socialise (either at home or outside it). The second factor – the propinquity of family – was in many respects a positive attribute of the localness of life. It enabled people to feel a tie to the area and generally (although not universally) gave them a source of support locally. But there was also a sense of retreating from the outside world on the part of some respondents and their families. This retreat had several roots. One was the constraints imposed by lack of money – one cannot move widely without some spending being involved and in this context people preferred to stay at home. Another reason for turning inwards was to escape the lack of status and respect that respondents were frequently faced with outside the home, especially in encounters with officialdom.

A final word

Poverty and low income, then, especially as they manifest themselves as a familial phenomenon, are theorised to take effect through structural, cultural, relational and representational dimensions. The causality involved is complex, in three regards. First, the factors or dimensions have to be seen as interacting, feeding into each other in complex ways. The fact that causal effects are interwoven is another reason why none of the dimensions can be rigidly separated for analytic purposes. Second, the causal effect of the different elements may vary (temporally but also in substance). At some periods and for some aspects of poverty and low income, structural factors are to the fore – such as the size of family and the numbers of able-bodied adults. Family relationships – especially in the context of whether family members are a source of support – also vary in their significance at any one point of time and over time. A third element of complexity is introduced by the positioning of cultural and representational factors. These also may confer or deplete resources – like when people have to defend themselves against negative expectations – but they also act like filters affecting the use of other resources. Some classic examples include people feeling the need to compensate their children for their situation and hence directing expenditure their way. A less concrete example is the energy and work that has to be put into making a good impression and having to establish one's legitimacy.

We have used the framework especially to understand poverty and low income as associated with processes, practices and relationships in everyday family life. There are things we have not focused on – like power relationships within families and how the linkages between class, race, ethnicity and gender among other lines of division are constitutive of, and lead to, poverty and low income. These, too, could be accommodated within the framework, although this would necessitate some reframing. We are hopeful that others might take this forward. The matter of the role and significance of family in a context of poverty and low income needs further work and further theorising. All the indications are that this, a relatively neglected area in existing work, deserves a prominent place in future research. If the results of this study hold elsewhere, people on low income cannot afford to be independent of family. And indeed it may be the case that they do not necessarily want to be.

References

Allan, G. (1996) *Kinship and friendship in modern Britain*, Oxford: Oxford University Press.

Anderson, W., White, V. and Finney, A. (2010) *'You just have to get by.' Coping with low income and cold homes*, Bristol: Centre for Sustainable Energy.

Athwal, B., Brill, L., Chesters, G. and Quiggin, M. (2011) *Recession, poverty and sustainable livelihoods in Bradford*, York: Joseph Rowntree Foundation.

Atkinson, W. (2014) 'A sketch of "family" as a field: from realized category to space of struggle', *Acta Sociologica*, vol 57, no 3, pp 223-35.

Baillie, R. (2011) 'An examination of the public discourse on benefit claimants in the media', *Journal of Poverty and Social Justice*, vol 19, no 1, pp 67-70.

Barnes, H., Garratt, E., McLennan, D. and Noble, M. (2011) *Understanding the worklessness dynamics and characteristics of deprived areas*, Department for Work and Pensions Research Report 779, London: Department for Work and Pensions.

Barnes, M., Butt, S. and Tomaszewski, W. (2008) *The dynamics of bad housing: The impact of bad housing on the living standards of children*, London: National Centre for Social Research.

Barrett, M. and McIntosh, M. (1982) *The anti-social family*, London: Verso.

Batty, E. and Cole, I. (2010) *Resilience and the recession in six deprived communities: Preparing for worse to come?*, York: Joseph Rowntree Foundation.

Beatty, C. and Fothergill, S. (2013) *The impact of welfare reform on Northern Ireland*, Sheffield: Centre for Regional Economic and Social Research, Sheffield Hallam University.

Bennett, F. and Daly, M. (2014) *Poverty through a gender lens: Evidence and policy review on gender and poverty*, Barnett Papers in Social Research, Oxford: University of Oxford.

Bennett, F. and Sung, S. (2013) 'Dimensions of financial autonomy in low-/moderate-income households from a gender perspective and implications for welfare reform', *Journal of Social Policy*, vol 42, no 4, pp 701-19.

Berger, B. and Berger, P. (1983) *The war over the family: Capturing the middle ground*, New York, NY: Anchor Press.

Bourdieu, P. (1996) 'On the family as a realized category', *Theory, Culture & Society*, vol 13, no 1, pp 19-26.

Bourdieu, P. (2001) *Masculine domination*, Cambridge: Polity Press.

Bradshaw, J. (ed) (2011) *The well-being of children in the United Kingdom*, Bristol: The Policy Press.

Brannen, J. and Wilson, G. (1987) *Give and take in families: Studies in resource distribution*, London: Allen & Unwin.

Browne, J. (2010) *The impact of tax and benefit reforms to be introduced between 2010-11 and 2014-15 in Northern Ireland*, IFS Briefing Note 114, London: Institute for Fiscal Studies.

Browne, J. and Roantree, B. (2013) *Universal Credit in Northern Ireland: What will its impact be, and what are the challenges?*, IFS Report 477, London: Institute for Fiscal Studies.

Browne, J., Hood, A. and Joyce, R. (2014) *Child and working-age poverty in Northern Ireland over the next decade: An update*, IFS Briefing Note 144, London: Institute for Fiscal Studies.

Burchardt, T. (2008) *Time and income poverty*, London: Centre for Analysis of Social Exclusion, London School of Economics and Political Science.

Canvin, K., Marttila, A., Burstrom, B. and Whitehead, M. (2009) 'Tales of the unexpected? Hidden resilience in poor households in Britain', *Social Science and Medicine*, vol 69, no 2, pp 238-45.

Cappellini, B. and Parsons, E. (2012) 'Practising thrift at dinnertime: mealtime leftovers, sacrifice and family membership', *The Sociological Review*, 60, S2, pp 121-34.

Centre for Social Justice (2012) 'Rethinking child poverty', www. centreforsocialjustice.org.uk/publications/rethinking-child-poverty

Chambers, D. (2012) *A sociology of family life*, Cambridge: Polity Press.

Chase, E. and Walker, R. (2013) 'The co-construction of shame in the context of poverty: beyond a threat to the social bond', *Sociology*, vol 47, no 4, pp 739-54.

Child Poverty Action Group (2012) *Ending child poverty by 2020: Progress made and lessons learned*, London: Child Poverty Action Group.

Churchill, H. (2013) 'Retrenchment and restructuring: family support and children's services reform under the coalition', *Journal of Children's Services*, vol 8, no 3, pp 209-22.

Committee for Social Development (2012) *Report on fuel poverty*, Northern Ireland Assembly Report, NIA 36/11-15, Belfast: Northern Ireland Assembly.

Cornford, J., Baines, S. and Wilson, R. (2013) 'Representing the family: how does the state "think family"?', *Policy & Politics*, vol 41, no 1, pp 1-19.

Crisp, R. and Robinson, D. (2010) *Family, friends and neighbours: Social relations and support in six low income neighbourhoods*, Research Paper 9, Sheffield: Centre for Regional and Economic Research, Sheffield Hallam University.

Culliney, M., Haux, T. and McKay, S. (2013) *Family structure and poverty*, York: Joseph Rowntree Foundation.

Daly, M. (2004) 'Family relations and social networks in Northern Ireland', in K. Lloyd, P. Devine, A.M. Gray and D. Heenan (eds) *Social attitudes in Northern Ireland*, London: Pluto, pp 53–66.

Daly, M. (2010a) 'Shifts in family policy in the UK under New Labour', *Journal of European Social Policy*, vol 20, no 5, pp 433–43.

Daly, M. (2010b) 'Assessing the EU approach to poverty and social exclusion over the last decade', in E. Marlier and D. Natali (eds) with R. Van Dam, *Europe 2020: Towards a more social EU?*, Brussels: P.I.E. Peter Lang, pp 143–61.

Daly, M. (2011) *Welfare*, Cambridge: Polity Press.

Daly, M. and Leonard, M. (2002) *Against all odds: Family life on a low income in Ireland*, Dublin: Institute of Public Administration/Combat Poverty Agency.

Dean, H. and Shah, A. (2002) 'Insecure families and low-paying labour markets: comments on the British experience', *Journal of Social Policy*, vol 31, no 1, pp 61–80.

Delfabbro, P. and Harvey, J. (2004) 'Psychological resilience in disadvantaged youth: a critical overview', *Australian Psychologist*, vol 39, no 1, pp 3–13.

Department for Social Development Northern Ireland (2010) *Family Resources Survey (2010)*, Belfast: Department for Social Development Northern Ireland.

Department for Social Development Northern Ireland (2011a) 'Households below average income Northern Ireland 2009/10: an analysis of the income distribution in Northern Ireland', www.dsdni.gov.uk/hbai_2009-10__03-08-2012_-2.pdf

Department for Social Development Northern Ireland (2011b) 'Warmer healthier homes: a new fuel poverty strategy for Northern Ireland', www.dsdni.gov.uk/fuel_poverty

Department for Social Development Northern Ireland (2013a) 'Northern Ireland benefit cap information booklet', www.dsdni.gov.uk/impact-of-benefit-cap.pdf

Department for Social Development Northern Ireland (2013b) 'Northern Ireland personal independence payment information booklet', www.dsdni.gov.uk/ni-pip-information-booklet.pdf

Department for Work and Pensions (2012) *Universal Credit: The impact on passported benefits*, Cm 8332.

Department of Energy and Climate Change (2013) *Annual report on fuel poverty statistics 2013*, London: Department of Energy and Climate Change.

Department of Health, Social Services and Public Safety (2011) *Health Survey Northern Ireland: First results from the 2010/11 survey*, Belfast: Department of Health, Social Services and Public Safety.

Department of Health, Social Services and Public Safety (2012) 'Northern Ireland health and social care inequalities monitoring system', www.dhsspsni.gov.uk/inequalities_monitoring_update4-2.pdf

Dermott, E. and Seymour, J. (eds) (2011) *Displaying families: A new concept for the sociology of family life*, Basingstoke: Palgrave Macmillan.

DeVault, M.L. (1999) 'Comfort and struggle: emotion work in family life', *The Annals of the American Academy of Political and Social Science*, vol 561, no 1, pp 52-63.

Dorsett, R., Lui, S. and Weale, M. (2011) *Estimating the effect of lifelong learning on women's earnings using a switching model*, LLAKES Research Paper 30, London: Centre for Learning and Life Chances in Knowledge Economies and Societies.

Duffy, S. (2014) 'Counting the cuts', www.centreforwelfarereform.org/library/by-date/counting-the-cuts.html

Duncan, S. and R. Edwards (1999) *Lone mothers, paid work and gendered moral rationalities*, Basingstoke: Macmillan.

Dyson, A., Hertzman, C., Roberts, H., Tunstill, J. and Vaghri, Z. (2010) *Childhood development, education and health inequalities*, London: Institute of Health Equity.

Edwards, R. and Gillies, V. (2005) *Resources in parenting: Access to capitals project report*, Families and Social Capital ESRC Research Group Working Paper 14, London: South Bank University.

Edwards, R., Ribbens McCarthy, J. and Gillies, V. (2012) 'The politics of concepts: family and its (putative) replacements', *British Journal of Sociology*, vol 63, no 4, pp 730-46.

Field, F. (2010) *The foundation years: Preventing poor children becoming poor adults*, London: Cabinet Office.

Finch, J. (1989) *Family obligations and social change*, Cambridge: Polity Press.

Finch, J. and Mason, J. (1993) *Negotiating family responsibilities*, London: Routledge.

Fine, M. and Glendinning, C. (2005) 'Dependence, independence or inter-dependence? Revisiting the concepts of "care" and "dependency"', *Ageing and Society*, vol 25, no 4, pp 601-21.

Flaherty, J. (2008) *Getting by, getting heard: Poverty and social exclusion in the Borders: Listening to the voices of experience*, Glasgow: Poverty Alliance.

Flint, J. (2010) *Coping strategies? Agencies, budgeting and self-esteem amongst low income households*, York: Joseph Rowntree Foundation.

Fram, M.S. (2003) *Managing to parent: Social support, social capital, and parenting practices among welfare-participating mothers with young children*, Institute for Research on Poverty Discussion Paper 1263-03, Madison, WI: University of Wisconsin.

Frydenberg, E. (2002) *Beyond coping: Meeting goals, visions and challenges*, Oxford: Oxford University Press.

Gardiner, K. and Hills, J. (1999) 'Policy implications of new data on income mobility', *The Economic Journal*, vol 109, no 453, F91-F111.

Garmezy, N. (1991) 'Resilience and vulnerability to adverse developmental outcomes associated with poverty', *American Behavioral Scientist*, vol 34, pp 416-30.

Gazso, A. and McDaniel, S. (2013) 'Families by choice and the management of low income through social supports', *Journal of Family Issues*, DOI: 10.1177/0192513X13506002.

Ghate, D. and Hazel, N. (2002) *Parenting in poor environments: Stress, support and coping*, London: Jessica Kingsley Publishers.

Gillies, V. (2008) 'Childrearing, class and the new politics of parenting', *Sociology Compass*, vol 2, no 3, pp 1079-95.

Gillies, V. (2012) 'Personalising poverty: parental determinism and the Big Society agenda', in W. Atkinson, S. Roberts and M. Savage (eds) *Class inequality in austerity Britain, power difference and suffering*, Basingstoke: Palgrave Macmillan, pp 90-110.

Gosling, V.K. (2008) '"I've always managed, that's what we do": social capital and women's experiences of social exclusion', *Sociological Research Online*, vol 13, no 1, pp 1-18.

Gray, P. and McAnulty, U. (2009) *Living in the private rented sector: Socio-economic profile of tenants in the private rented sector*, Belfast: Northern Ireland Housing Executive.

Green, S. and Hickman, P. (2010) *Residents' stories from six challenging neighbourhoods*, Research Paper 12, Sheffield: Centre for Regional Economic and Social Research, Sheffield Hallam University.

Gubrium, J. and Holstein, J. (1990) *What is family?* Mountain View, CA: Mayfield Publishing.

Hamilton, K. (2012) 'Low-income families and coping through brands: Inclusion or stigma?', *Sociology*, vol 46, no 1, pp 74-90.

Harkness, S., Gregg, P. and Macmillan, l. (2012) *Poverty: The role of institutions, behaviours and cultures*, York: Joseph Rowntree Foundation.

Harrison, E. (2013) 'Bouncing back? Recession, resilience and everyday lives', *Critical Social Policy*, vol 33, no 1, pp 97-113.

Harrison, L.E. and Huntington, S. (eds) (2000) *Culture matters: How values shape human progress*, New York, NY: Basic Books.

Herrnstein, R. and Murray, C. (1994) *The bell curve: Intelligence and class structure in American life*, New York, NY: Free Press.

Hickman, P., Batty, E., Dayson, C. and Muir, J. (2014) *'Getting by', coping and resilience in difficult times initial findings*, Research Paper 1, Recession, Resilience and Rebalancing Social Economies in Northern Ireland's Neighbourhoods: A Research Project Funded by the Office of the First Minister and Deputy First Minister, Sheffield: Sheffield Hallam University.

Hills, J., Brewer, M., Jenkins, S., Lister, R., Lupton, R., Machin, S., Mills, C., Modood, T., Rees, T. and Riddell, S. (2010) *An anatomy of economic inequality in the UK: Report of the National Equality Panel*, Case Report 60, London: Government Equalities Office, London School of Economics and Political Science, http://eprints.lse.ac.uk/28344/1/CASEreport60.pdf

HM Treasury (2010) *Spending Review 2010*, Cm 7942, London: The Stationery Office.

HM Treasury (2013) *Spending Round 2013*, Cm 8639, London: The Stationery Office.

Hohnen, P. (2007) 'Having the wrong kind of money. A qualitative analysis of new forms of financial, social and moral exclusion in consumerist Scandinavia', *The Sociological Review*, vol 55, no 4, pp 748-67.

Hooper, C.A., Gorin, S., Cabral, C. and Dyson, C. (2007) *Living with hardship 24/7: The diverse experiences of families in poverty in England*, London: NSPCC/The Frank Buttle Trust.

Horgan, G. (2007) '"They are not looking at the cost of living": a study of income adequacy in Northern Ireland', *Benefits*, vol 15, no 1, pp 59-68.

Horgan, G. and Monteith, M. (2009) *What can we do to tackle child poverty in Northern Ireland?*, JRF Viewpoint, York: Joseph Rowntree Foundation.

Howard, S., Dryden, J. and Johnson, B. (1999) 'Childhood resilience: review and critique of literature', *Oxford Review of Education*, vol 25, pp 307-23.

Irwin, S. (2005) *Reshaping social life*, London: Routledge.

Jenkins, S.P. and Rigg, J.A. (2001) *The dynamics of poverty in Britain*, Department for Work and Pensions Research Report 157, Leeds: Corporate Document Services.

Jones, C. and Novak, T. (1999) *Poverty, welfare and the disciplinary state*, London: Routledge.

Katz, M.B. (1989) *The undeserving poor*, New York, NY: Pantheon Books.

Katz, I., Corlyon, J., La Placa, V. and Hunter, S. (2007) *The relationship between parenting and poverty*, York: Joseph Rowntree Foundation.

Kelly, G., Tomlinson, M., Daly, M., Hillyard, P., Nandy, S. and Patsios, D. (2012) *The necessities of life in Northern Ireland*, PSE: Working Paper – Analysis Series No. 1, Poverty and Social Exclusion in the UK Study, available at: www.poverty.ac.uk/pse-research/pse-uk/results-analysis.

Kempson, E. (1996) *Life on a low income*, York: Joseph Rowntree Foundation.

Kempson, E., Bryson, A. and Rowlingson, K. (1994) *Hard times? How poor families make ends meet*, London: Policy Studies Institute.

Kochuyt, T. (2004) 'Giving away one's poverty. On the consumption of scarce resources within the family', *The Sociological Review*, vol 52, no 2, pp 139-61.

Kohli, M. (1999) 'Private and public transfers between generations: linking the family and the state', *European Societies*, vol 1, no 1, pp 81-104.

Komter, A. and Vollebergh, W. (2002) 'Solidarity in Dutch families: family ties under strain?', *Journal of Family Issues*, vol 23, pp 171-88.

Krumer-Nevo, M. and Benjamin, O. (2010) 'Critical poverty knowledge: contesting othering and social distancing', *Current Sociology*, vol 58, no 5, pp 693-714.

Lamont, M. and Small, M.S. (2010) 'Cultural diversity and anti-poverty policy', *International Social Science Journal*, vol 61, no 199, pp 169-80.

Lareau, A. (2003) *Unequal childhoods: Class, race and family life*, Oakland, CA: University of California Press.

Law Centre (NI) (2014) July 2014 e-newsletter, www.lawcentreni.org/news/recent-news.html

Levitas, R. (2012) *There may be 'trouble' ahead: What we know about those 120,000 'troubled families'*, PSE: Policy Response Series No. 3, Poverty and Social Exclusion in the UK Study, available at: http://poverty.ac.uk/pse-research/pse-uk/policy-response

Levitas, R. (2014) *Troubled families in a spin*, Poverty and Social Exclusion in the UK Study, available at: http://poverty.ac.uk/editorial/troubled-families-spin

Lewis, O. (1959) *Five families: Mexican case studies in the culture of poverty*, New York, NY: Basic Books.

Liddell, C. (2008) *The impact of fuel poverty on children*, Save the Children Policy Briefing, Belfast: University of Ulster.

Lister, R. (2004) *Poverty*, Cambridge: Polity Press.

Luthar, S. and Zelazo, L.B. (2003) 'Research on resilience: an integrative review', in S. Luthar (ed) *Resilience and vulnerability: Adaptation in the context of childhood adversities*, Cambridge/New York, NY: Cambridge University Press, pp 510-49.

Lynd, H.M. (1958) *On shame and the search for identity*, New York, NY: Harcourt Brace.

MacInnes, T., Aldridge, H., Bushe, S., Kenway, P. and Tinson, A. (2013) *Monitoring poverty and social exclusion 2013*, York: Joseph Rowntree Foundation.

Marmot Review (2010) *Fair society, healthy lives: Strategic review of health inequalities in England post-2010 (The Marmot Review)*, London: UCL Institute of Health Equity.

Marsh, A. and Vegeris, S. (2004) *The British lone parent cohort and their children 1991 to 2001*, Department for Work and Pensions Research Report 209, London: Department for Work and Pensions.

Marx Ferree, M. (2010) 'Filling the glass: gender perspectives on families', *Journal of Marriage and Family*, vol 72, pp 420-39.

Mason, J. (2008) 'Tangible affinities and the real life fascination of kinship', *Sociology*, vol 42, no 1, pp 29-45.

Mauss, M. (1966) *The gift: Forms and functions of exchange in archaic societies*, London: Cohen & West.

McCausland, N. (2012) 'Tailoring welfare reforms for Northern Ireland', Northern Ireland Executive News Release, 22 October.

McCormick, J. (2013) *Ending poverty: A review of devolved approaches across the UK*, York: Joseph Rowntree Foundation.

McIntyre, L., Officer, S. and Robinson, L. (2003) 'Feeling poor: the felt experience of low-income lone mothers', *Affilia-Journal of Women and Social Work*, vol 18, no 3, pp 316-31.

McKendrick, J.H., Cunningham-Burley, S. and Backett-Milburn, K. (2003) *Life in low income families in Scotland: Research report*, Edinburgh: Scottish Executive Social Research.

McLaughlin, E. (1993) 'Women and the family in Northern Ireland: a review', *Women's Studies International Forum*, vol 16, no 6, pp 553-68.

Millar, J. (2007) 'The dynamics of poverty and employment: the contribution of qualitative longitudinal research to understanding transitions, adaptations and trajectories', *Social Policy and Society*, vol 6, no 4, pp 533-44.

Miller, P. (2005) 'Useful and priceless children in contemporary welfare states', *Social Politics*, vol 12, no 1, pp 3-41.

Miller, S. (1996) 'The great chain of poverty explanations', in E. Oyen, S.M. Miller and S. Abdus Samad (eds) *Poverty: A global review: Handbook on international poverty research*, Stockholm: Scandinavian University Press, pp 569-86.

Mitchell, W. and Green, E. (2002) '"I don't know what I'd do without our Mam": motherhood, identity and support networks', *The Sociological Review*, vol 50, no 1, pp 1-22.

Monteith, M., Lloyd, K. and McKee, P. (2008) *Persistent child poverty in Northern Ireland*, Belfast: Save the Children.

Morgan, D.H.J. (1996) *Family connections: An introduction to family studies*, Cambridge: Polity Press.

Morgan, D.H.J. (2010) *Rethinking family practices*, Basingstoke: Palgrave Macmillan.

Murray, C. (1984) *Losing ground: American social policy 1950-1980*, New York, NY: Basic Books.

Murray, C. (1996) *Charles Murray and the underclass: The developing debate*, London: IEA Health and Welfare Unit.

Narayan, D., Chambers, R., Shah, M. and Petesch, P. (2000) *Crying out for change*, New York, NY: Oxford University Press/World Bank.

National Audit Office (2013) *Universal Credit: Early progress, HC 621*, London: The Stationery Office.

National Centre for Social Research (2012) *Welfare, British Social Attitudes 29*, London: National Centre for Social Research, www.bsa-29.natcen.ac.uk

Northern Ireland Executive (2014) *Bright start: The NI Executive's programme for affordable and integrated childcare*, Belfast: Northern Ireland Executive.

Northern Ireland Housing Executive (2011) *House conditions survey 2009*, Belfast: Northern Ireland Housing Executive.

Norton, A., with Bird, B., Brock, K., Kakander, M. and Turk, C. (2001) *A rough guide to PPAS*, London: Overseas Development Institute.

Ofcom (2010) 'Ofcom seventh annual communications market report', www.ofcom.org.uk

Office of the First Minister and Deputy First Minister (2012) *Towards a childcare strategy: A consultation document*, Belfast: OFMDFM.

Office of the First Minister and Deputy First Minister (2014) *Delivering social change for children and young people consultation document*, Belfast: OFMDFM.

Olagnero, M., Meo, A. and Corcoran, M.P. (2005) 'Social support networks in impoverished European neighbourhoods: case studies from Italy and Ireland', *European Societies*, vol 7, no 1, pp 53-79.

O'Reilly, D. and Stevenson, M. (2003) 'Mental health in Northern Ireland: have "the Troubles" made it worse?', *Journal of Epidemiology and Community Health*, vol 57, no 7, pp 488-92;

Padley, M. and Hirsch, D. (2014) *Households below a minimum income standard: 2008/9 to 2011/12*, York: Joseph Rowntree Foundation.

Pahl, J. (1989) *Money and marriage*, London: Macmillan.

Pahl, R. and Spencer, L. (2004) 'Personal communities: not simply of "fate" or "choice"', *Current Sociology*, vol 52, no 2, pp 199-221.

Parsons, T. and Bales, R. (1955) *Family socialisation and interaction processes*, Flencoe, IL: Free Press.

Patrick, R. (2014) 'Working on welfare: findings from a qualitative, longitudinal study into the lived experiences of welfare reform in the UK', *Journal of Social Policy*, DOI: 10.1017/S0047279414000294.

Paull, G. and Patel, T. (2012) *An international review of skills, jobs and poverty: Implications for the UK*, York: Joseph Rowntree Foundation.

Peacock, M., Bissell, P. and Owen, J. (2013) 'Shaming encounters: reflections on contemporary understandings of social inequality and health', *Sociology*, vol 48, no 2, pp 387-402.

Pemberton, S., Sutton, E. and Fahmy, E. (2013) *A review of the qualitative evidence relating to the experience of poverty and social exclusion*, PSE: Working Paper – Methods Series No. 22, Poverty and Social Exclusion in the UK Study, available at: http://poverty.ac.uk/pse-research/pse-uk/methods-development

Pickard, L. (2011) *The supply of informal care in Europe*, ENEPRI Research Report 94, Brussels: Centre for European Policy Studies.

Pickett, K., James, O. and Wilkinson, R. (2006) 'Income inequality and the prevalence of mental illness: a preliminary international analysis', *Journal of Epidemiology and Community Health*, vol 60, no 7, pp 646-47.

Platts-Fowler, D. and Robinson, D. (2013) *Neighbourhood resilience in Sheffield*, Sheffield: Centre for Regional and Economic Research, Sheffield Hallam University.

Ramaekers, S. and Suissa, J. (2011) *The claims of parenting: Reasons, responsibility and society*, Duesseldorf: Springer.

Reay, D. (2012) '"We never get a fair chance": working-class experiences of education in the twenty-first century', in W. Atkinson, S. Roberts and M. Savage (eds) *Class inequality in austerity Britain, power difference and suffering*, Basingstoke: Palgrave Macmillan, pp 33-50.

Ribbens, J. (1994) *Mothers and their children: A feminist sociology of childrearing*, London: Sage.

Ribbens McCarthy, J. (2012) 'The powerful relational language of "family": togetherness, belonging and personhood', *The Sociological Review*, vol 60, no 1, pp 68-90.

Ridge, T. (2002,) *Childhood poverty and social exclusion: From a child's perspective*, Bristol: The Policy Press.

Ridge, T. and Millar, J. (2008) *Work and well-being over time: Lone mothers and their children*, Department for Work and Pensions Research Report 536, London: Department for Work and Pensions.

Ritchie, J. and Lewis. J. (eds) (2003) *Qualitative research practice: A guide for social science students and researchers*, London: Sage Publications.

Rosenthal, C.J. (1985) 'Kinkeeping in the familial division of labour', *Journal of Marriage and the Family*, vol 47, no 4, pp 965-74.

Runciman, W.G. (1966) *Relative deprivation and social justice*, London: Routledge and Kegan Paul.

Savage, M. (2010) *Identities and social change in Britain since 1940: The politics of method*, Oxford: Oxford University Press.

Savage, M. (2012) 'Broken communities?', in W. Atkinson, S. Roberts and M. Savage (eds) *Class inequality in austerity Britain, power difference and suffering*, Basingstoke: Palgrave Macmillan, pp 145-62.

Sayer, A. (2005) *The moral significance of class*, Cambridge: Cambridge University Press.

Scheff, T.J. (2000) 'Shame and the social bond: a sociological theory', *Sociological Theory*, vol 18, no 1, pp 84-99.

Schofield, G. (1994) *The youngest mothers – the experience of pregnancy and motherhood among young women of school age*, Aldershot: Avebury.

Sen, A. (1983) 'Poor, relatively speaking', *Oxford Economic Papers*, vol 35, no 2, pp 153-67.

Sen, A. (1984) *Resources, values and development*, Oxford: Basil Blackwell.

Sgritta, G.B. (1989) 'Towards a new paradigm: family in the welfare state crisis', in K. Boh, M. Bak and C. Clason (eds) *Changing patterns of European family life: A comparative analysis of 14 European countries*, London: Routledge, pp 71-92.

Shildrick, T., MacDonald, R., Webster, C. and Garthwaite, K. (2012) *Poverty and insecurity: Life in low-pay, no-pay Britain*, Bristol: The Policy Press.

Sissons, P., Barnes, H. and Stevens, H. (2011) *Routes into Employment and Support Allowance*, Department for Work and Pensions Research Report 774, London: Department for Work and Pensions.

Small, M.L., Harding, D.J. and Lamont, M. (2010) 'Reconsidering culture and poverty', *The Annals of the American Academy of Political and Social Science*, vol 629, pp 6-27.

Smart, C. (2007) *Personal life*, Cambridge: Polity Press.

Spencer, L., Ritchie, J. and O'Connor, W. (2003) 'Analysis: practices, principles and processes', in J. Ritchie and J. Lewis (eds) (2003) *Qualitative research practice: A guide for social science students and researchers*, London: Sage Publications, pp 199-218.

Standing, G. (2011) 'Behavioural conditionality: why the nudges must be stopped – an opinion piece', *Journal of Poverty and Social Justice*, vol 19, no 1, pp 27-38.

Tomlinson, M. and Walker, R. (2010) *Recurrent poverty: The impact of family and labour market changes*, York: Joseph Rowntree Foundation.

Townsend, P. (1979) *Poverty in the United Kingdom*, Harmondsworth: Penguin.

Trades Union Congress (2012) 'Under-employment crisis: a TUC analysis of under-employment across the UK', available at: www.allofusfirst.org/commonweal/assets/File/Underemployment-report.pdf

Vandsburger, E., Harrigan, M. and Biggerstaff, M. (2008) 'In spite of all, we make it: themes of stress and resiliency as told by women in families living in poverty', *Journal of Family Social Work*, vol 11, no 1, pp 17-35.

Vincent, C., Ball, S.P. and Braun, A. (2010) 'Between the estate and the state: struggling to be a "good" mother', *British Journal of Sociology of Education*, vol 31, no 2, pp 123-38.

Walker, K. (1995) '"Always there for me": friendship patterns and expectations among middle- and working-class men and women', *Sociological Forum*, vol 10, no 2, pp 273-96.

Walker, R. and Collins, C. (2004) 'Families of the poor', in J. Scott, J. Treas and M. Richards (eds) *The Blackwell companion to the sociology of families*, Oxford: Blackwell, pp 193-217.

Weeks, J., Heaphy, B. and Donovan, C. (2001) *Same sex intimacies: Families of choice and other life experiments*, London: Routledge.

Whitty, L. (2012) *Energising Northern Ireland*, Belfast: Consumer Council.

Wilkinson, R.G. and Pickett, K.E. (2006) 'Income inequality and population health: a review and explanation of the evidence', *Social Science and Medicine*, vol 62, no 7, pp 1768-84.

Wilkinson, R.G. and Pickett, K.E. (2009) *The spirit level: Why more equal societies almost always do better*, London: Allen Lane.

Williams, F. (2004) *Rethinking families*, London: Gulbenkian Foundation.

Wilson, W.J. (1987) *The truly disadvantaged: The inner city, the underclass and public policy*, Chicago, IL: University of Chicago Press.

Zelizer, V.A. (1985) *Pricing the priceless child: The changing social value of children*, New York, NY: Basic Books.

Zelizer, V.A (1994) *The social meaning of money*, New York, NY: Basic Books.

APPENDIX A

Interview schedule

Family life in Northern Ireland in 2012

When I ask you about your family, who do you think of/include?

And when it comes to your immediate family, the family that you live with, it would be helpful at this stage to know a little bit about the household structure – the number of people who live in the family, their ages and relationship to you.

We would now like to hear about the things that make up and matter to your family, what it's like, the things you would say if you were describing this family to somebody who didn't know you.

When you think of your family, what words or phrases come to your mind?

What struggles does the family face? (prompt: health, income, accessing services)

Would you say that you face these struggles as a family together or is it one or a few people who do all the worrying/adjustment?

Would you like to change anything about your family life?

(If yes) What three things would you most like to change?

Do you think that people in your situation can generally change things if they want to?

    (prompt: empowerment)

What makes you most proud about your family?

Who are the people that rely on you in life?

We're also interested in how families support each other, where that support comes from and what form it takes. The next few questions are about the give and take of family life.

Living on a tight budget can put a strain on families but sometimes it can also bring families closer together. Can you tell me how living on a tight budget affects your family?

Tell us about your good days and your bad days – what would a good day be like and a bad one?

Have you ever felt embarrassed because you have a low income?

Where do you get your own support or help from, especially when you have difficult decisions to make?

Who, if anybody, is particularly good to you when you're up against it in financial terms?

And are there other types of help or support that they give to you?

Who, if anybody, are you particularly good to when they're up against it in financial terms?

Are there any other types of support that you give to others?

What would happen if family support wasn't available?

Support can also come from other sources – like friends and neighbours. We'd like to hear about that too.

Would you say you are a person with a lot of close friends?

How important are friends as a source of help?

In what way?

Do you do anything for them in return?

Has lack of income affected your friendships?

And what about neighbours – how important are they to you and/ or the family?

High/medium/low

If they help, how do they help or assist?

Do you do anything for them in return?

Would you say there's a sense of community in this area?

Do you see yourself as having links to the community? (prompt: involved in groups or organisations)

How would you rate the level of this family's involvement in the local community?

High/medium/low

We would now like to move to the way the family runs on a day-to-day basis, how the demands and pressures of family life are handled, how decisions are made and generally how things are managed.

What are the priorities in the family when it comes to deciding about money?

How does your situation this year compare with this time last year?

Are there things that you could cut back on if you needed to?

And are there things that cannot be cut back on?

Are there things you miss not being able to have? What, for example?

For you, what is a luxury?

Who in the family has the biggest say when it comes to making decisions about money – for example, everyday decisions about food shopping and bigger decisions like the electric bill?

(If not the respondent) Could you have a bigger say in these if you wanted to?

(Only if non-dependent children living at home) Does ... contribute financially to help with the household expenses?

Are there days of the week (or fortnight/month) when there's no money left? What do you do then?

How do you manage to make ends meet?

How much of a struggle is it for you?

What is your safety net (if you have one)?

What happens in emergencies, for example, if the cooker breaks down or you lose a purse?

What happens for things that need additional cash, for example, birthdays?

And Christmas?

Do you worry about the money situation?

Is debt an issue?

Has your peace of mind been affected?

Have you ever felt ashamed because of having a low income?

What would you say your family is rich in?

What makes you most happy about family life?

Do you feel under pressure to buy particular brands for your children?

How do you try to get your children to manage their expectations?

If you were giving tips to someone else about managing family life in your situation, what would be your top three tips?

What are the things that help you cope?

And the barriers or roadblocks that make life difficult for you and the family?

What are the skills (or things that you are good at) that help you in your situation?

How does your family compare to other families, do you think?

How would you rate the quality of family life in this family on a scale from 1 to 5

(1 being poor and 5 being excellent), not talking about the things that cost money?

(Follow up with – Why's that?)

How would you rate the standard of living in this family on a scale from 1 to 5

(1 being poor and 5 being excellent) – this is more material things?

(Follow up with – Why's that?)

What are the family priorities at the moment?

Do you think about how things will work out down the line?

(If so) Do you have plans for the future?

And what about expectations or hopes?

How do you think these will work out?

Are there things you have faced as a family that you haven't mentioned?

(If so) Would you like to tell us about them?

What about as a parent? What challenges face you there?

What services in your local area do you get support from or use regularly and how satisfied are you with each?

a) Your GP

Highly satisfied, moderately satisfied/OK, dissatisfied, very dissatisfied

b) Local dentist

Highly satisfied, moderately satisfied/OK, dissatisfied, very dissatisfied

c) Priest/minister/faith community

Highly satisfied, moderately satisfied/OK, dissatisfied, very dissatisfied

d) Advice centre/Citizens Advice Bureau (If yes, is it easy to get an appointment/to see somebody)

Highly satisfied, moderately satisfied/OK, dissatisfied, very dissatisfied

e) Credit union

Highly satisfied, moderately satisfied/OK, dissatisfied, very dissatisfied

f) Social worker/social services

Highly satisfied, moderately satisfied/OK, dissatisfied, very dissatisfied

g) School-related services/Sure Start

Highly satisfied, moderately satisfied/OK, dissatisfied, very dissatisfied

Which would you say is the most important to you?

APPENDIX B

Details of response rate and equivalisation of income

Table B.1: Response rate from Family Resources Survey list and reasons for non-response

Original contact list		90
Returned for incorrect address	5	
Refused	27	
Unobtainable (phone number changed/answer machine/no answer)	34	
Uncontactable	10	
Interviews completed		14

Equivalisation of income

Tables B.2 and B.3 set out the equivalence scales used to take into consideration economies of scale and to adjust for differences in size and type of family before and after housing costs. While they adjust for the number of adults in the household and also for children aged under and over 14 years, they do not take into consideration extra costs associated with disability or indebtedness. The tables also show the weekly equivalent monetary values by family type, in Northern Ireland, at the 60% median threshold for 2009-2010.

Table B.2: Equivalising income (before housing costs)

Unit	Value	60% median (2009/10)[1]
First adult	0.67	£148
Spouse	0.33	£72.90
Other adult	0.33	£72.90
Child (< 14 years)	0.20	£44.20
Child (> 14 years)	0.33	£72.90

[1] Also see Department for Social Development (2010) for statistics relating to the overall net disposable income distribution and equivalent monetary values by family type in Northern Ireland.

Table B.3: Equivalising income (after housing costs)

	Value	60% median (2009/10)
Unit	0.58	£114.20
Spouse	0.42	£82.70
Other adult	0.42	£82.70
Child (< 14 years)	0.20	£39.40
Child (> 14 years)	0.42	£82.70

Index